A PORTRAIT OF
LIVERPOOL

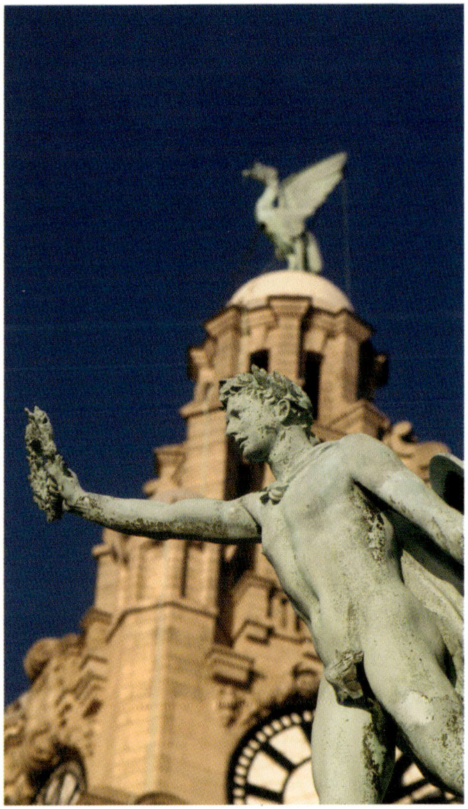

PAUL MCMULLIN
Text by Mike McNamee

HALSGROVE

First published in Great Britain in 2004

Title page image: *Cunard War Memorial*

British Library Cataloguing-in-Publication Data
A CIP record for this title is available from the British Library

ISBN 1 84114 379 0

HALSGROVE
Halsgrove House
Lower Moor Way
Tiverton, Devon EX16 6SS
Tel: 01884 243242
Fax: 01884 243325
email: sales@halsgrove.com
website: www.halsgrove.com

Printed and bound by D'Auria Industrie Grafiche Spa, Italy

Dedication
To Liz and Peter for putting up with early mornings, late evenings and constant weather watching.

Foreword

By Lord David Alton of Liverpool

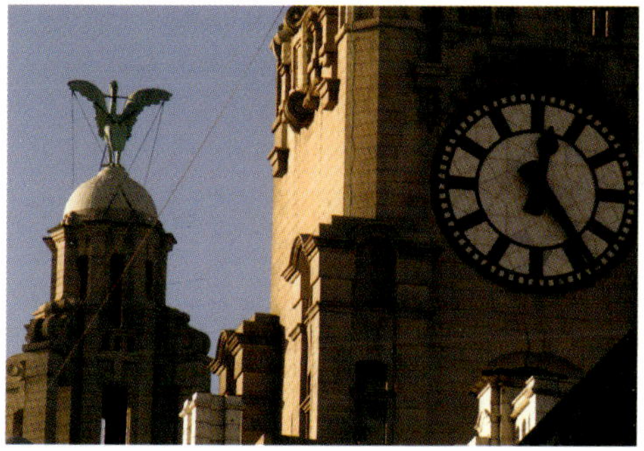

Cities need vision. They need to understand how they can create and sustain wealth and growth. They need to understand how to build a sustainable environment which can embrace the natural while adding the exceptional. Tomorrow's cities need to be built for people. A statement of the obvious, yet it was lost in the fog and smog which filled the planners' minds of the past.

People are returning to the urban centres vacated a few decades earlier, they are choosing to live, work and enjoy the sense of belonging which great cities engender. Nobody doubts that New Yorkers love their city, nobody doubts the joy the Parisians get from the streets, the cafés and the music of the French capital and you don't have to be a Londoner to admire the majesty and history of the English capital. You just have to look all around you.

Liverpool's startling attribute is its river – its river and its people. For most of the last two centuries, the river was seen as the economic lifeblood from which grandeur and money flowed out and into the magnificent architecture and designs which filled the streets. That money helped to build the finest modern cathedral in England, adorned the Town Hall, created the breathtaking St George's Hall and constructed a waterfront which would become famous across the globe. But few looked out on the river from their own homes. It was a place to work not to live. Today the River Mersey is the vista more and more people choose from their lounges. It is the 'natural' and we must continue to add the 'exceptional' to make it more so as we remove the scars of the industrialised past.

The city is the place where more and more people now choose to find their entertainment and enjoyment. New homes, new businesses, new ideas and new confidence as well as new designs and constructions are adding to the history we acknowledge and admire. This book celebrates and captures the transition. A transition which should see the new being skilfully grafted on to the old to create a new energy, a new pride and a new sense of direction in an ever confident community. Design and tradition can be fused together and as the prophet said; 'Without vision, the people perish.'

The Capital of Culture award for 2008 should be just the beginning. It should be a celebration of the achievement to date and a recognition of the challenge ahead. The challenge is to finally persuade all doubters that in a modern post industrial world, the wealth generated from the new technologies, from the diversity we now enjoy in music, sport, the arts and the creative industries can flow as easily from the West coast as it can from the South East. True regeneration may start with buildings and development but to sustain itself it has to have hearts and minds close behind. Liverpool can be at the beginning of the next economic chapter as much as it has led and shaped the last few.

Paul McMullin's outstanding work clearly demonstrates that we have a canvas envied by many. Now we must have the leadership and vision to make the city the first choice for those seeking investment, development, joy and leisure. I know you will enjoy these images of our city: once great and now great once more.

David Alton
Liverpool, June 2004

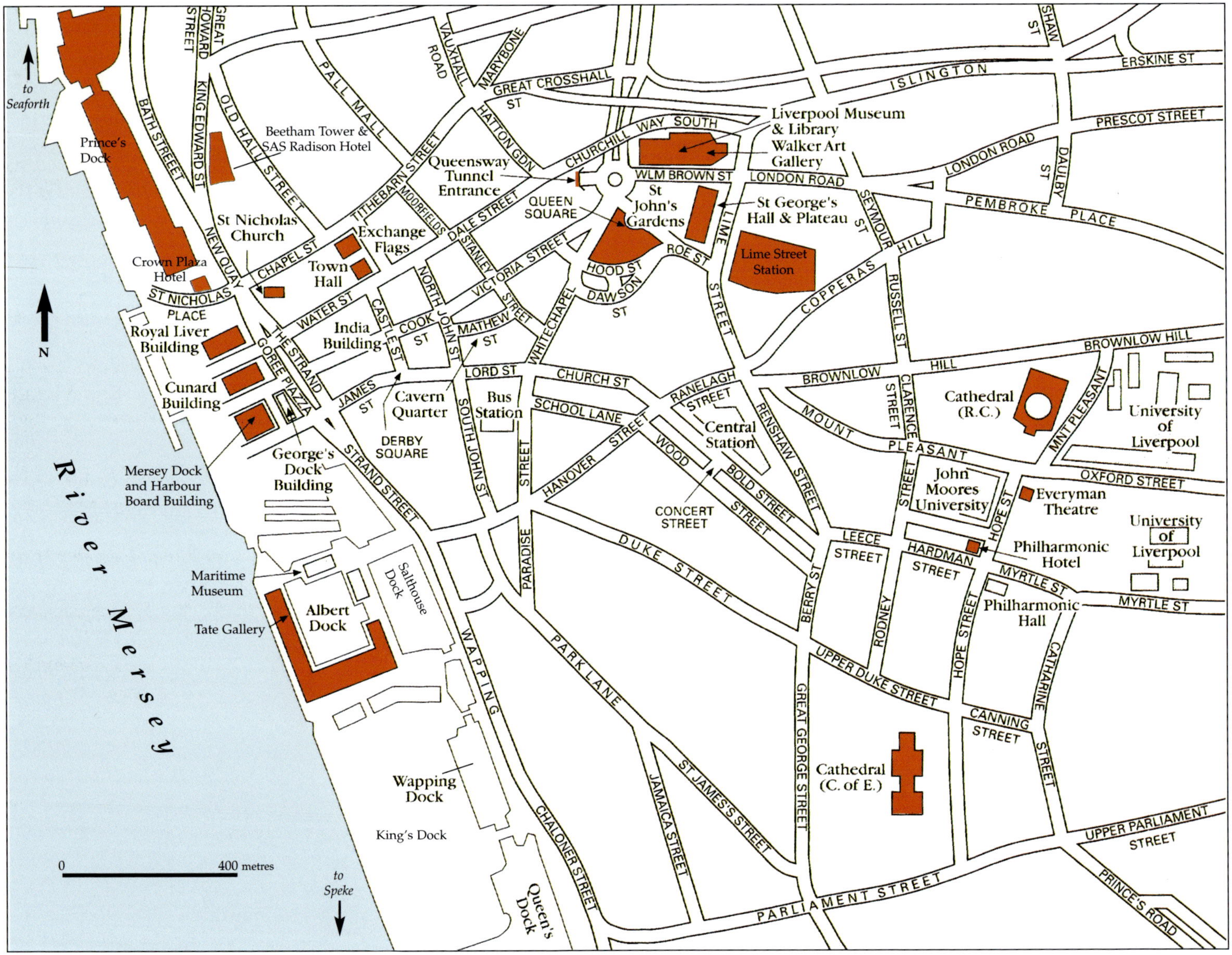
to Seaforth
Prince's Dock
N
River Mersey
Crown Plaza Hotel
Royal Liver Building
Cunard Building
Mersey Dock and Harbour Board Building
Maritime Museum
Tate Gallery
Albert Dock
Salthouse Dock
Wapping Dock
King's Dock
Queen's Dock
to Speke
0
400 metres
Beetham Tower & SAS Radison Hotel
St Nicholas Church
Town Hall
Exchange Flags
India Building
George's Dock Building
Queensway Tunnel Entrance
QUEEN SQUARE
St John's Gardens
Liverpool Museum & Library
Walker Art Gallery
St George's Hall & Plateau
Lime Street Station
Cavern Quarter
Bus Station
DERBY SQUARE
Central Station
CONCERT STREET
Cathedral (R.C.)
University of Liverpool
John Moores University
Everyman Theatre
Philharmonic Hotel
Philharmonic Hall
Cathedral (C. of E.)
GREAT HOWARD STREET
BATH STREET
KING EDWARD ST
OLD HALL STREET
PALL MALL
VAUXHALL ROAD
MARYBONE
GREAT CROSSHALL ST
HATTON GDN
TITHEBARN STREET
MOORFIELDS
DALE STREET
CHURCHILL WAY SOUTH
WLM BROWN ST
LONDON ROAD
ISLINGTON
ERSKINE ST
SHAW ST
PRESCOT STREET
DAULBY ST
PEMBROKE PLACE
SEYMOUR ST
NEW QUAY
CHAPEL ST
ST NICHOLAS PLACE
WATER ST
THE STRAND
GOREE PIAZZA
STANLEY
VICTORIA STREET
NORTH JOHN ST
CASTLE ST
COOK ST
MATHEW ST
STANLEY STREET
WHITECHAPEL
HOOD ST
DAWSON ST
ROE ST
LIME STREET
COPPERAS HILL
RUSSELL ST
BROWNLOW HILL
LORD ST
CHURCH ST
JAMES ST
SCHOOL LANE
RANELAGH STREET
SOUTH JOHN ST
STREET
HANOVER STREET
WOOD
BOLD STREET
RENSHAW STREET
MOUNT PLEASANT
CLARENCE STREET
MNT PLEASANT
OXFORD STREET
STRAND STREET
PARADISE
DUKE STREET
LEECE STREET
BERRY ST
HARDMAN STREET
HOPE ST
MYRTLE ST
RODNEY
HOPE STREET
CATHARINE STREET
UPPER DUKE STREET
CANNING STREET
WAPPING
PARK LANE
JAMAICA STREET
ST JAMES'S STREET
GREAT GEORGE STREET
CHALONER STREET
UPPER PARLIAMENT STREET
PARLIAMENT STREET
PRINCE'S ROAD

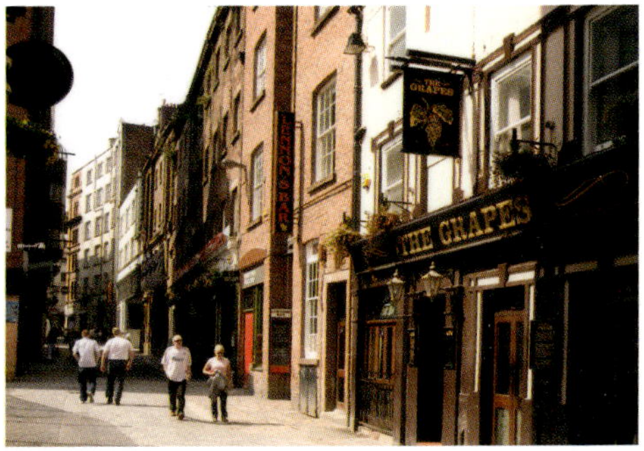

Introduction

Wherever I am in the world – often in the most remote parts – and I am asked where I am from, I always proudly say Liverpool. Just that; not Liverpool in England, just Liverpool. And I can say not once in all my years have I been asked: 'Where is that?'

Liverpool, you see, is known throughout the world – and for all the best reasons. Whether for its football, its music, its buildings, its fantastic waterfront, its river, cathedrals or, of course, for its humour.

I was in New York just over a year ago with a friend from 'over the water' in Wallasey (Mike Walker, who makes my cameras), and we were in a little Italian restaurant when the conversation turned to where we were from. The owner, on hearing that Liverpool was our home, came over with bottles of wine. His ship had called into the Port of Liverpool en-route to New York in the 1960s and he had always remembered his time there. I'm sure it wouldn't have happened if it had been any other city port.

When asked to do the images for *Portrait of Liverpool* late in 2003, I made quite a comprehensive list of the subjects which I thought ought to be included in the book. Initially I decided to concentrate on the inner city, but felt I should include other important areas, such as the Royal Seaforth Docks on the northern edge and Speke to the south.

I have tried to cover my list with as many up-to-date images as possible, and to show the city in its very many facets. However there will always be omissions, and I can only apologise if you feel I have missed a favourite building, place, statue or feature.

The photographs in this book are as recent as possible, the majority taken in 2004. Some have been originally shot for clients, and I thank them for allowing me to use them in this book on our great city, Liverpool.

Paul McMullin
June 2004

Acknowledgements

With thanks to all the companies and individuals who have helped with the making of this book:

Mersey Docks and Harbour Board; Liverpool Chamber of Commerce; Liverpool Business Centre; Liverpool City Council; Tweeds Construction Consultancy; The Mersey Partnership; Cains Brewery; Rob Mcloughlin; Mike Walker; Peter O'Brian; Philip Parker of the Atlantic Container Line; Liverpool Anglican Cathedral, and the Metropolitan Cathedral of Christ the King.

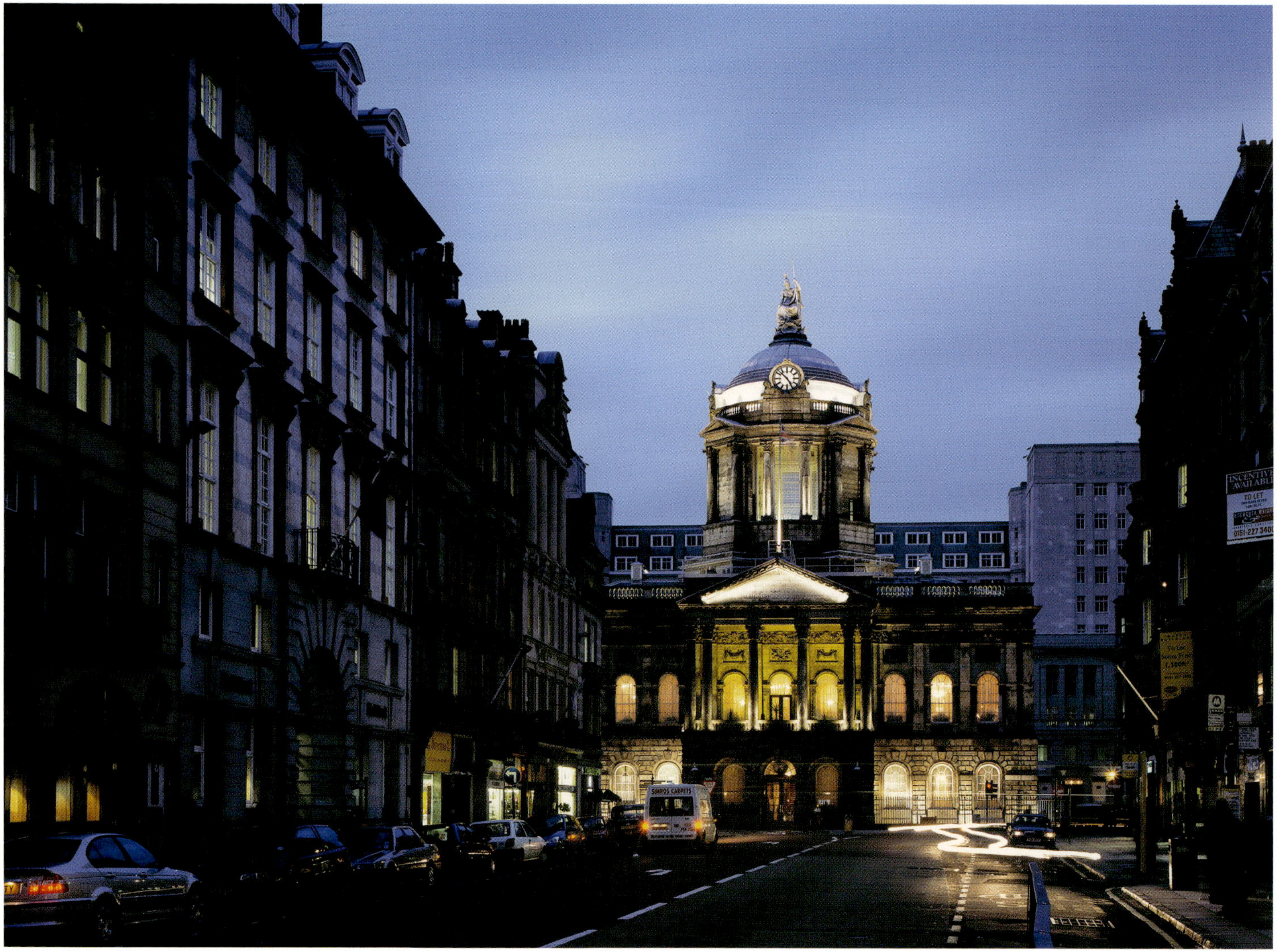

Liverpool Town Hall

Originally built in 1749 and reconstructed in 1807, the Town Hall is situated on Castle Street. The original architect was John Wood theYounger of Bath, James Wyatt and John Foster jnr. Originally intended for purely ceremonial purposes, the Town Hall is still used for grand functions, and it is even possible to get married here. Part of the ground floor was remodelled to form a grand Council Chamber.

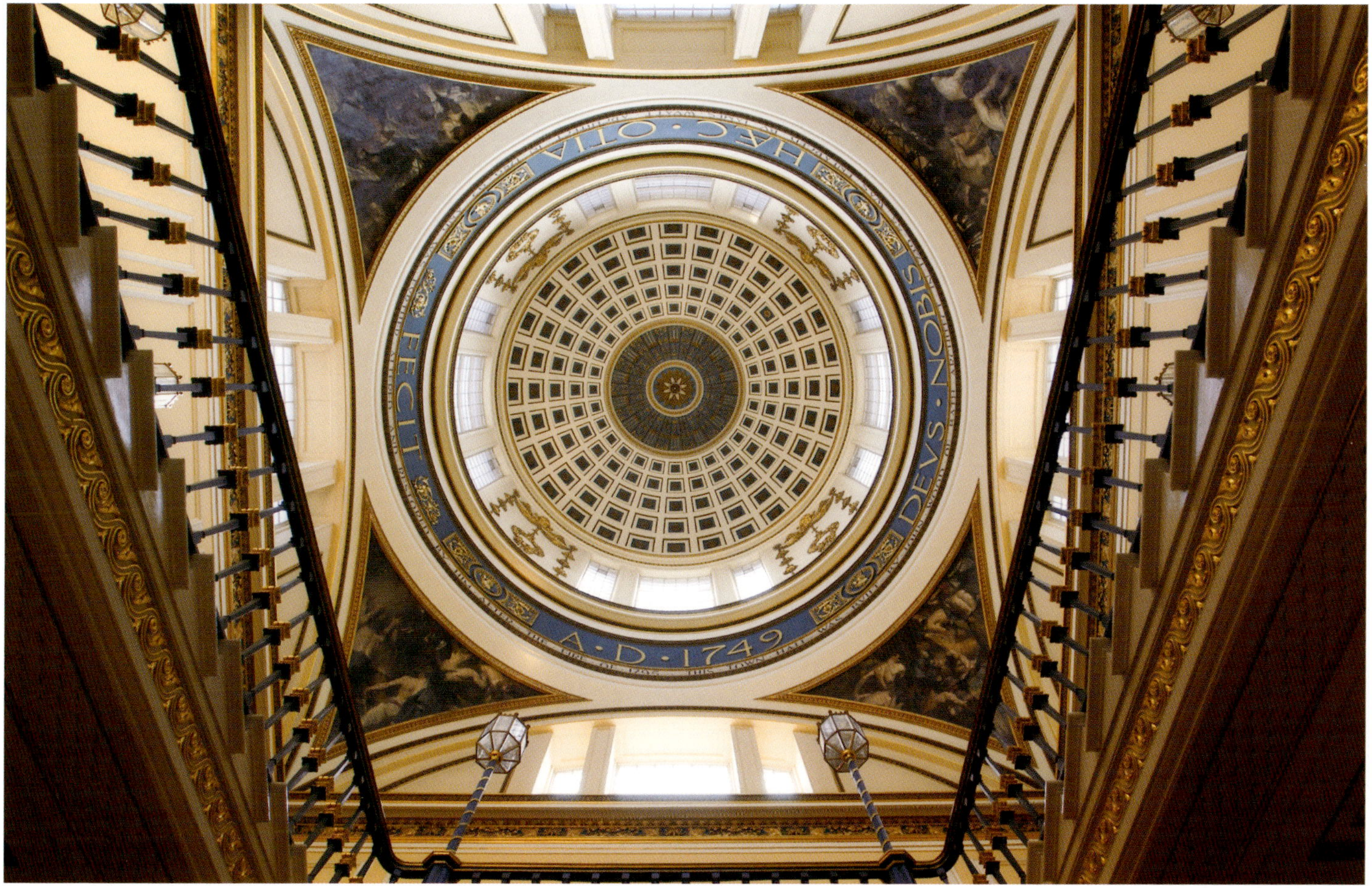

Liverpool Town Hall

The interior of the Town Hall, showing the ornate dome. Built between 1749 and 1754, this is one of the treasures of Liverpool. The spectacular interior décor was not completed until 1820 and is regarded as a prime example of Georgian taste and design. The four pictures at each corner are by Charles W. Furse and were painted in 1901.

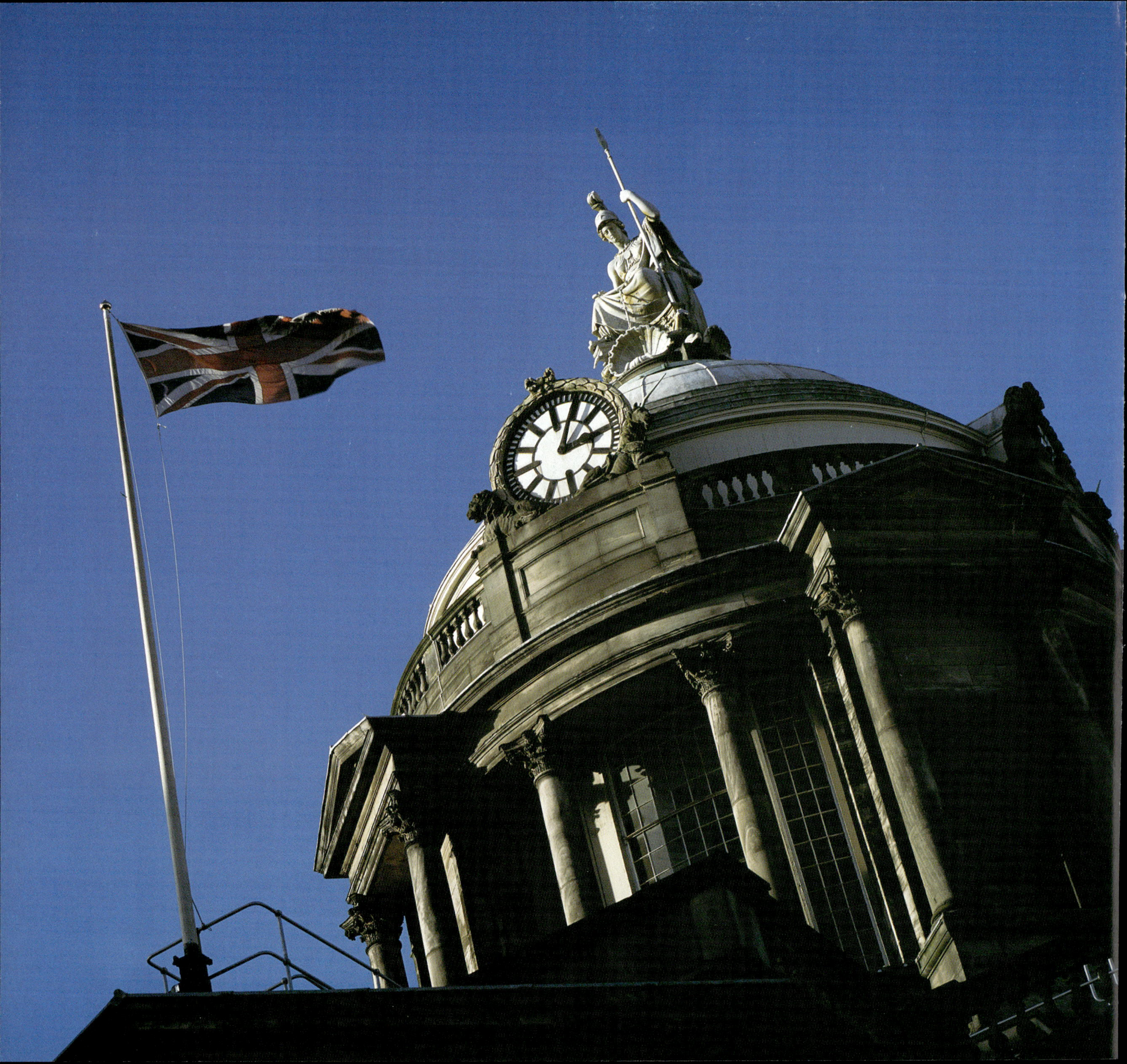

Minerva/Britannia ***(left)***

This figure sits on top of the dome of Liverpool Town Hall and was sculpted by John Charles Felix Rossi in the early nineteenth century. There has always been great debate as to whether the figure is Minerva or Britannia. The cost in 1802 was about £460.

Exchange Flags and Exchange Buildings

The monument to Lord Nelson and the Battle of Trafalgar was designed by Matthew Cotes Wyatt and the sculptor was Richard Westmacott. Unveiled in 1813, this impressive monument stands over 9 metres tall in the centre of the square, and is surrounded on three sides by the Exchange Buildings. These were completed in 1955, after construction had been interrupted by the war.

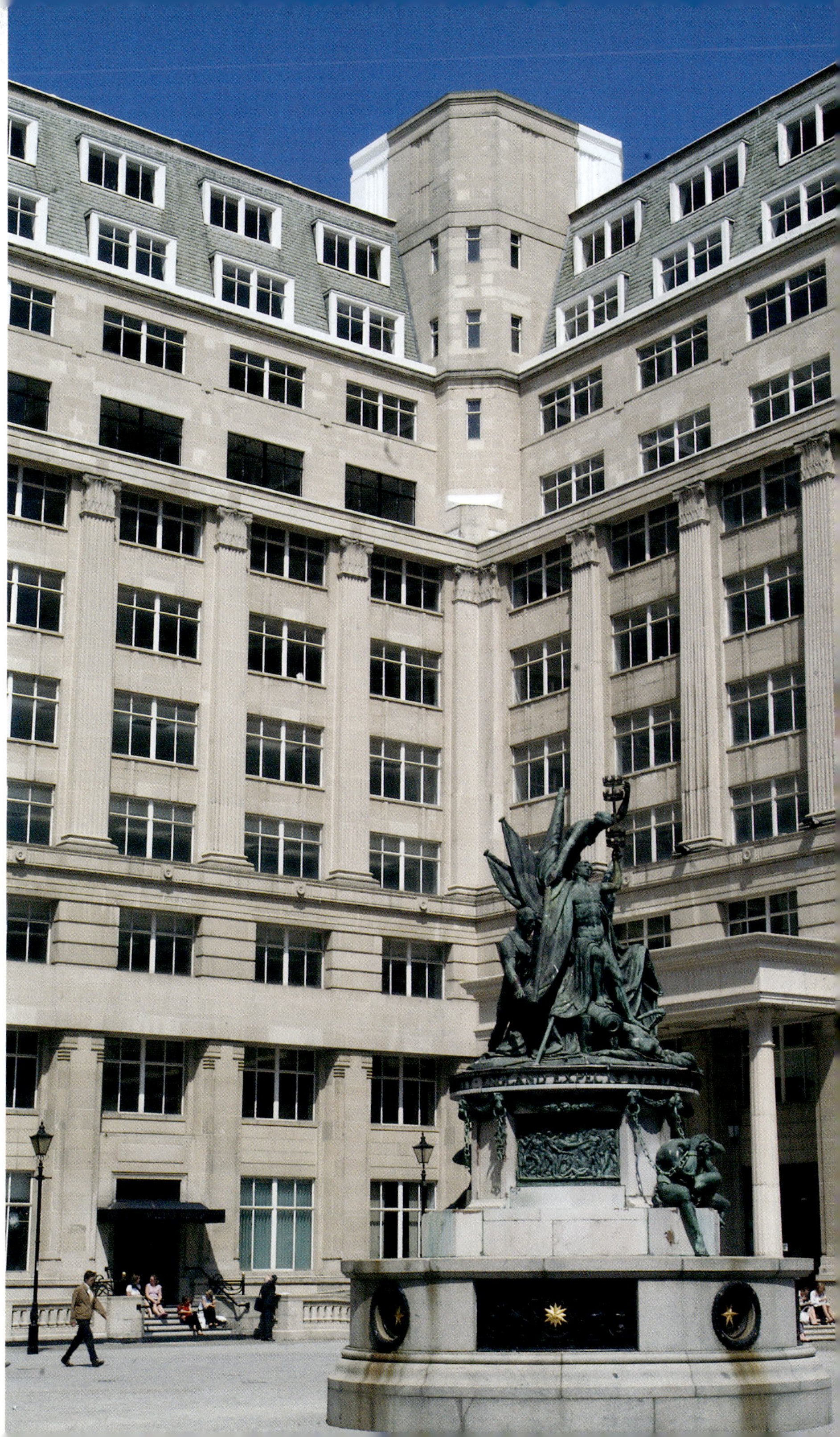

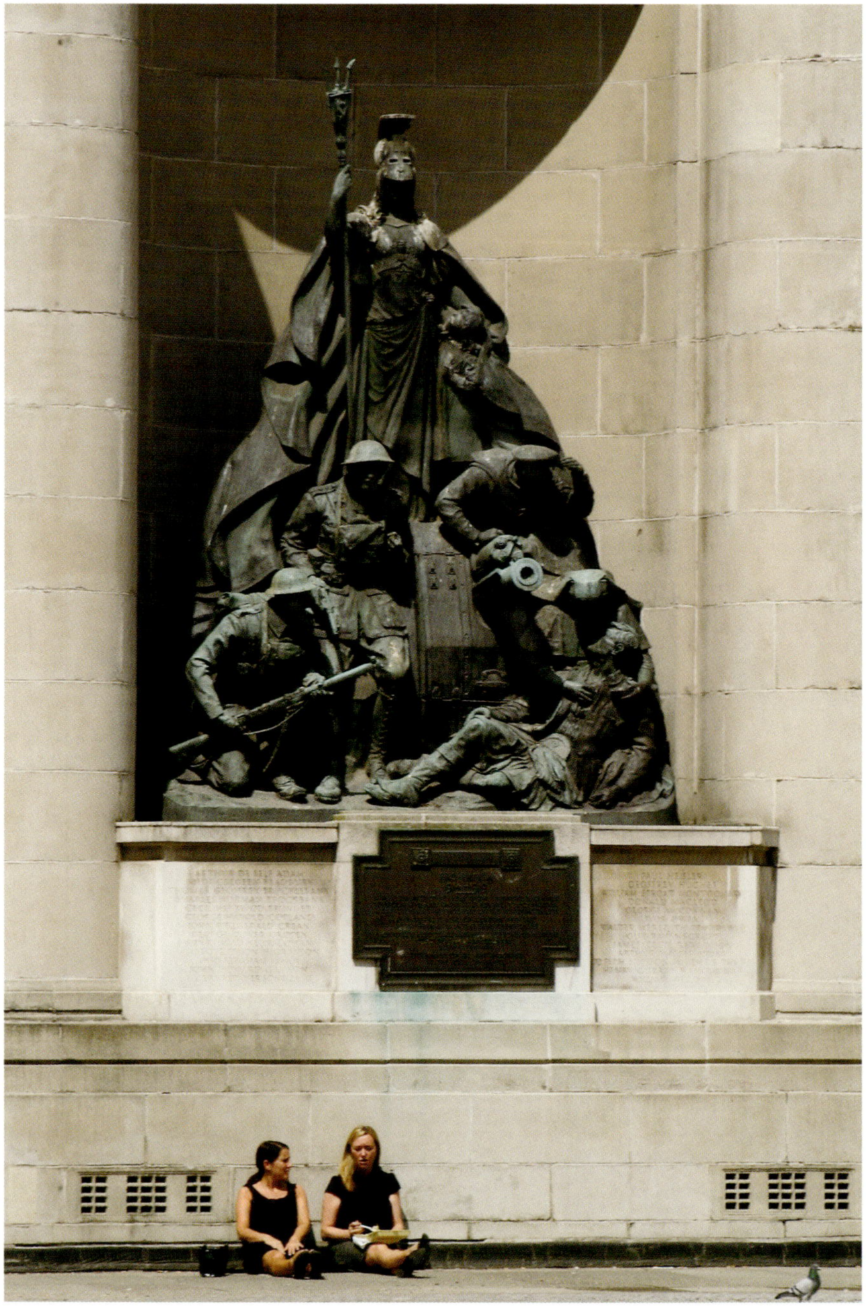

Exchange Flags

On hot, summer days, the square behind the Town Hall becomes an impromptu eating place at lunch time. The News Room war memorial was unveiled by the 17th Earl of Derby in the News Room of Derby House in 1924. It was moved to this position in between the entrances of the alley-ways leading to Tithebarn Street in 1953.

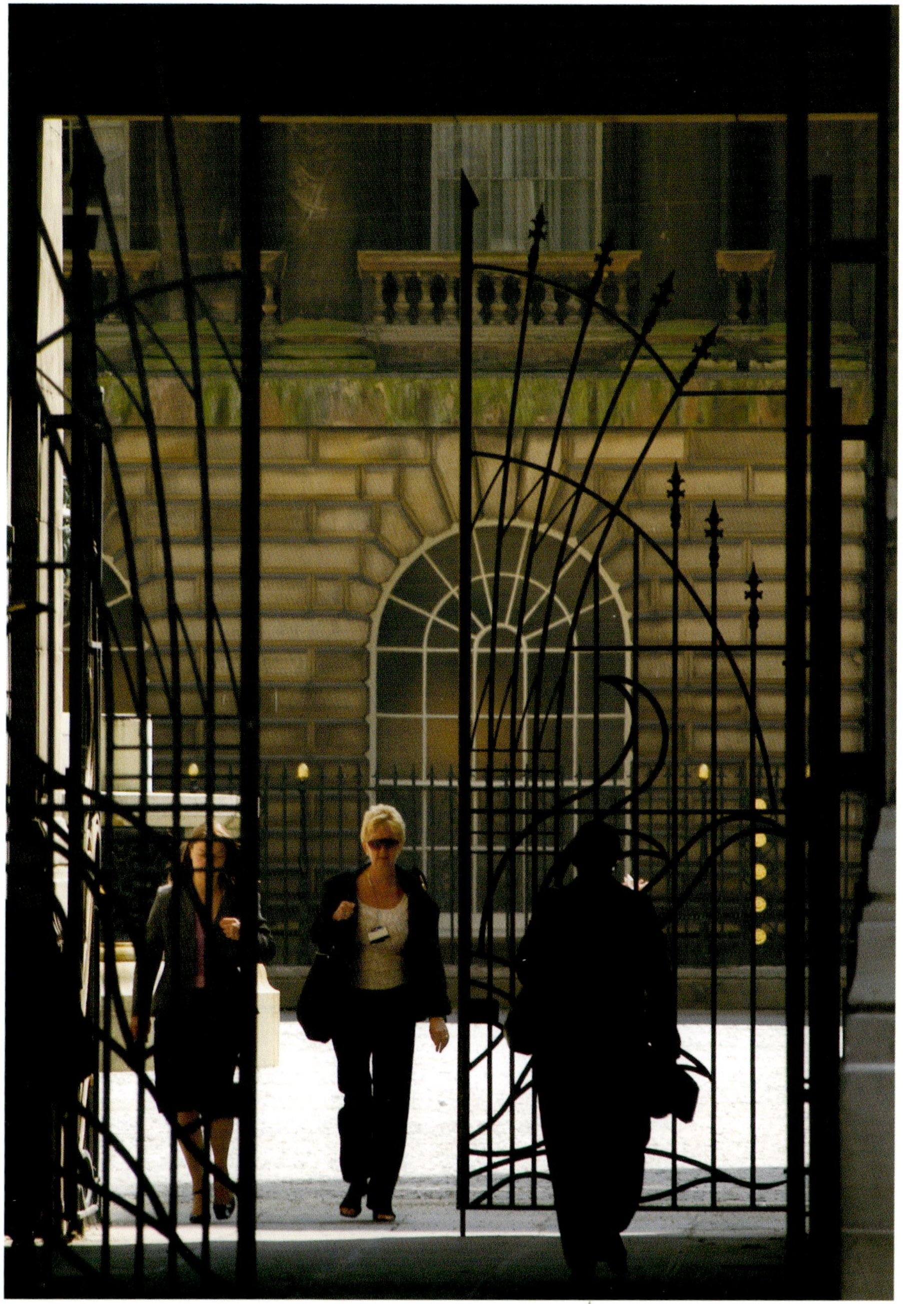

Gateway to commerce
One of the alleyways between Exchange Flags and Tithebarn Street. The wrought iron gates are rarely closed, because this is an important link between the two commercial parts of the city.

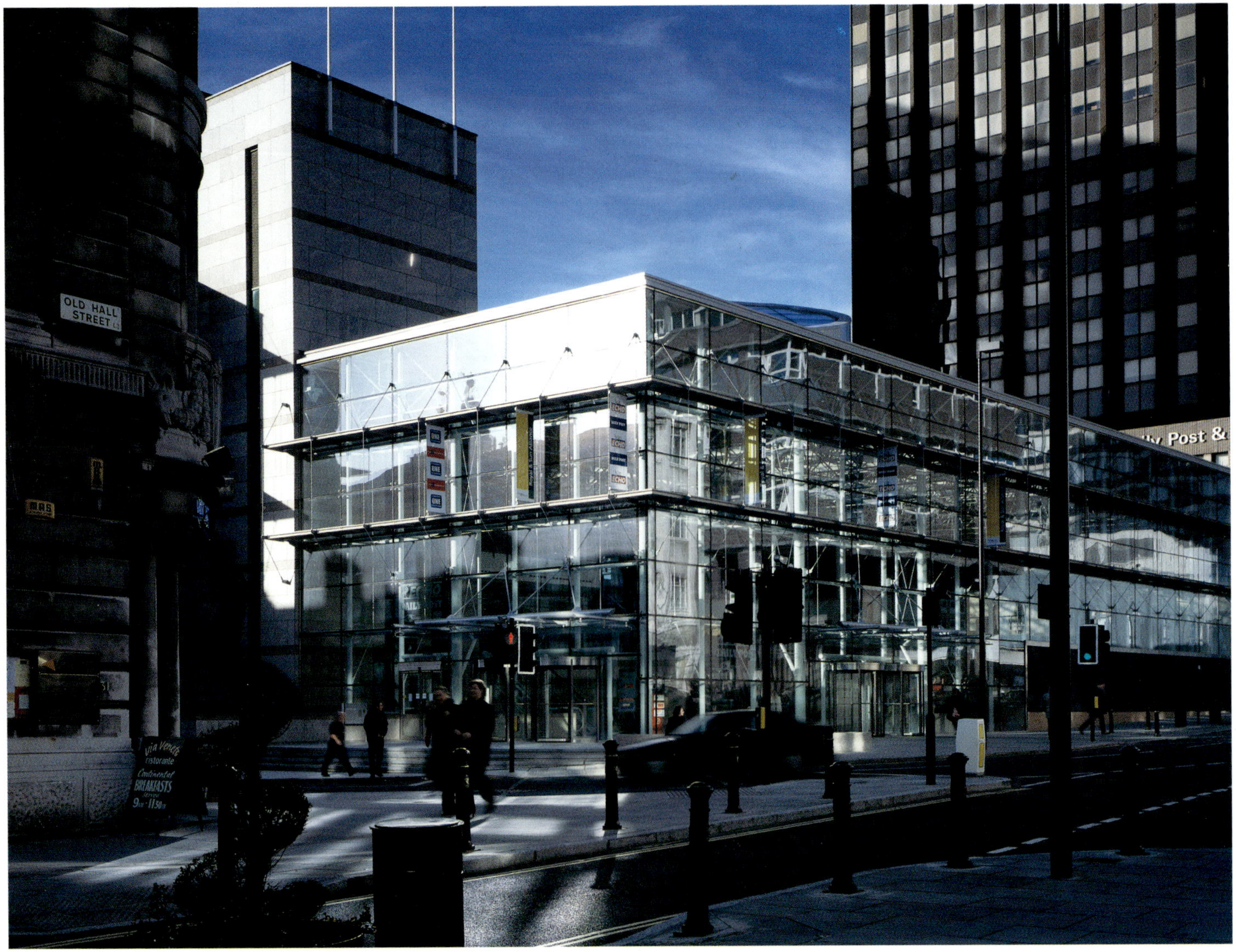

City Exchange

This new façade on the City Exchange was designed by architects KKA in 2001. This building houses the Royal Sun Alliance Insurance Company and the *Liverpool Daily Post and Echo* newspaper.

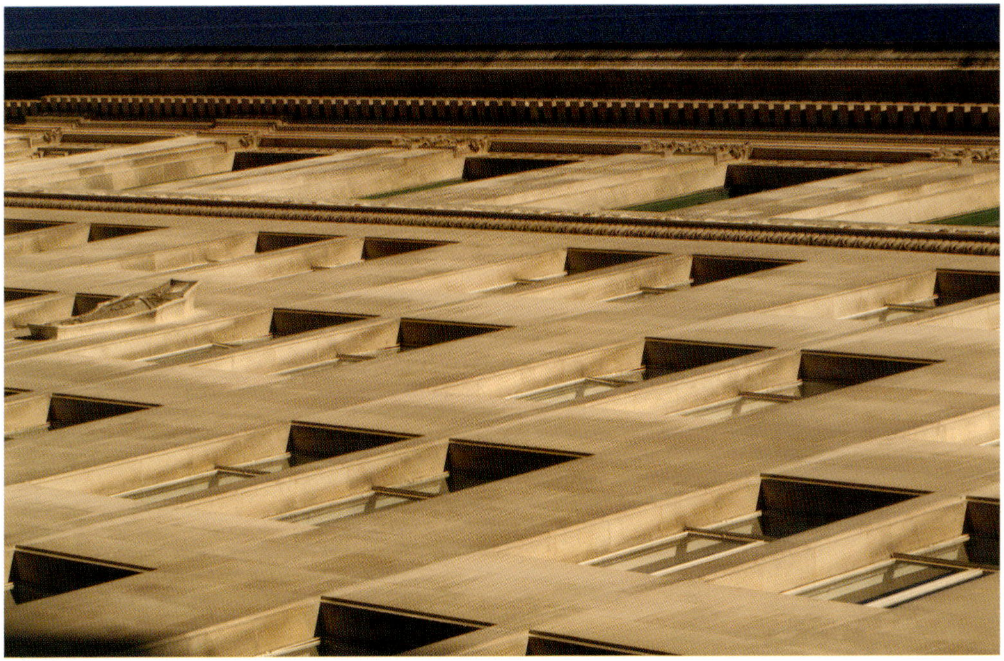

India Building

Designed in 1923 by Herbert Rowse, this is one of the largest office blocks in Liverpool, occupying an entire block between Water Street and Chapel Street. Originally, it was the offices of Alfred Holt & Co, owners of the famous Blue Funnel Line.

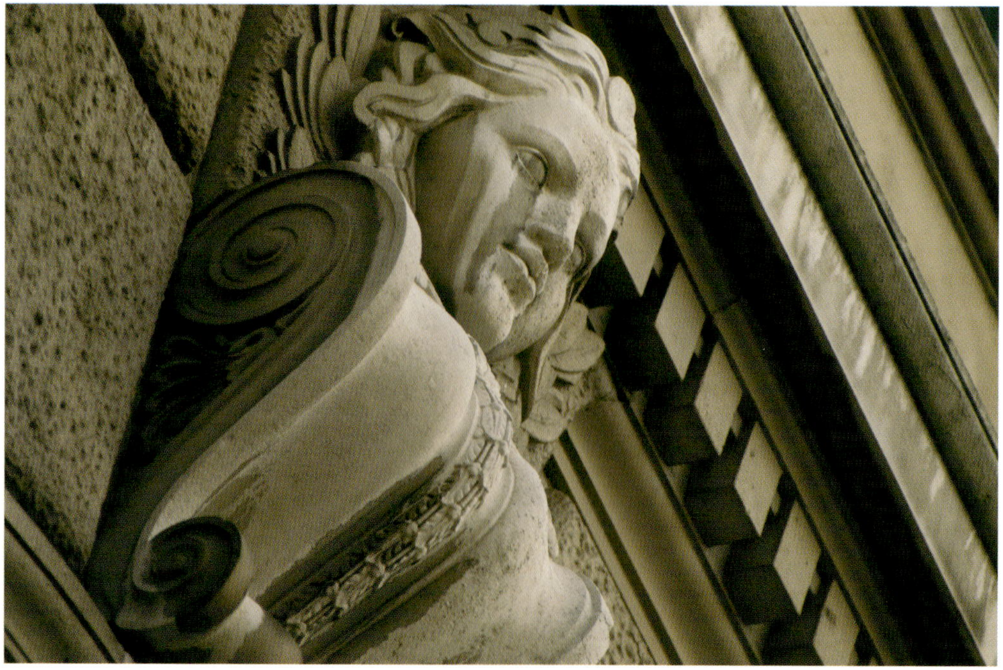

India Building

One of seven keystone heads on the India Building. This one is situated on Drury Lane, between Water Street and Chapel Street.

India Building Arcade
This vaulted arcade runs through the centre of the building from Water Street to Cook Street. Built between 1924 and 1932 for Alfred Holt & Co., owners of the Blue Funnel Line, the designers hedged their bets by incorporating the possibility of turning the building into a warehouse, should the offices have proved difficult to let.

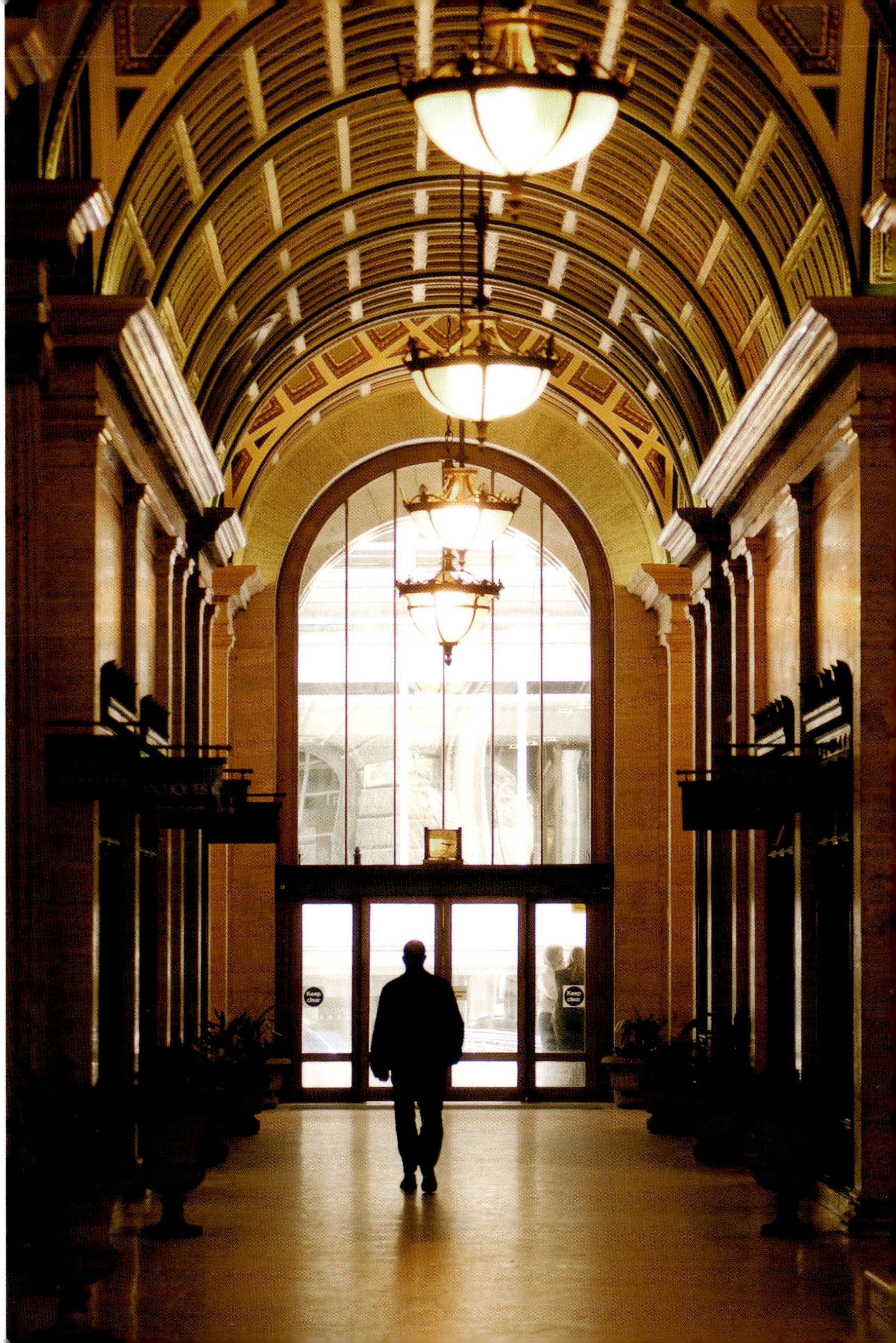

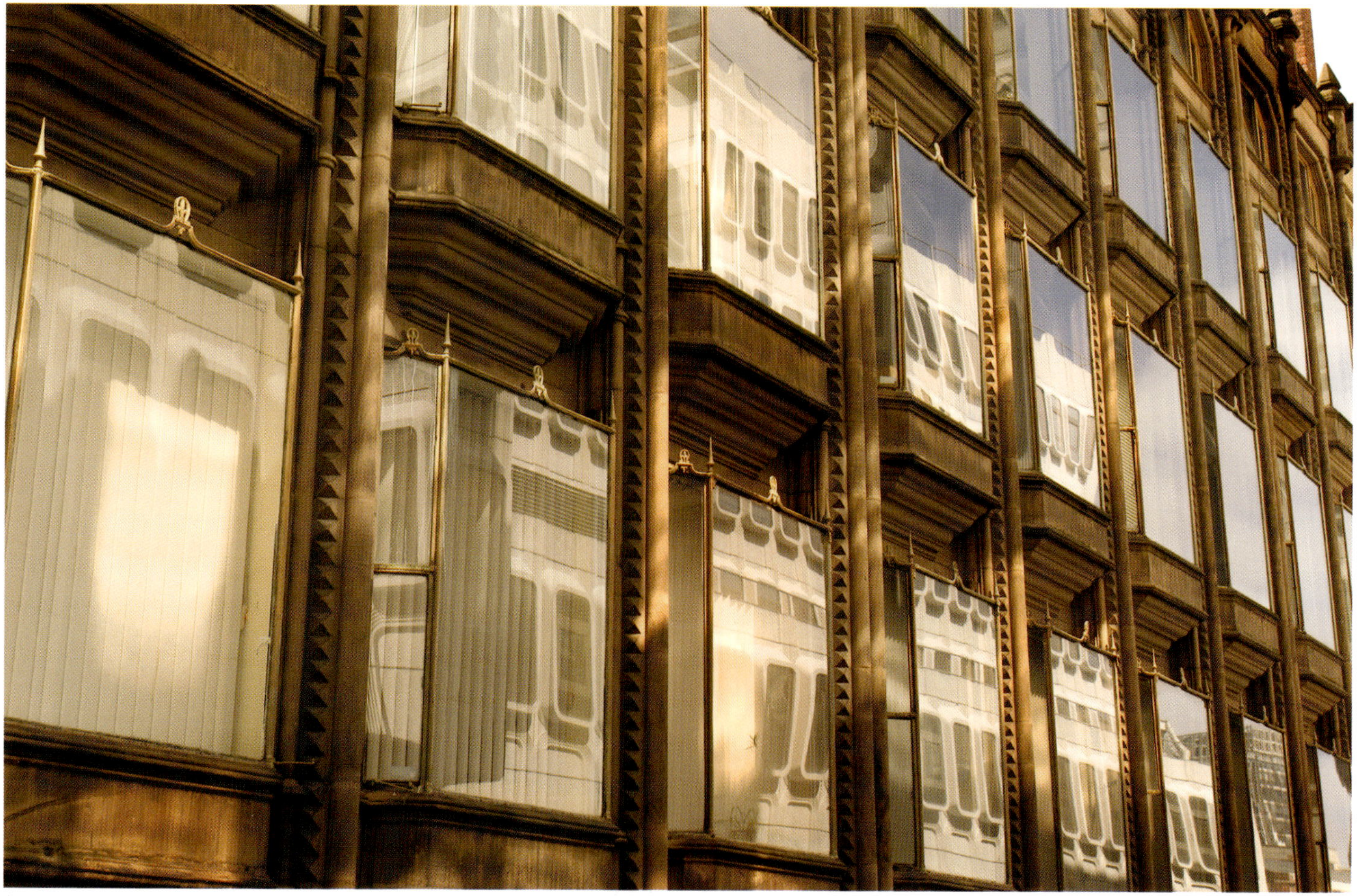

Oriel Chambers

Oriel Chambers stands opposite India Building on Water Street. It has been said that this building, built in 1864 to designs by Peter Ellis, is one of the most important in the world because of its structure. The façade is a very early example of cantilevered cladding design and although it was unpopular at the time of its completion, it predicted the Modern Movement in architecture.

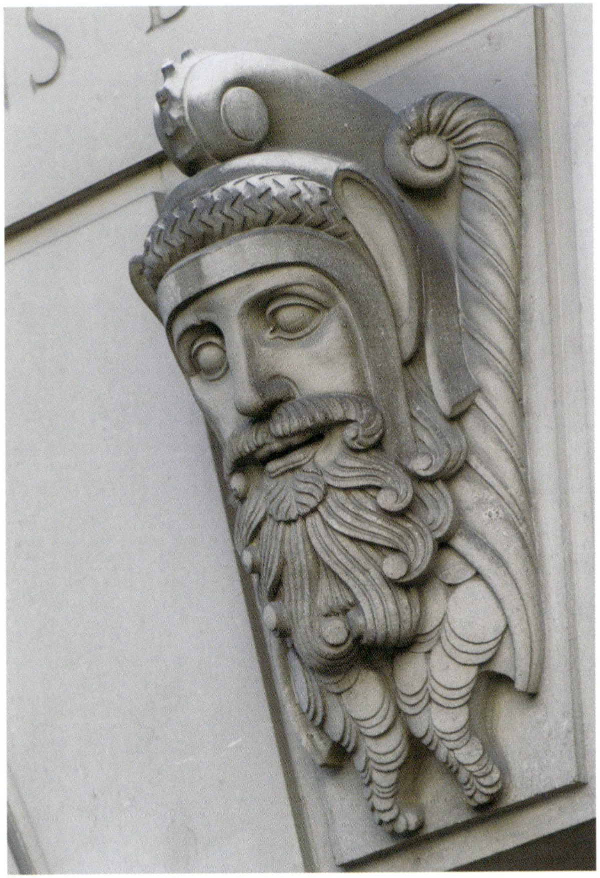

Keystone figure – Head of Midas

The head of Midas forms an appropriate keystone on the Martins Bank Building (built 1927/32) facing Exchange Flags and into the city.

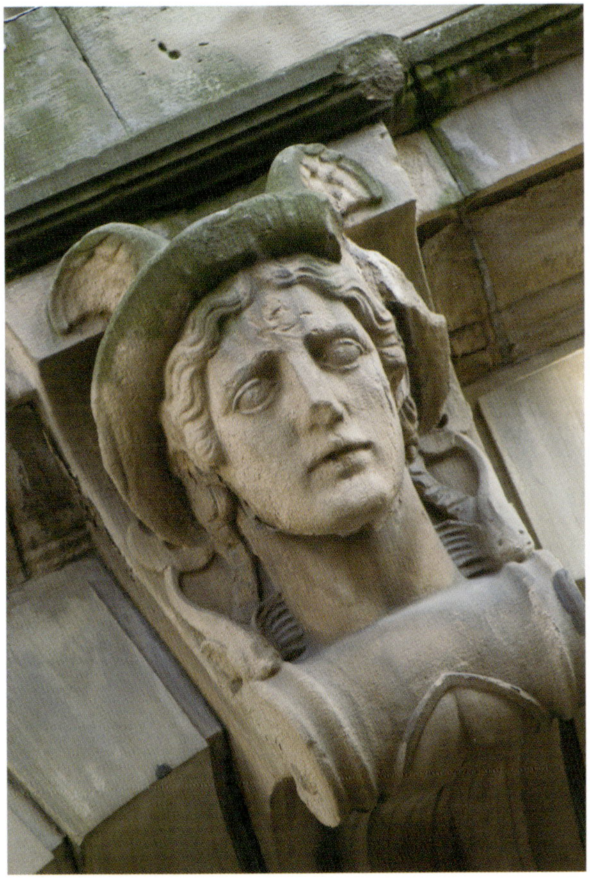

Figurehead on Liverpool & London Insurance Company building

This is now the Royal Bank of Scotland Building and faces Exchange Flags, looking towards the Waterfront and the Town Hall. The building was built between 1856-8 and the architect was C.R. Cockerell.

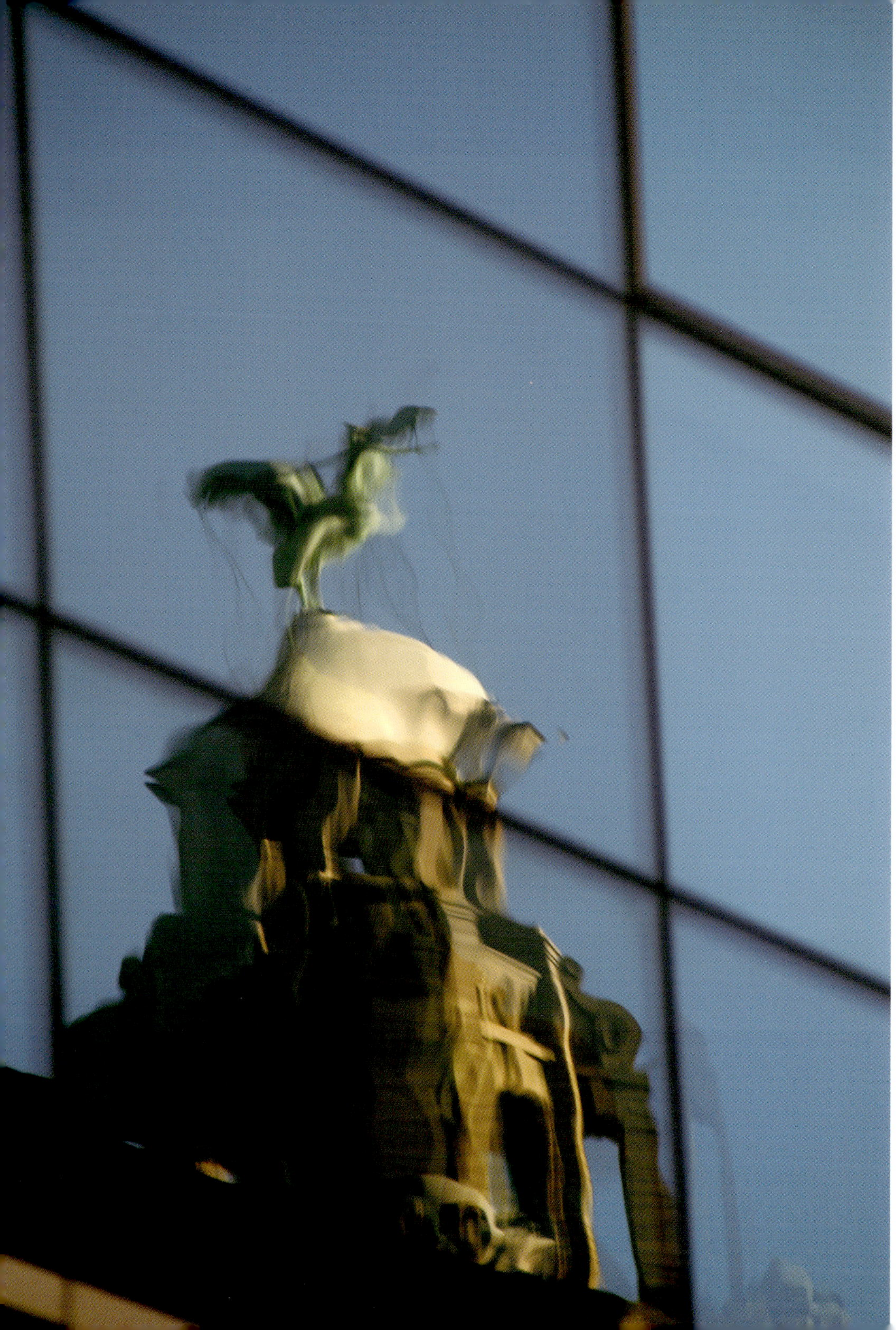

Abstract
The reflection of one of the Liver Birds in one of the many office and apartment windows around the waterfront.

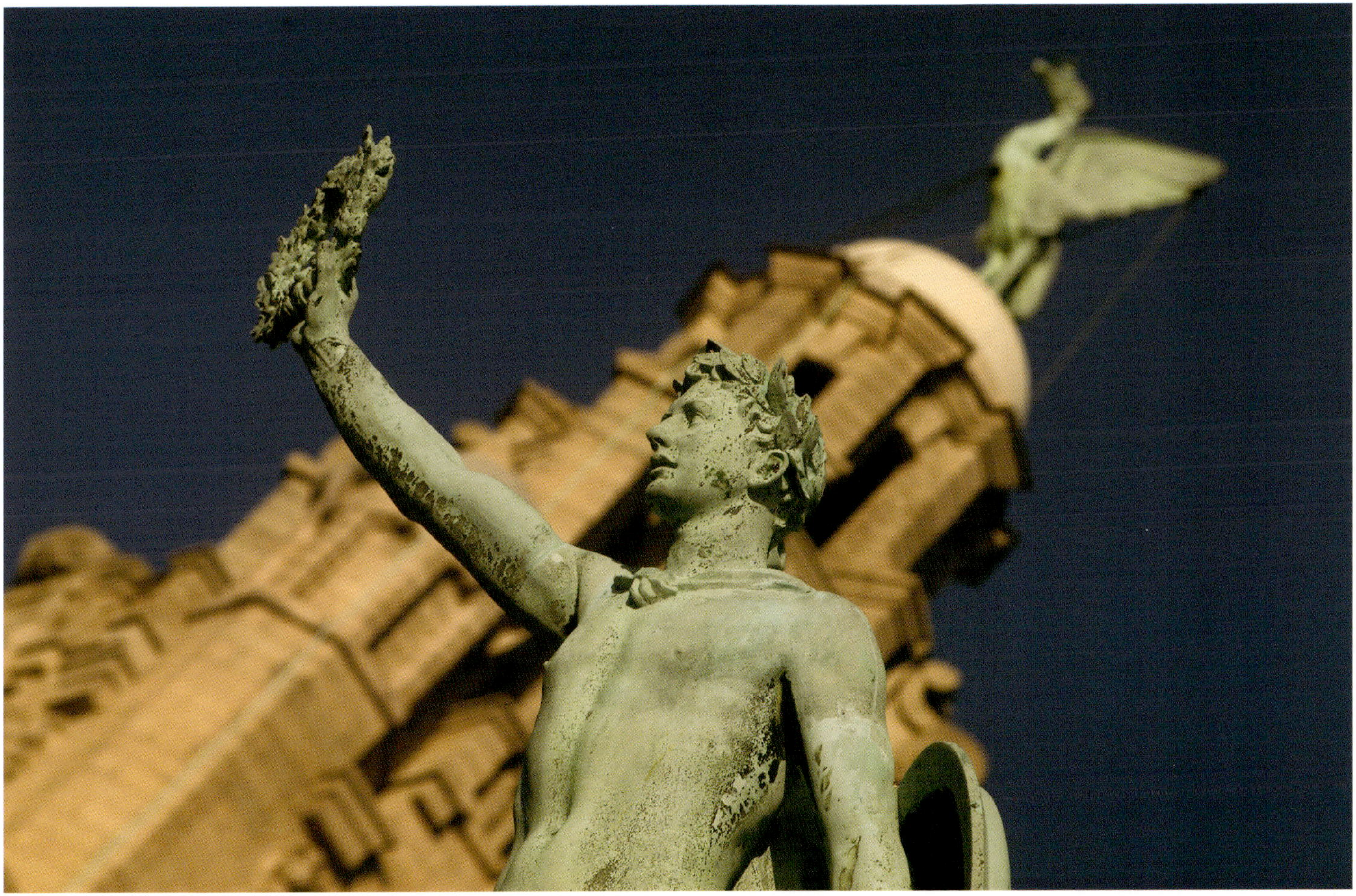

Cunard War Memorial

Unveiled in 1922 in front of the main entrance of the Cunard Building, this memorial not only commemorates the 134 Cunard employees who lost their lives in the Great War, it also remembers all those who served and survived. The memorial cost £4000 and was designed by A.J. Davis. The sculptor was Henry Pegram.

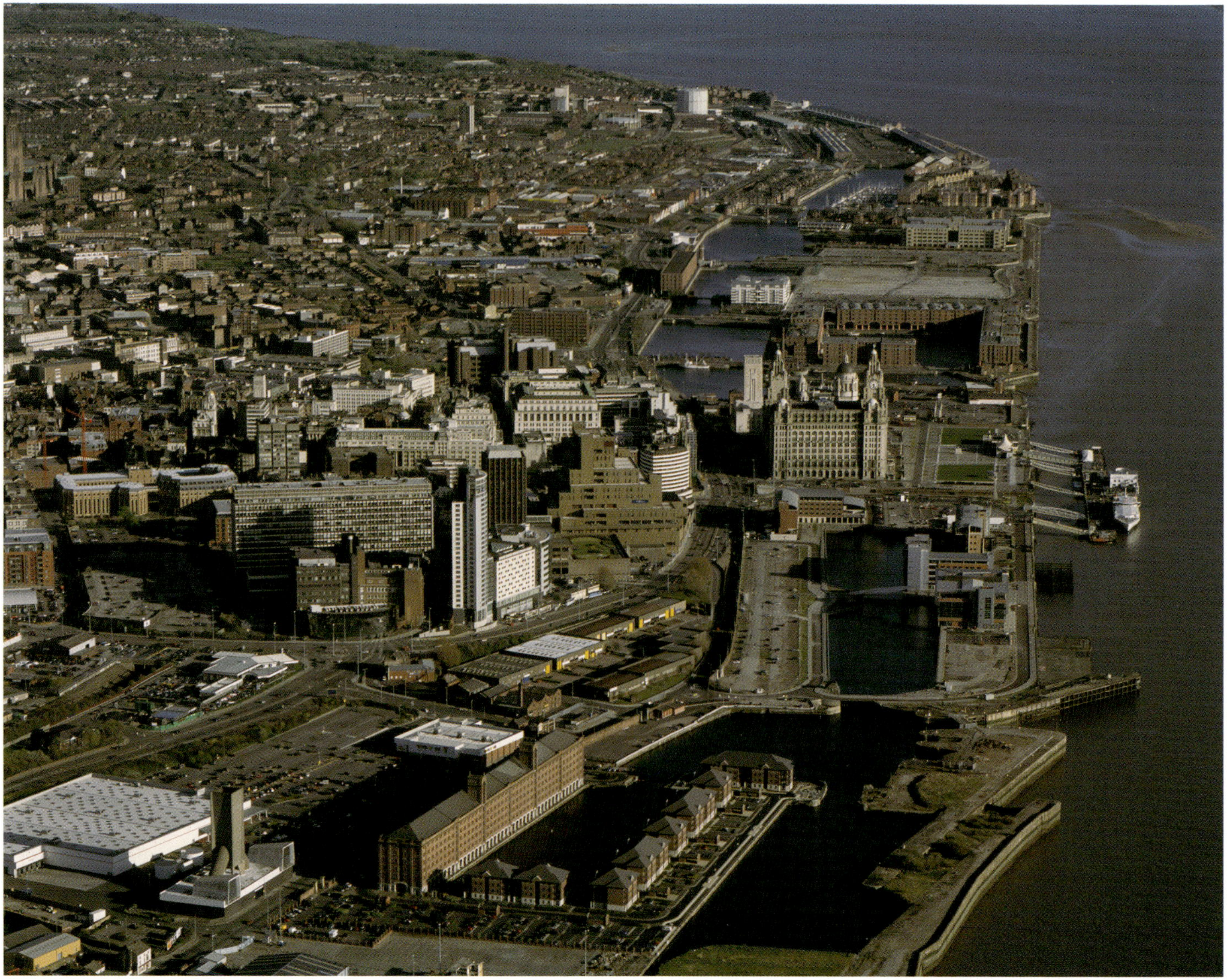

Aerial view of Liverpool from the North Docks

Waterloo Dock is in the middle foreground, followed by Prince's Dock then the Pier Head and beyond that Albert Dock, King's Dock and Coburg Dock. The whole of this area is currently undergoing extensive refurbishment for commerce, living and leisure.

Liver Bird
One of the two famous Liver Birds which stand at over 100 metres above the city on top of the towers of the Royal Liver Building. One faces into the city while the other faces across the Mersey to the Wirral. Each bird is identical and they both stand 6 metres high. The heads are just over a metre in length and the wings are 3 metres long. The mythical birds are made of hammered copper plates bolted together on a structure of rolled steel joists. The designer was Carl Bernard Bartels (1866 – 1955) and the maker was George Cowper and the Bromsgrove Guild. During the xenophobia of the First World War, Bartels' contribution was erased from the records because he was of German origin.

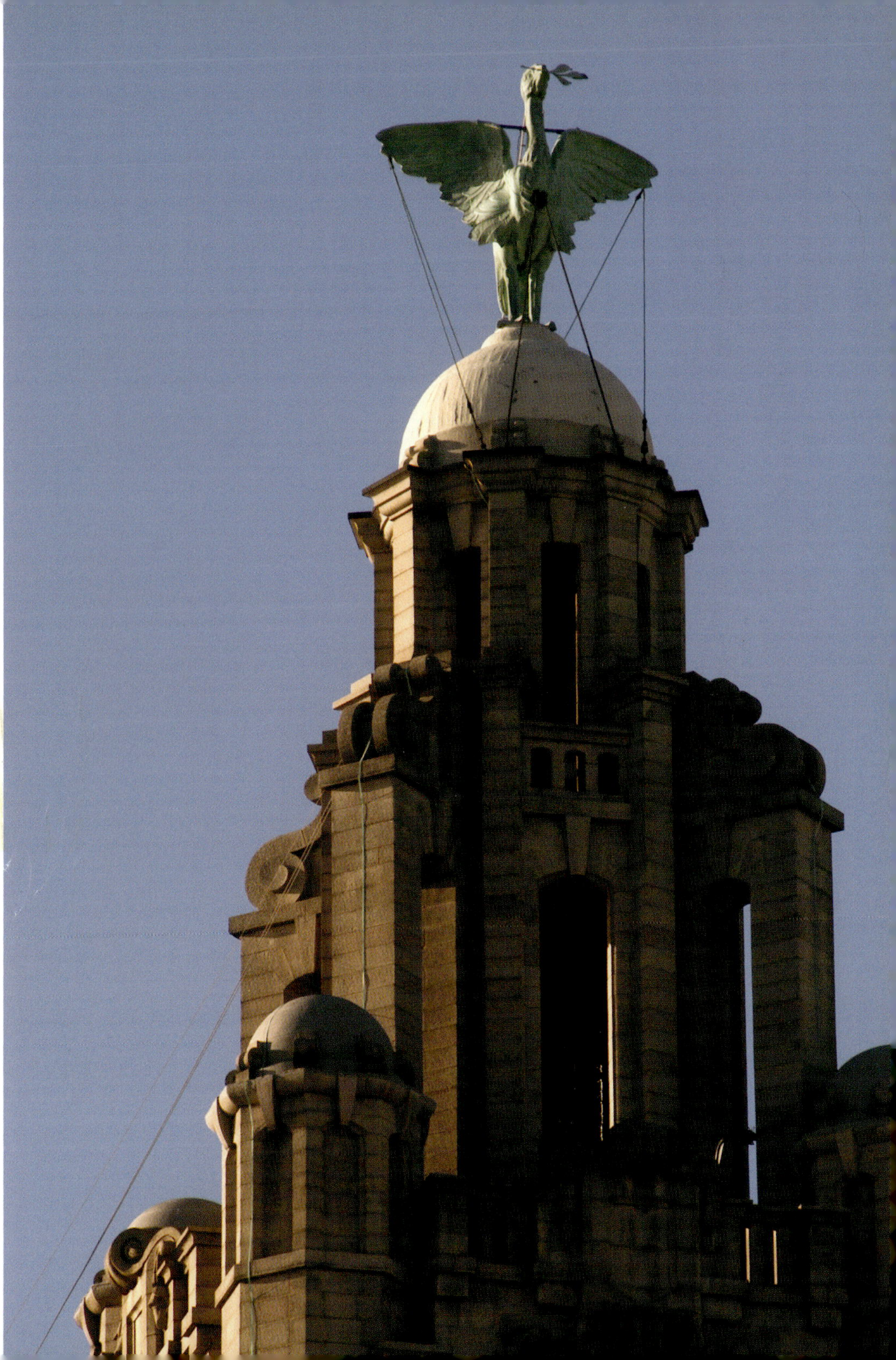

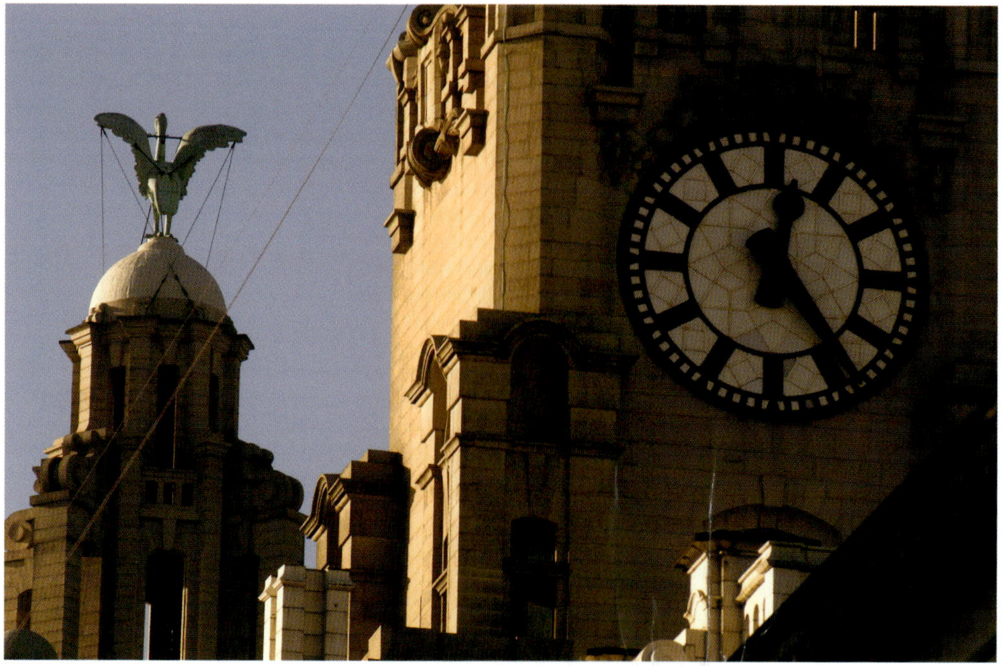

Royal Liver Building clock

Gents of Leicester were the builders of the famous clock. The face, which is over 25 feet in diameter, seated 40 guests at a dinner before its removal to Liverpool. The minute hand is over 14 feet long. At the time it was the largest electric clock in the UK. The clocks on the Royal Liver Building can be read from all parts of the city – and even from the Wirral on the other side of the Mersey. There are four clocks in total: three on the side facing the Mersey and the other one facing the city.

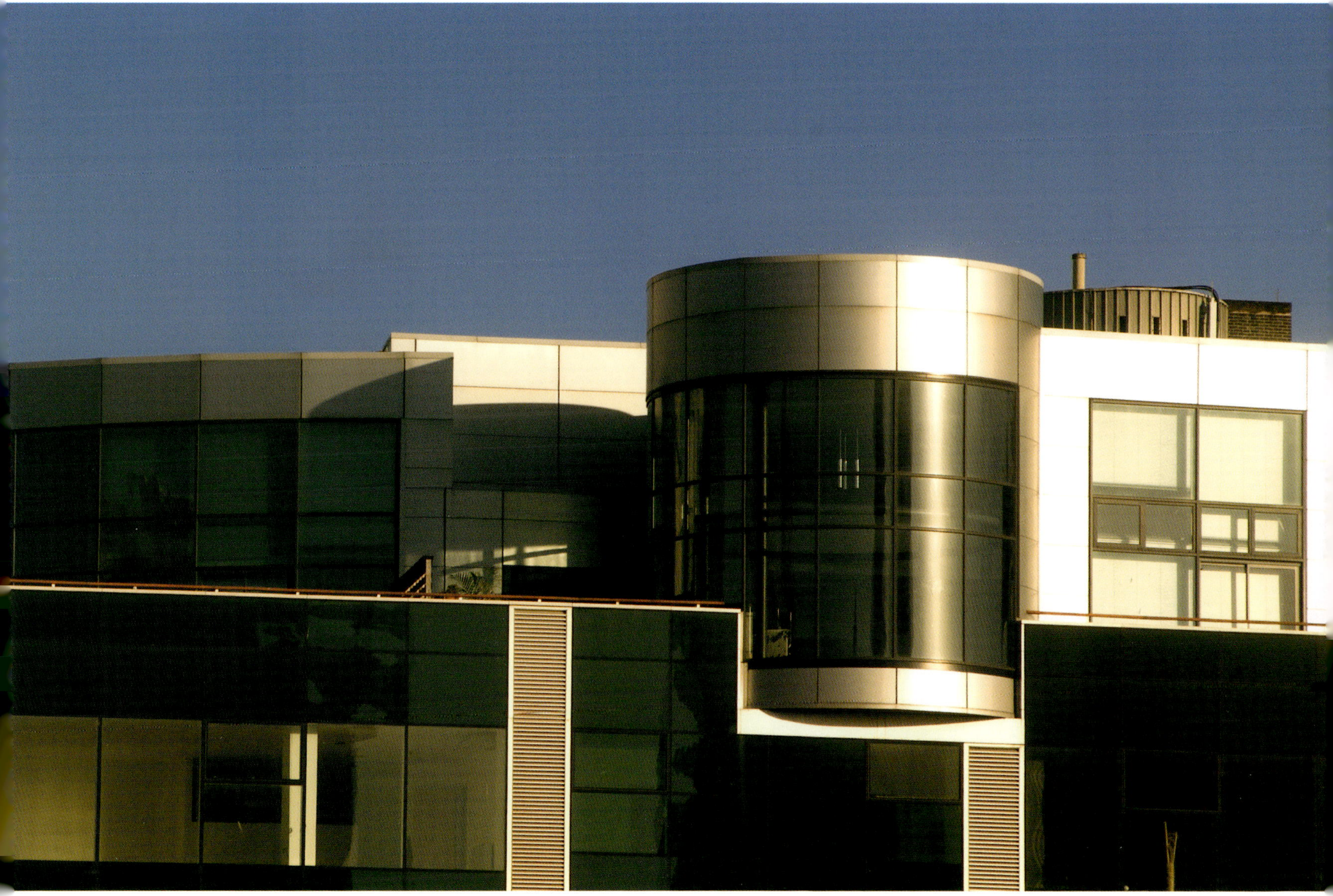

Beetham Plaza
One of the new luxury apartments above The Strand behind the Port of Liverpool and Cunard Buildings.
It was reputed to include the first £1million apartment in Liverpool when it was completed in 2001.

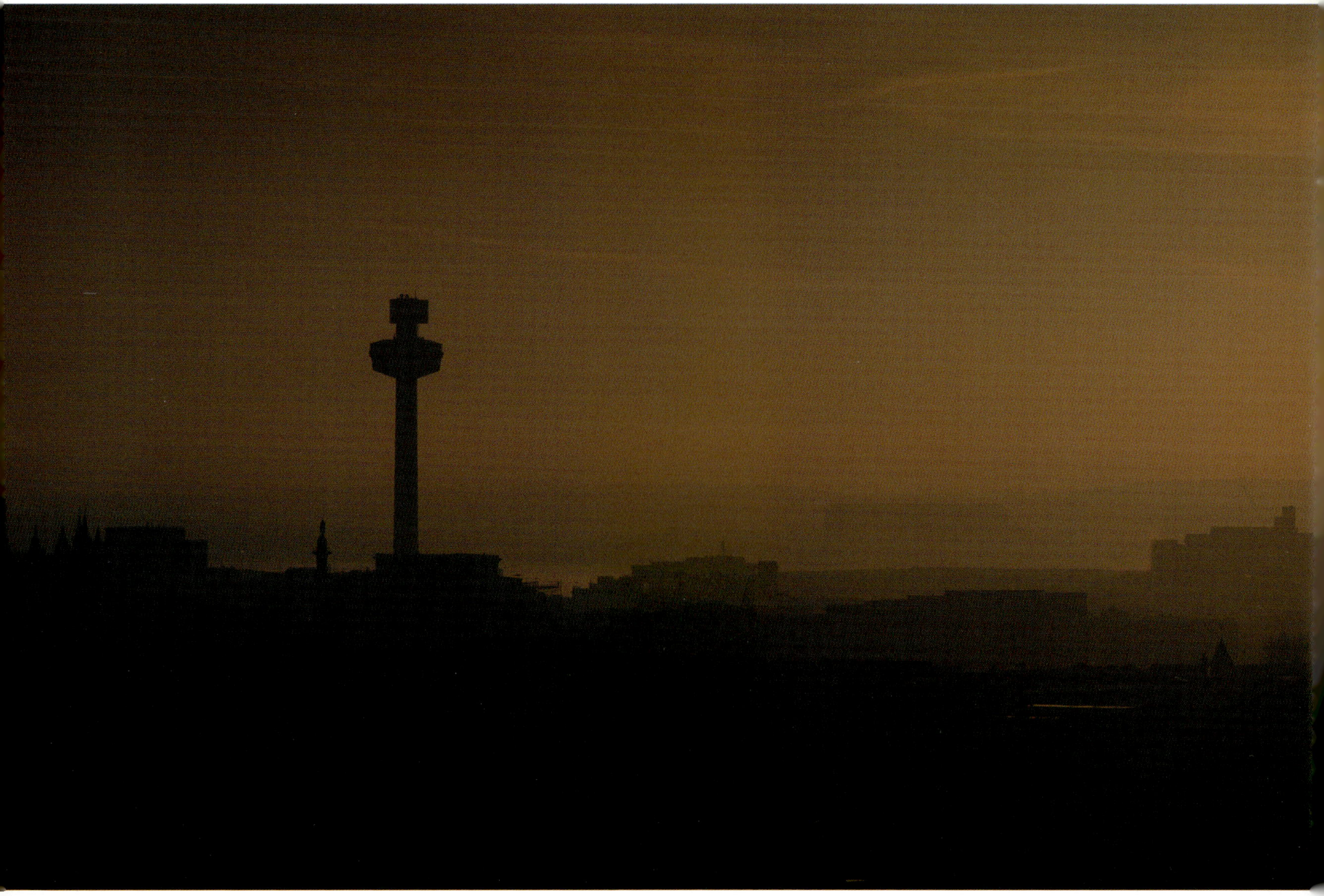

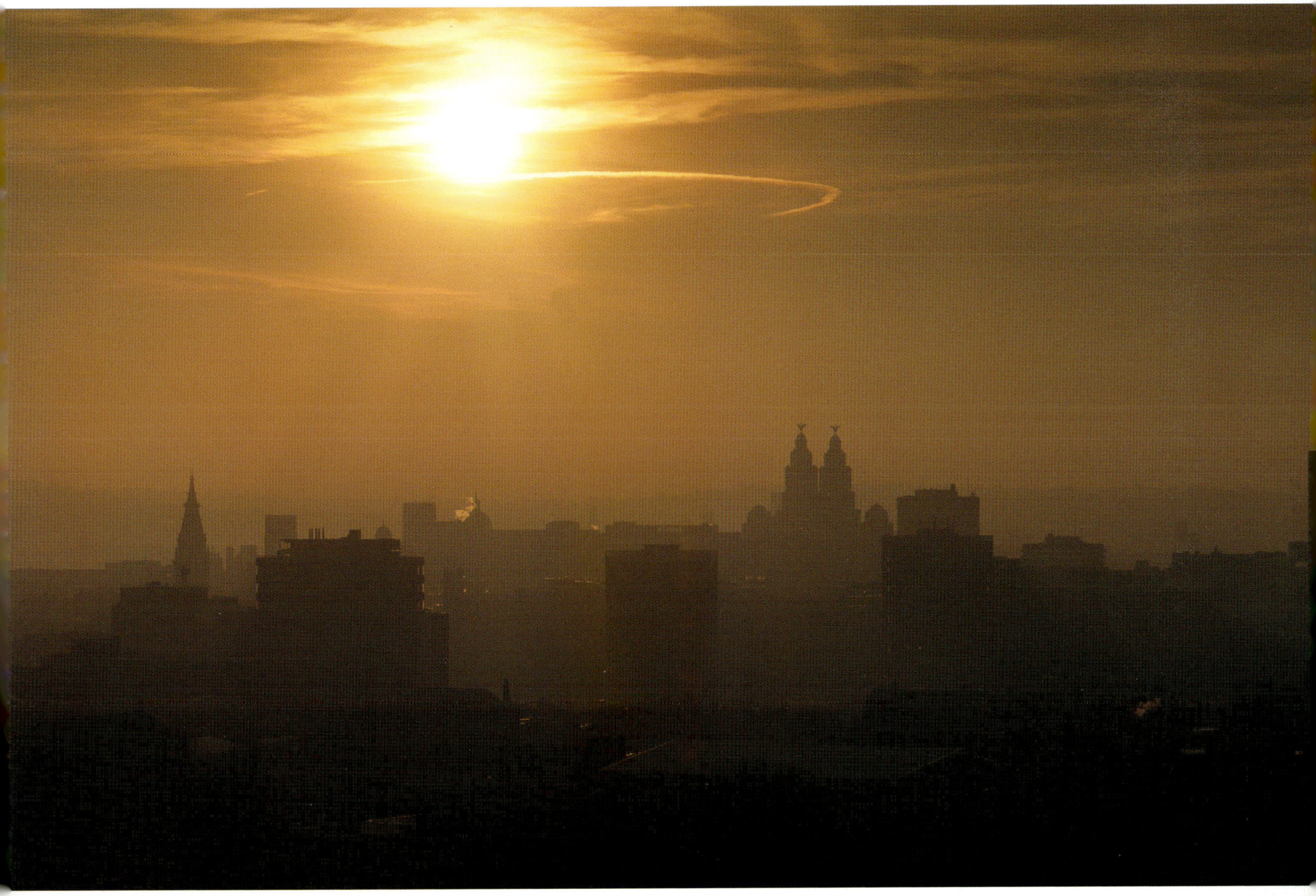

Winter sunset
A winter sun going down from Everton Brow on the outskirts of the city.

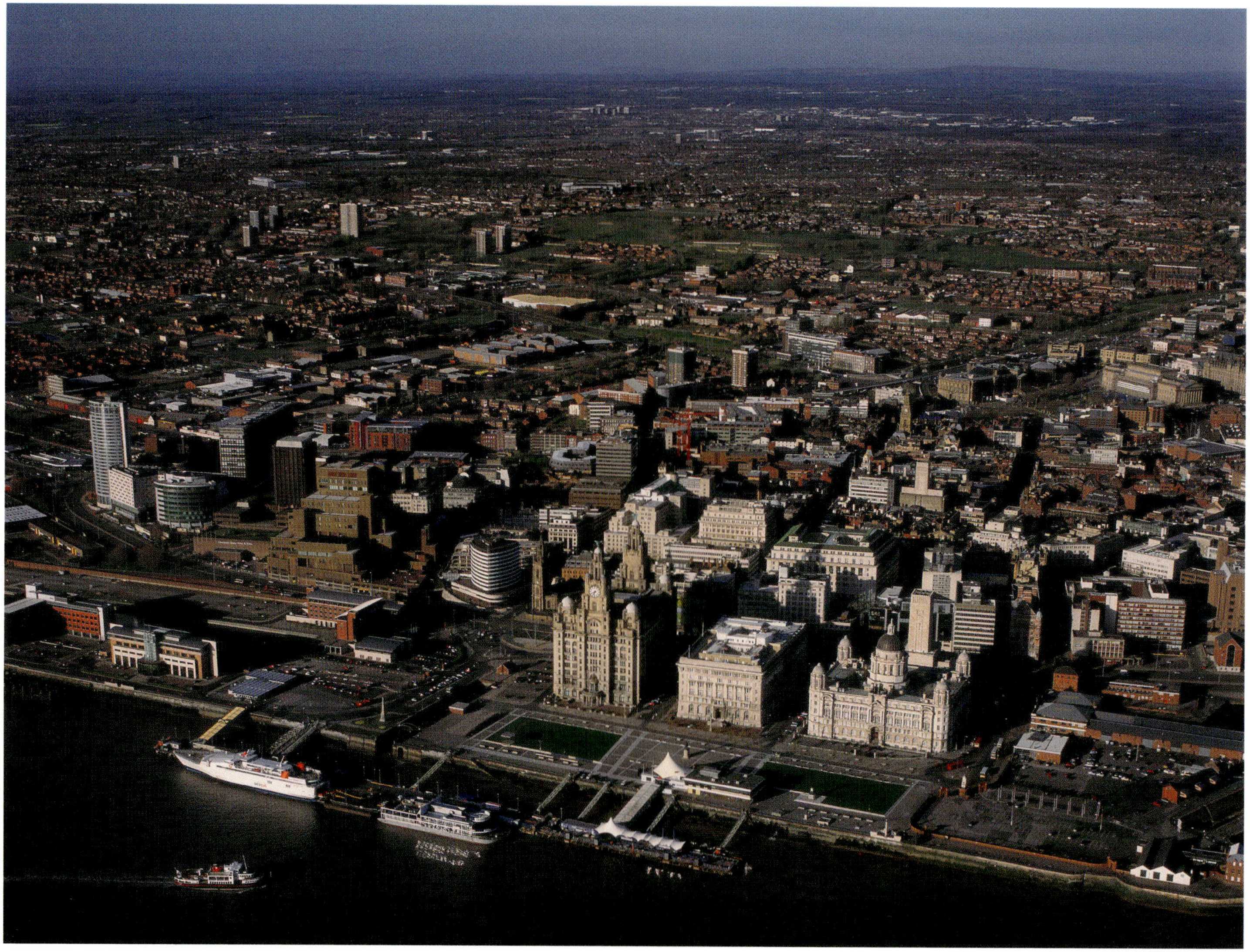

Aerial view of the Waterfront

With the outskirts of the city spreading eastwards into the county of Lancashire, the grounds of the city's two great football clubs, Everton and Liverpool, can be seen separated by Stanley Park.

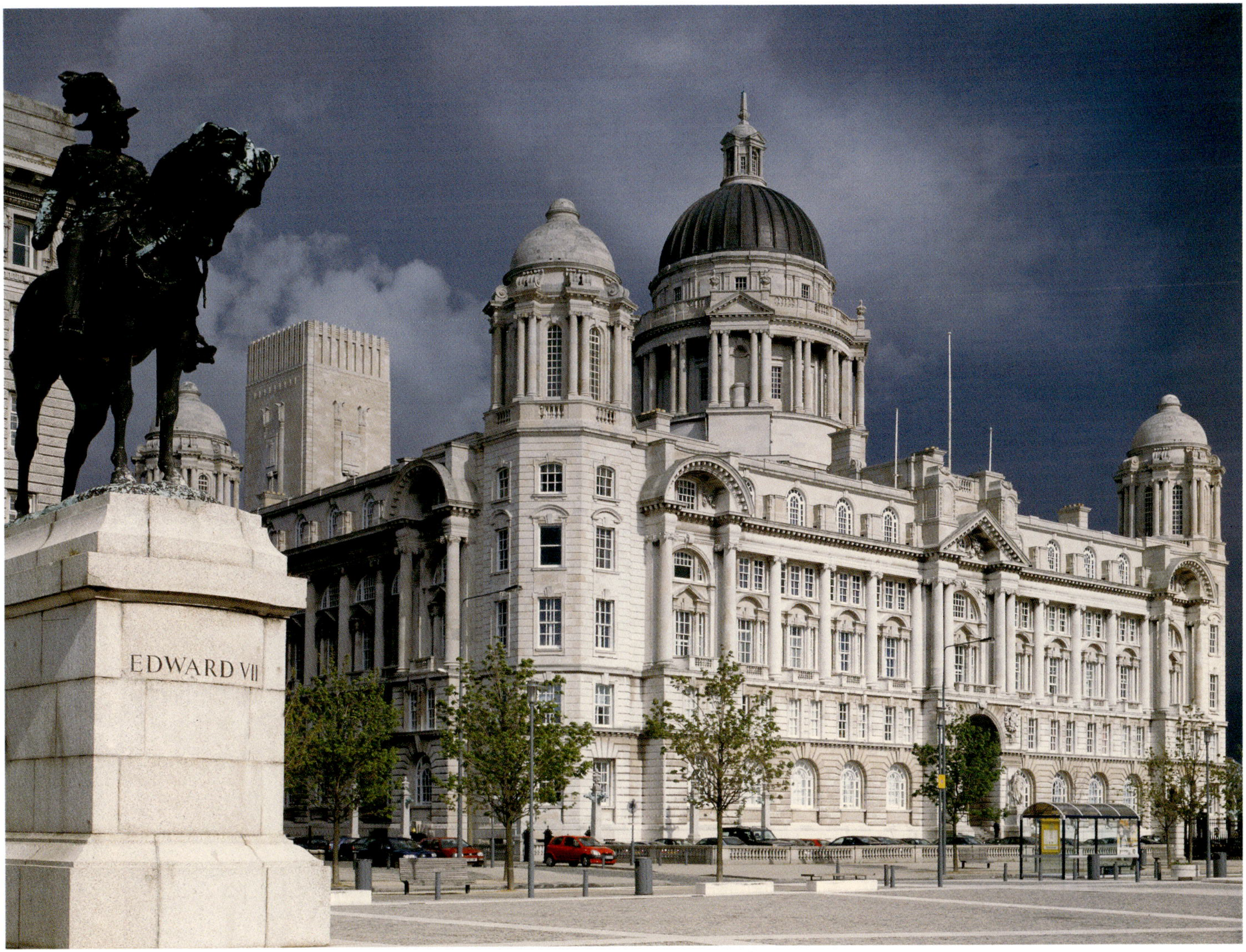

The Port of Liverpool Building

One of the famous Three Graces on the Liverpool Waterfront. Built for the Mersey Docks and Harbour Board, it was completed in 1907 and is now owned privately following MDHB's office move to Seaforth. The statue of King Edward VII was unveiled by his grandson, Edward, Prince of Wales in 1921.

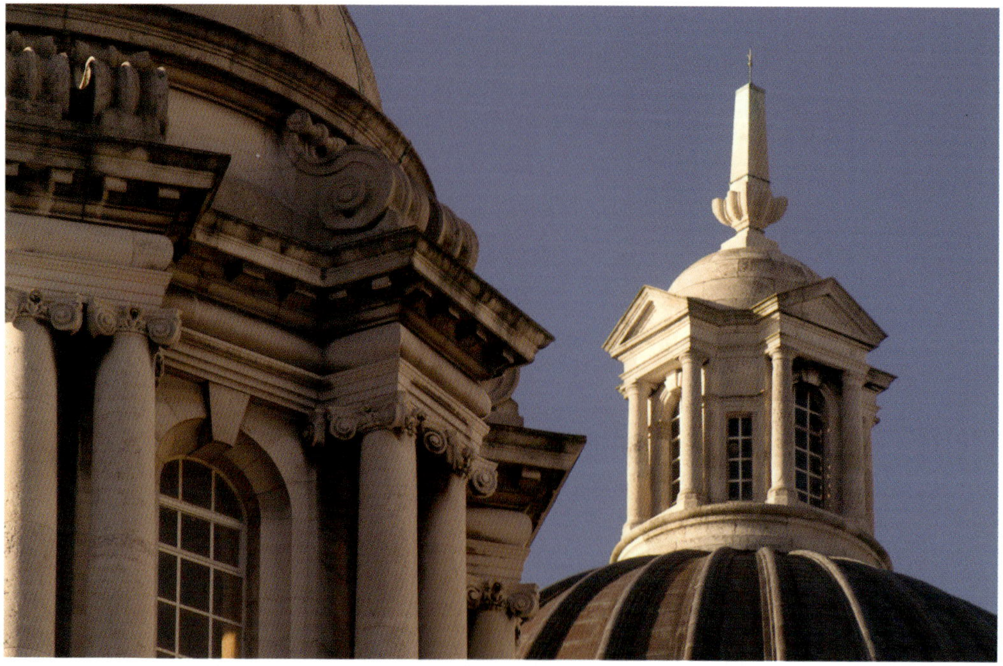

Mersey Docks and Harbour Board Building (detail)
Now the Port of Liverpool Building, it was built between 1903-07, and was the first of Liverpool's famous Three Graces. It bears a strong resemblance to Belfast City Hall.

The Port of Liverpool Building ***(right)***
The view into the dome from the ground floor. Around the lower floor level reads the inscription: 'They that go down to the sea in ships, that do business in great waters. These see the works of the lord and his wonders in the deep. Anno Domini MCMVII.'

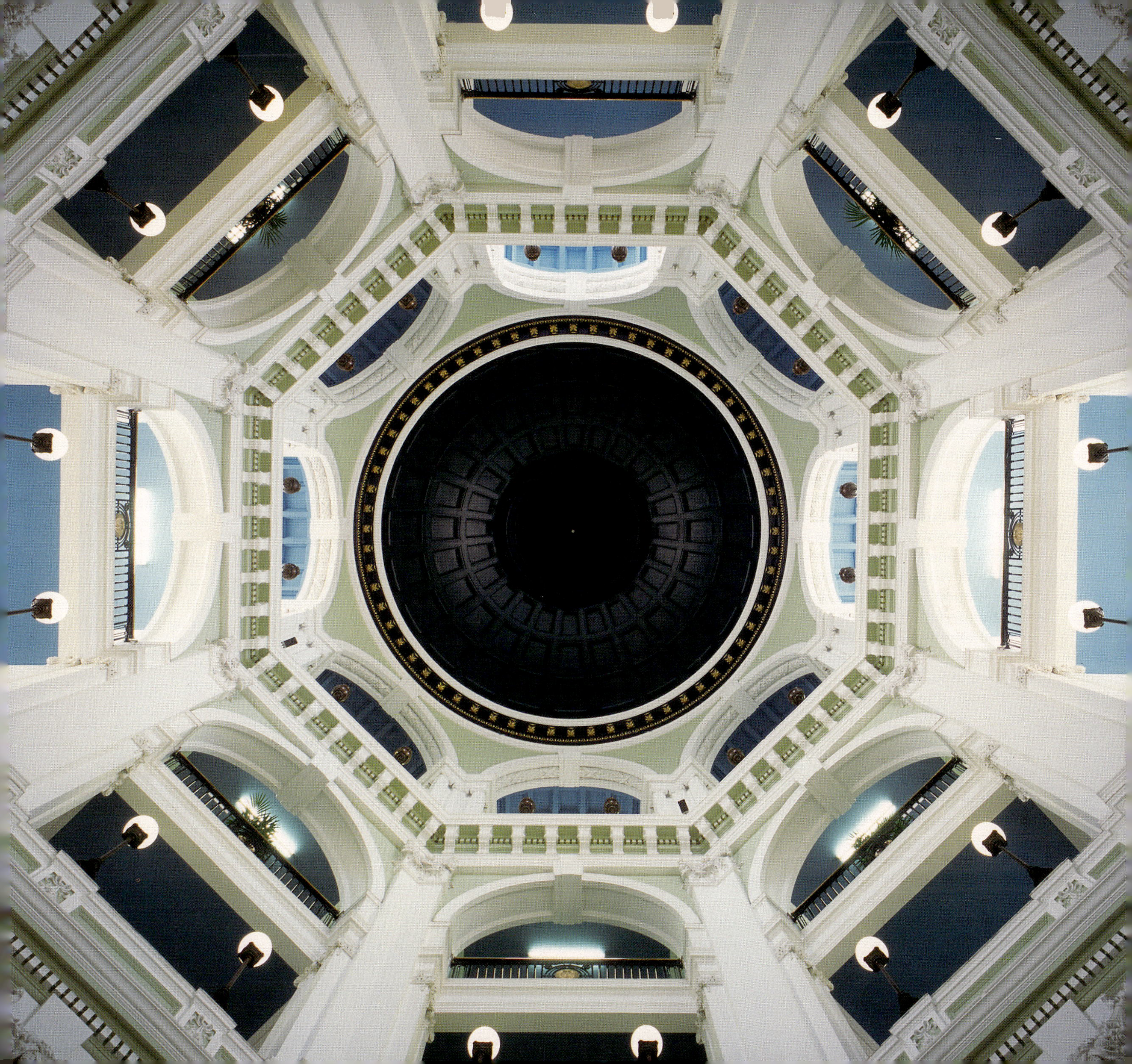

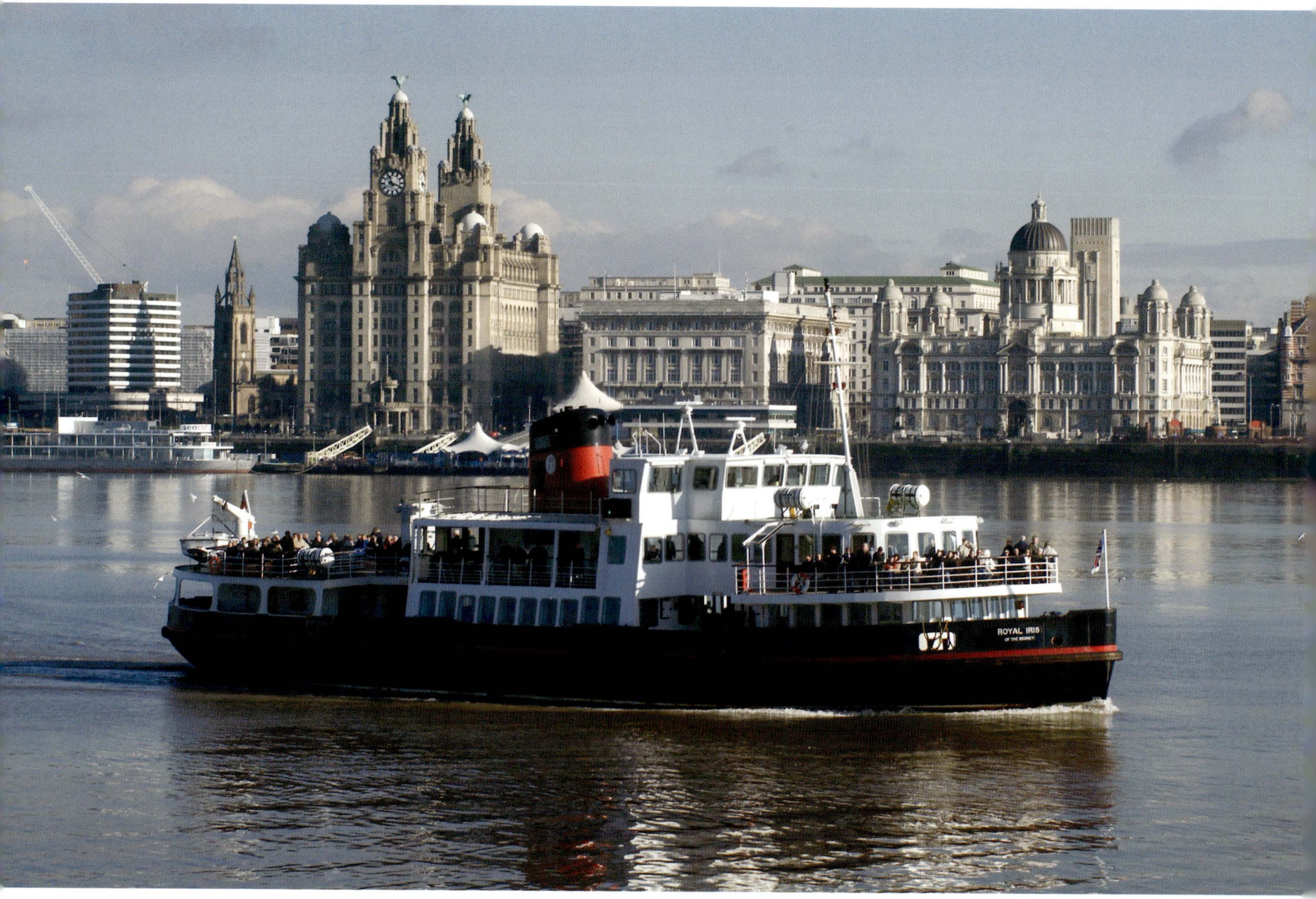

The *Royal Iris*

The *Royal Iris* glides gently on a still winter morning towards the Woodside Landing Stage. The Mersey Ferry Company operates all the year round, whatever the weather, and it also runs special cruises around the Mersey with an onboard commentary.

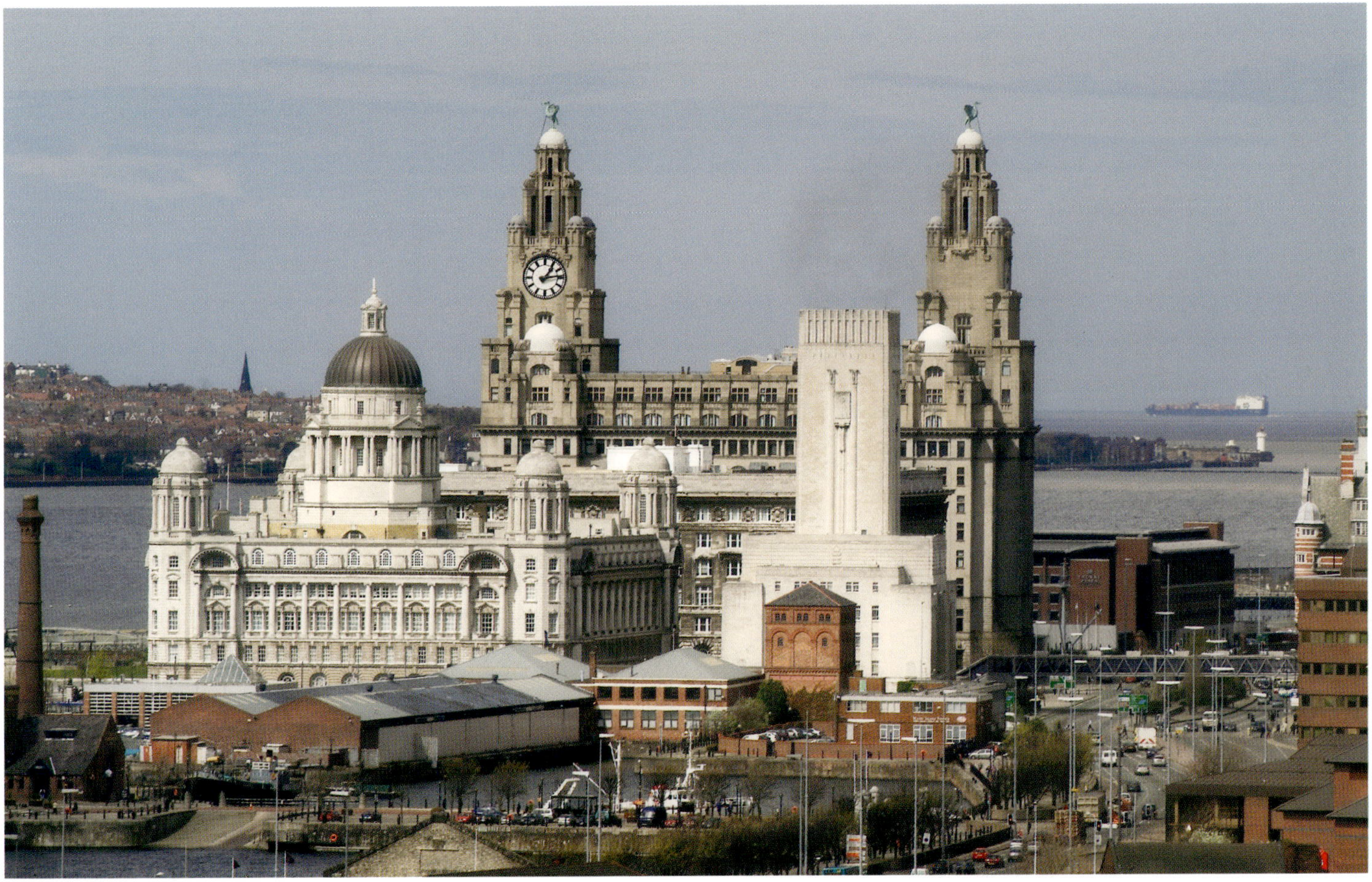

Liverpool Pier Head

Behind the Port of Liverpool Building stands the George's Dock Building, which covers the main ventilating shaft for the Mersey Tunnel. In the far distance you can just see the New Brighton Lighthouse at the mouth of the River Mersey, and beyond that is one of the ACL ships heading towards North America, having just left Royal Seaforth Dock.

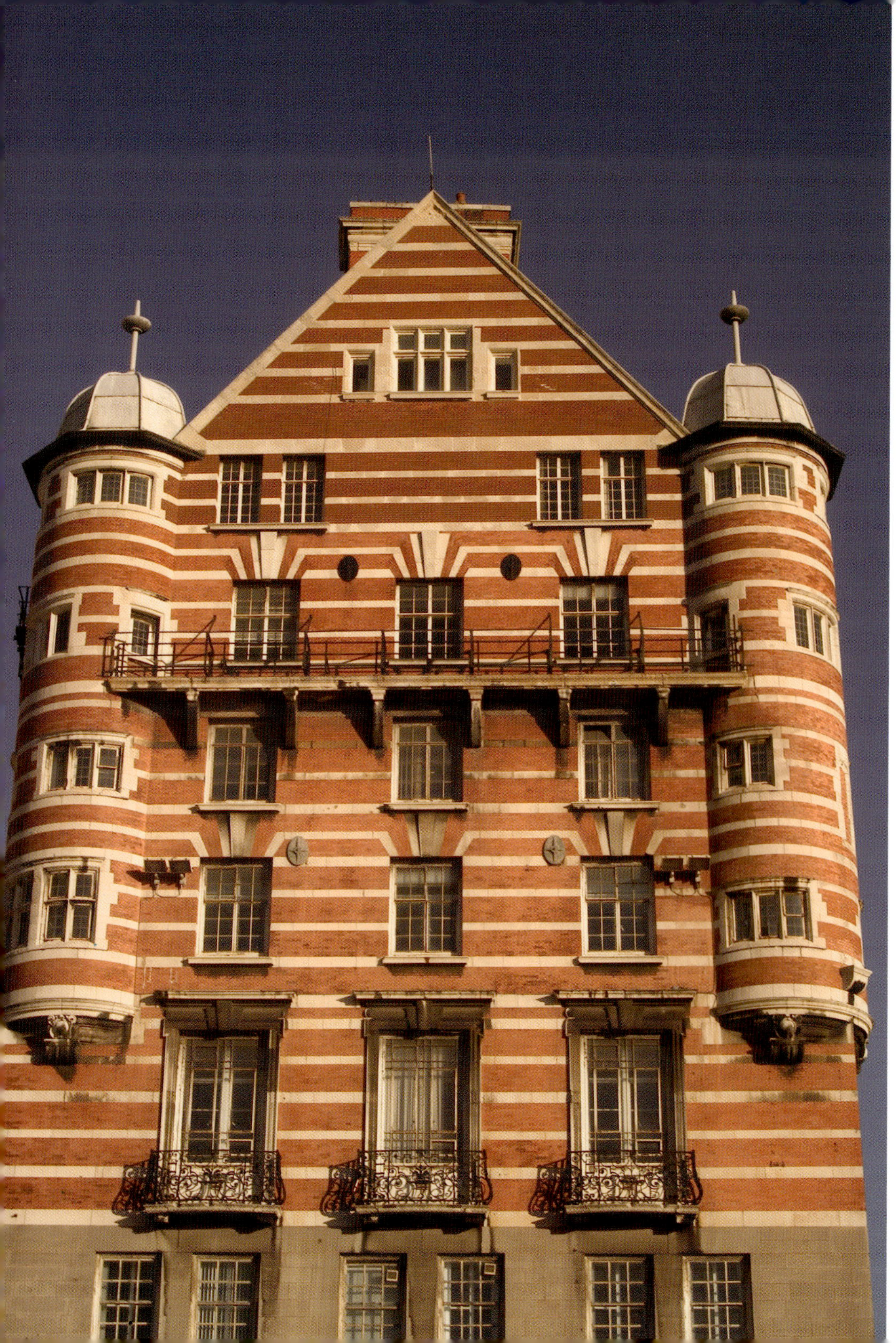

Albion House

Once famous as the White Star Shipping Line Offices, Albion House stands on the corner of James Street and The Strand. Designed by architects Shaw and Doyle, the building closely resembles New Scotland Yard in London. On hearing the news of the sinking of the *Titanic* in April, 1912, massive crowds gathered outside this building, and the clerks, concerned about their own safety, wrote the names of the surviving passengers and tossed the slips into the crowd.

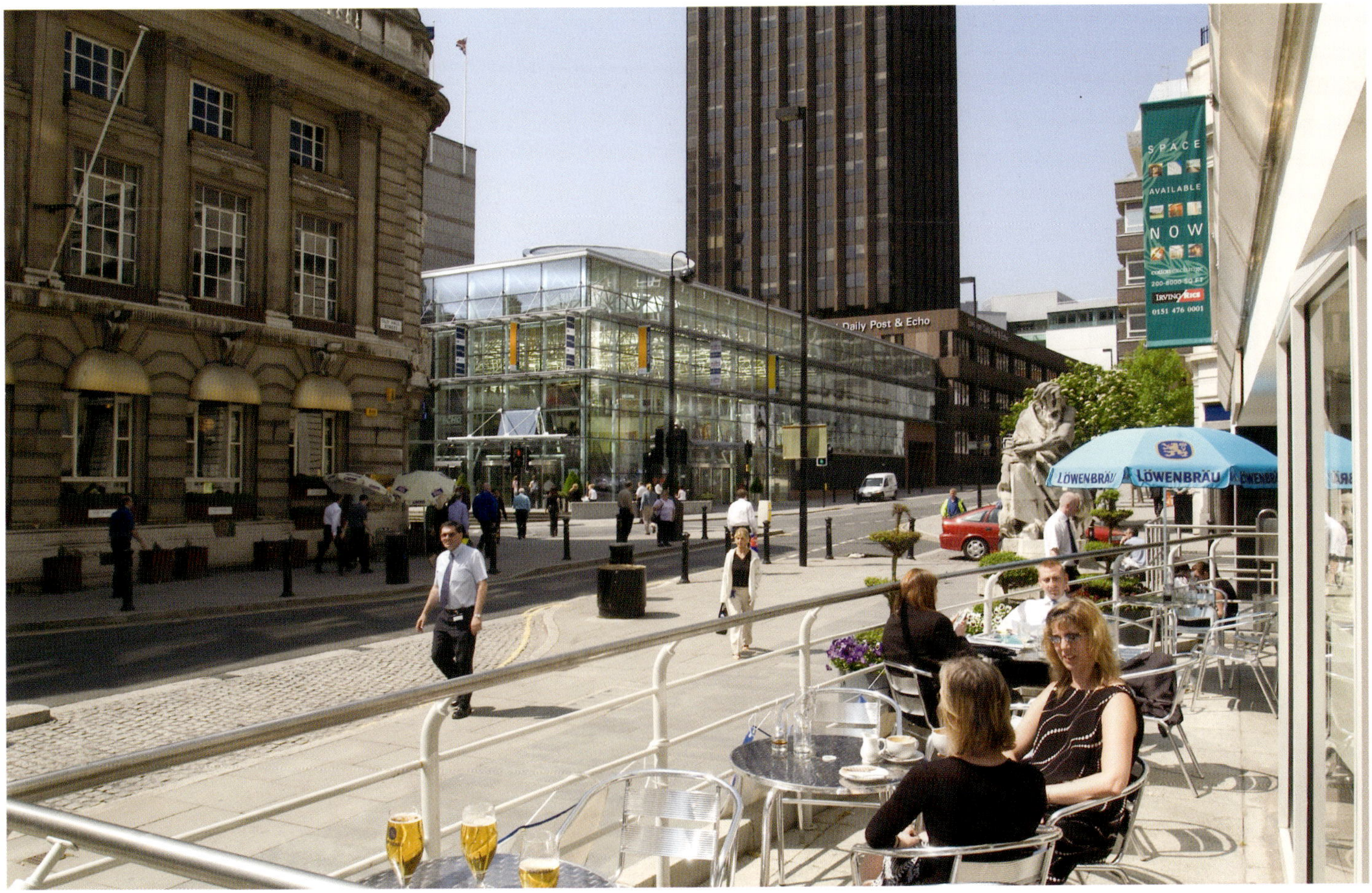

Café Bar on Old Hall Street

Looking towards the Royal and Sun Alliance Building and *Liverpool Daily Post & Echo* building. Liverpool now has an abundance of bistros and coffee bars, often offering open-air eating, especially at lunchtime in the summer months.

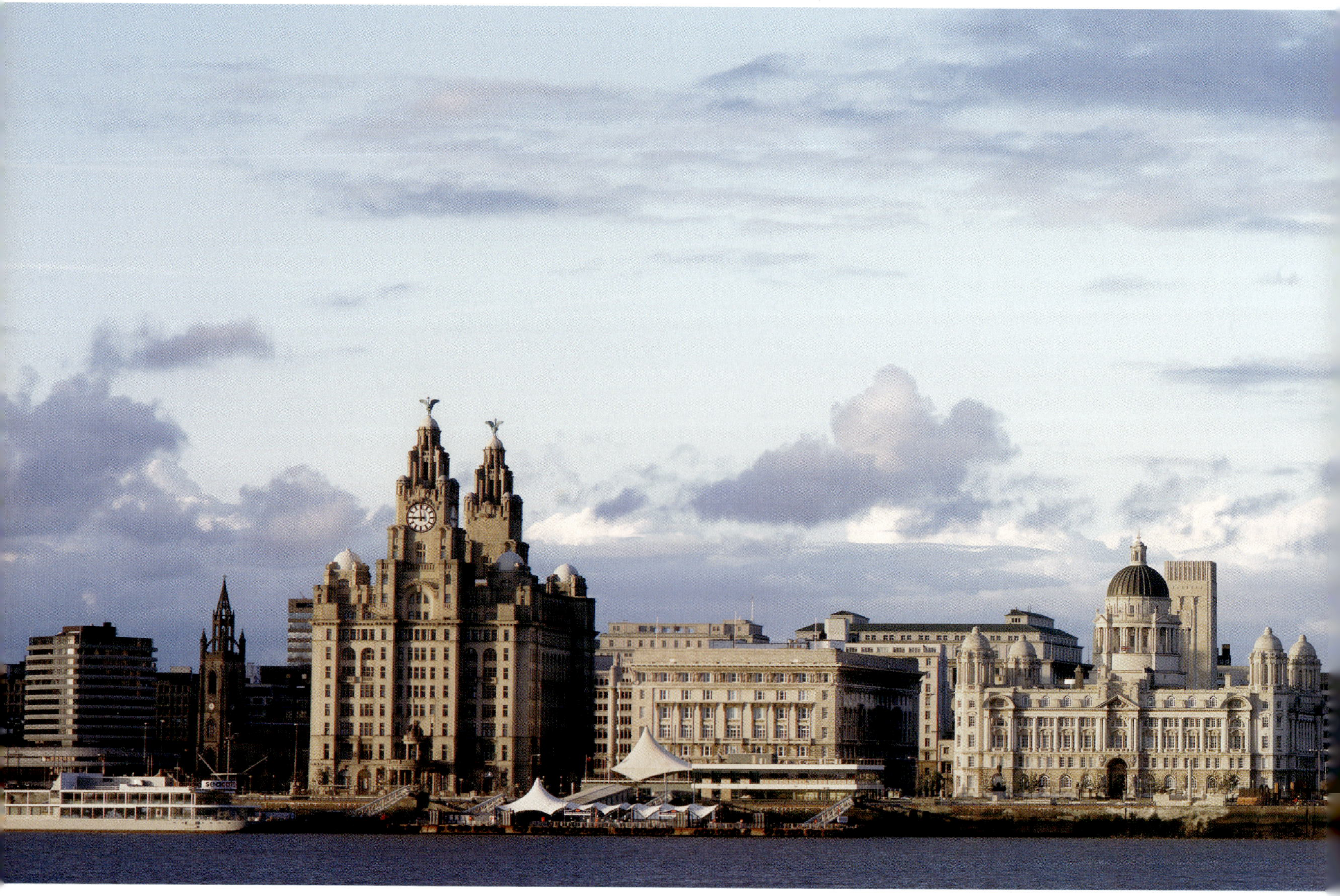

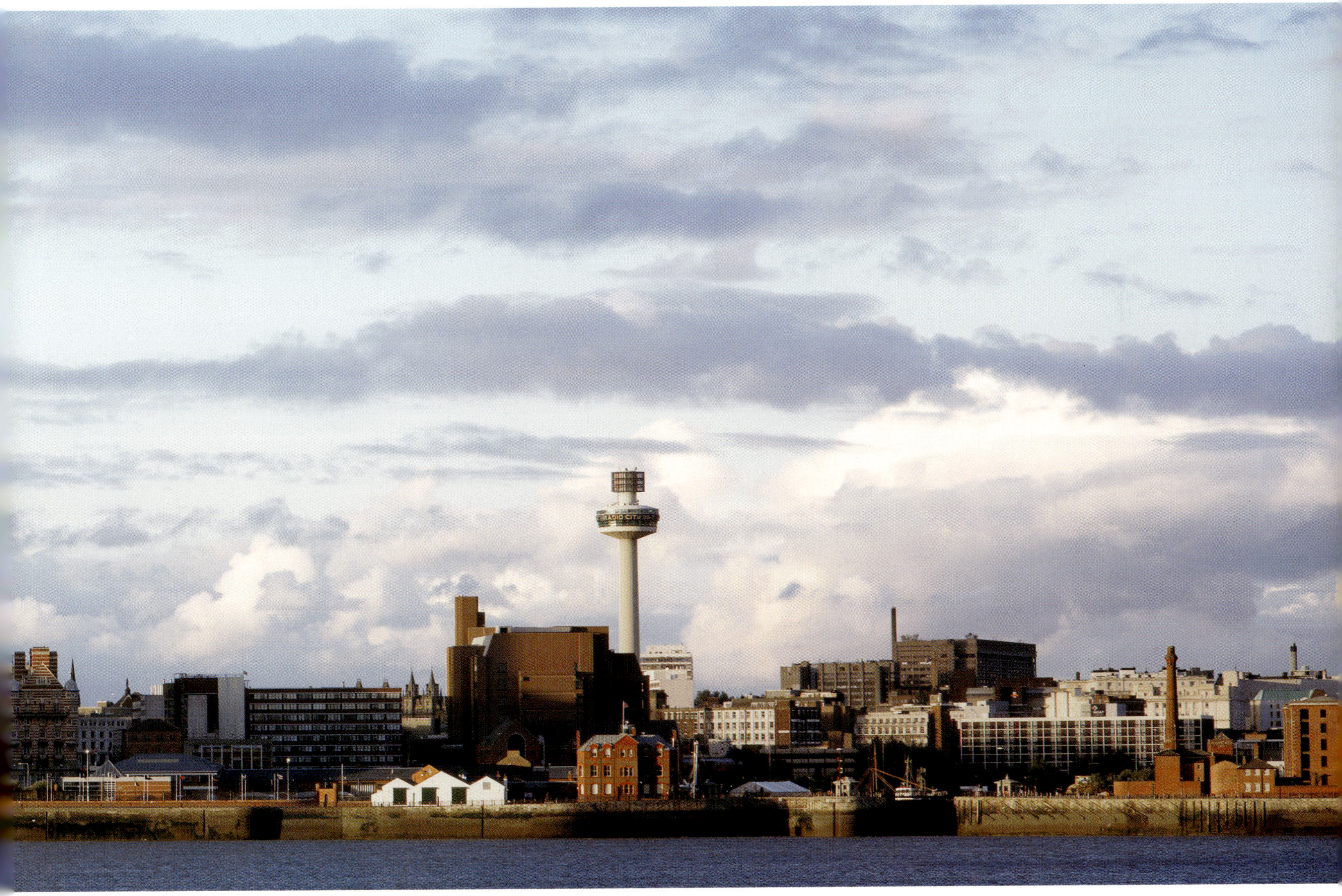

Late evening, Liverpool

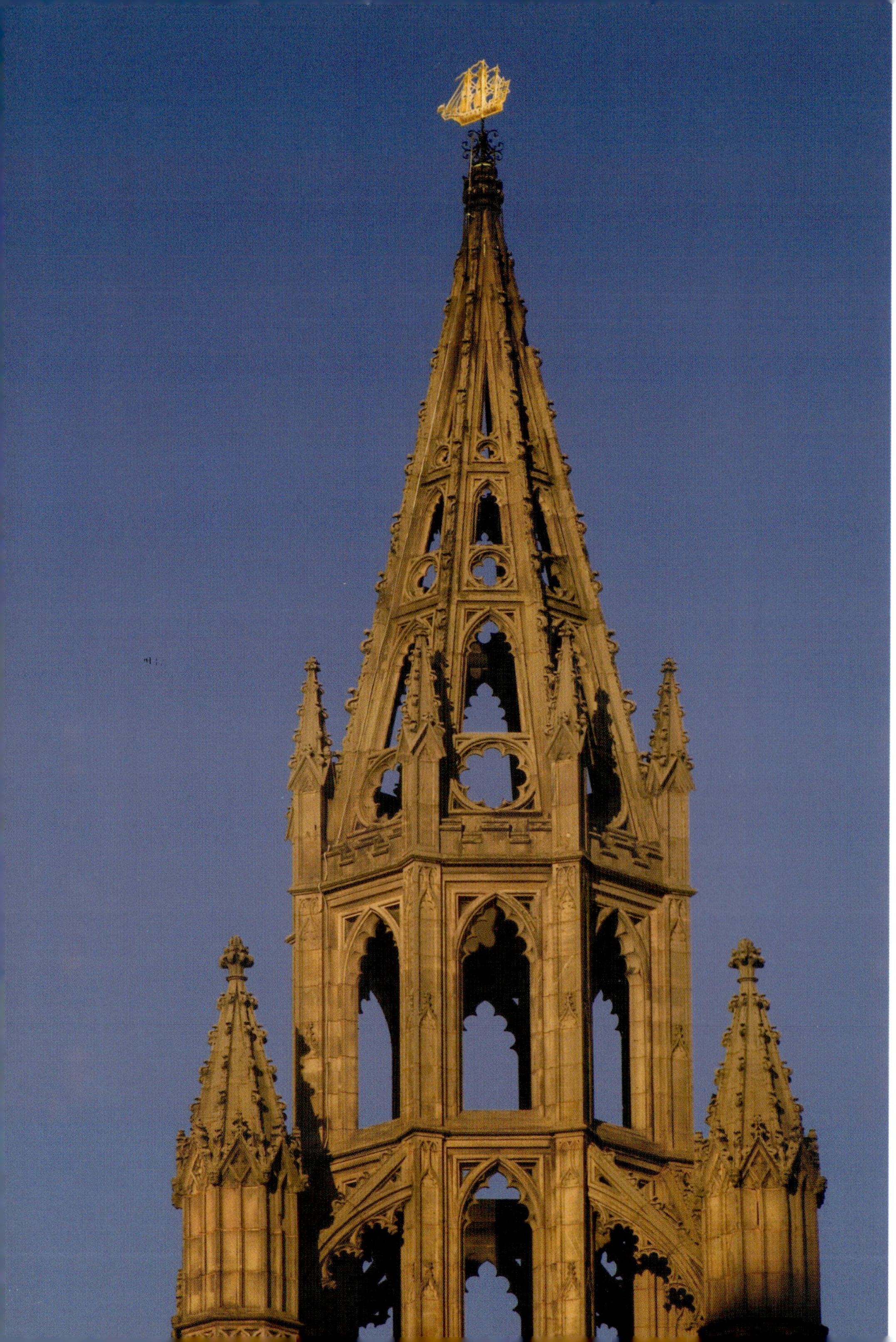

Spire of the Church of our Lady and St Nicholas

On the corner of Chapel Street and George's Dock Gate and colloquially known as 'St Nicks', this is reputed to be the oldest ecclesiastical foundation in Liverpool. The present building only dates from 1815, but it has been rebuilt many times since 1699. In 1810 the tower collapsed onto worshippers due to poor construction, killing 23 girls from the Moorfields Charity School.

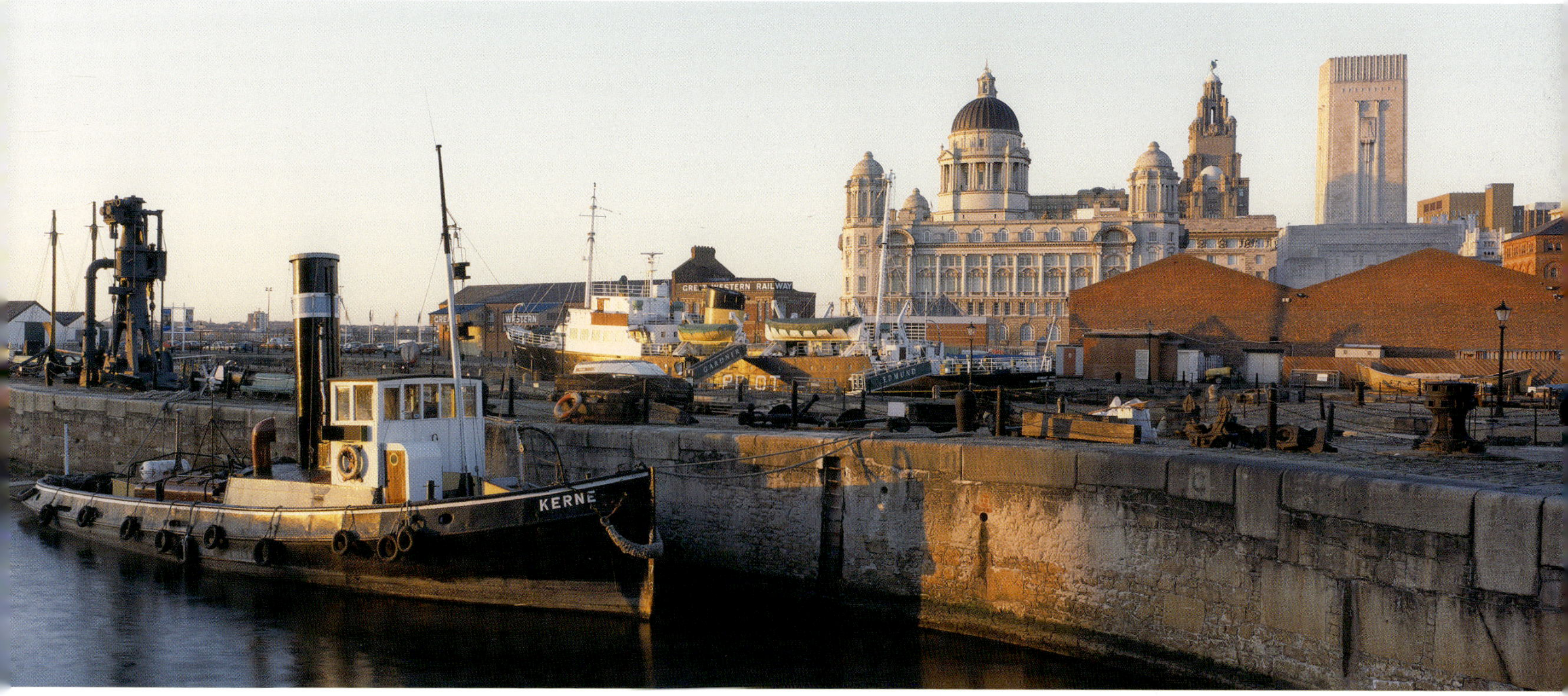

S.T. *Kerne*

The coal-fired steam tug *Kerne* moored adjacent to the Albert and Salthouse Docks in the Canning Half Tide dock. The *Kerne* was built in 1913, and was originally named *Viking*, then *Terrier*. She was initially used as an Admiralty tug around Chatham and the Medway. The *Kerne* was a regular feature around the Mersey from the late 1940s until her retirement in 1971, and she is now privately-owned by a group of enthusiasts – The North Western Steamship Company.

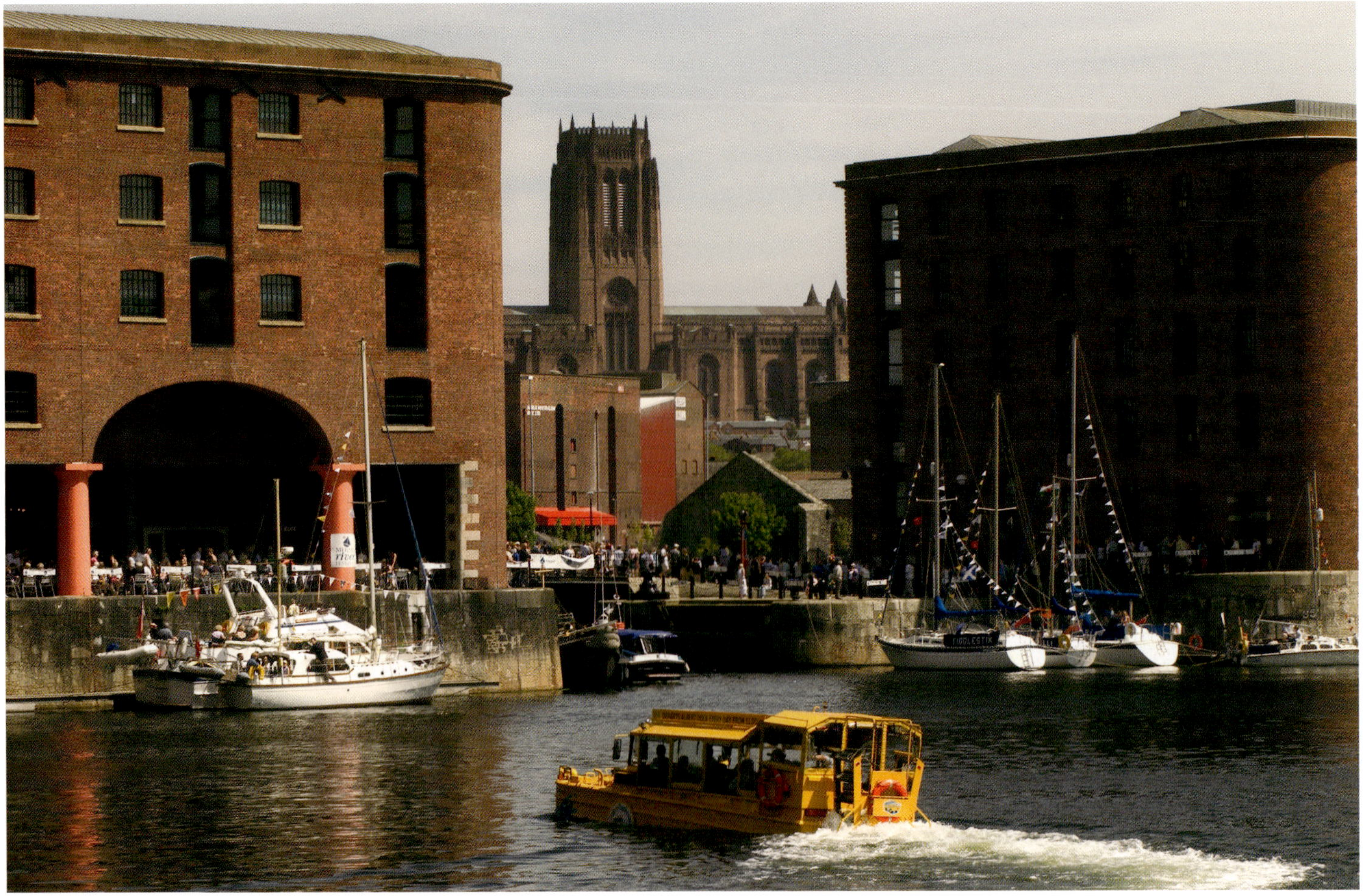

The Albert Dock and Duck

These 'ducks' were originally Second World War landing craft. Now known as 'the Wacker Quackers I & II', they take tourists on land and river trips around the sights of the docks and the city.

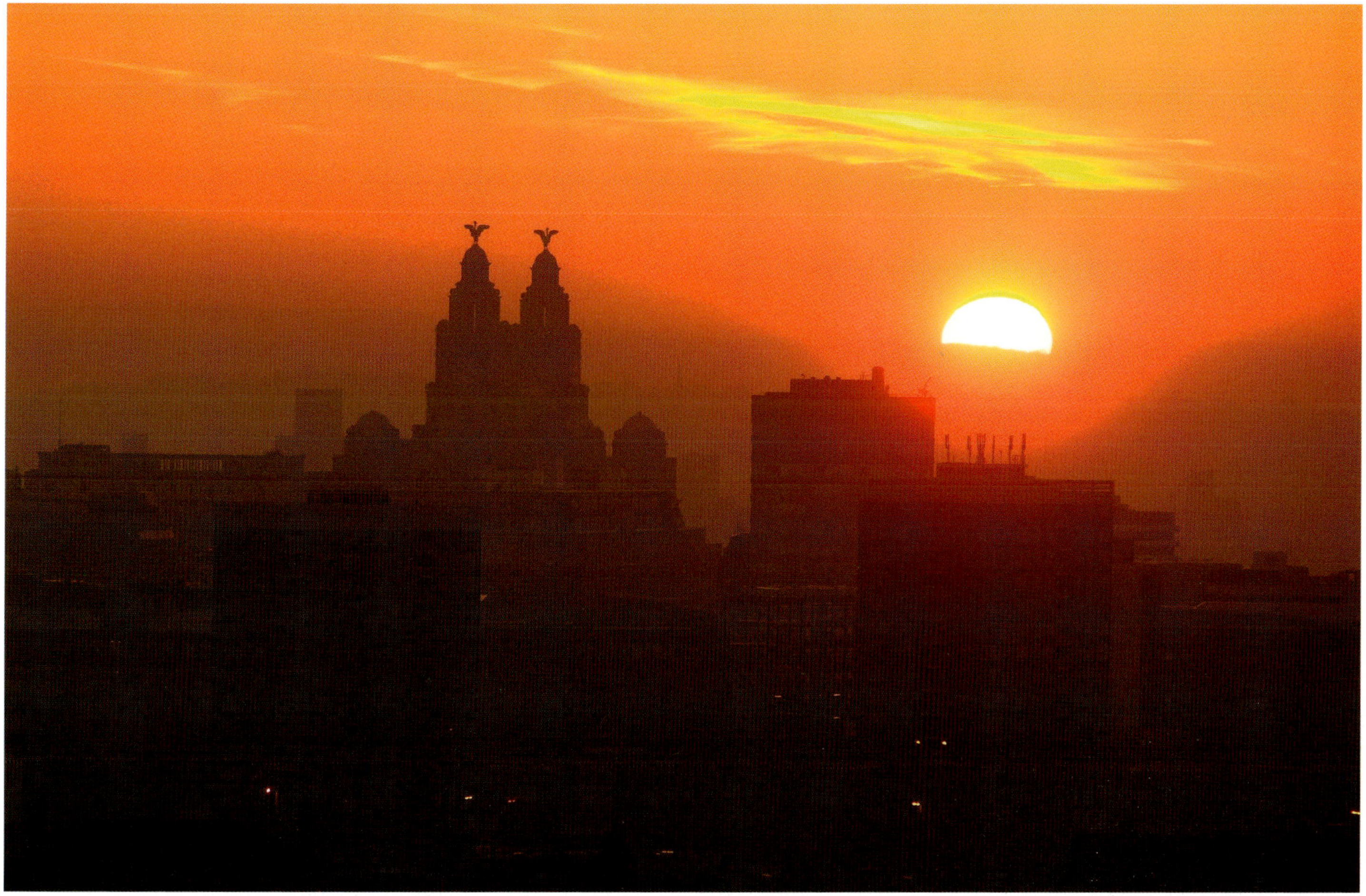

Sunset over Liverpool

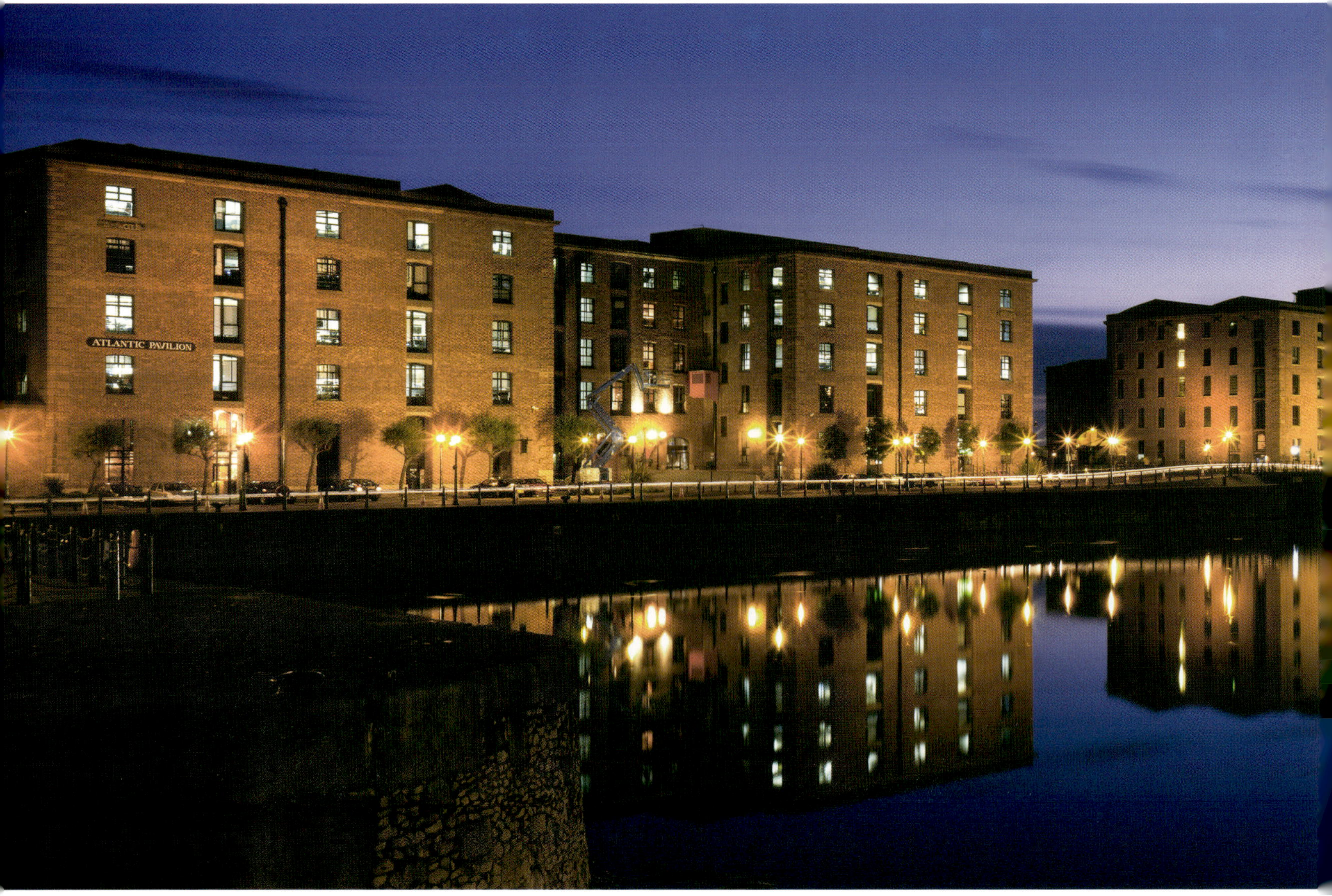
ATLANTIC PAVILION

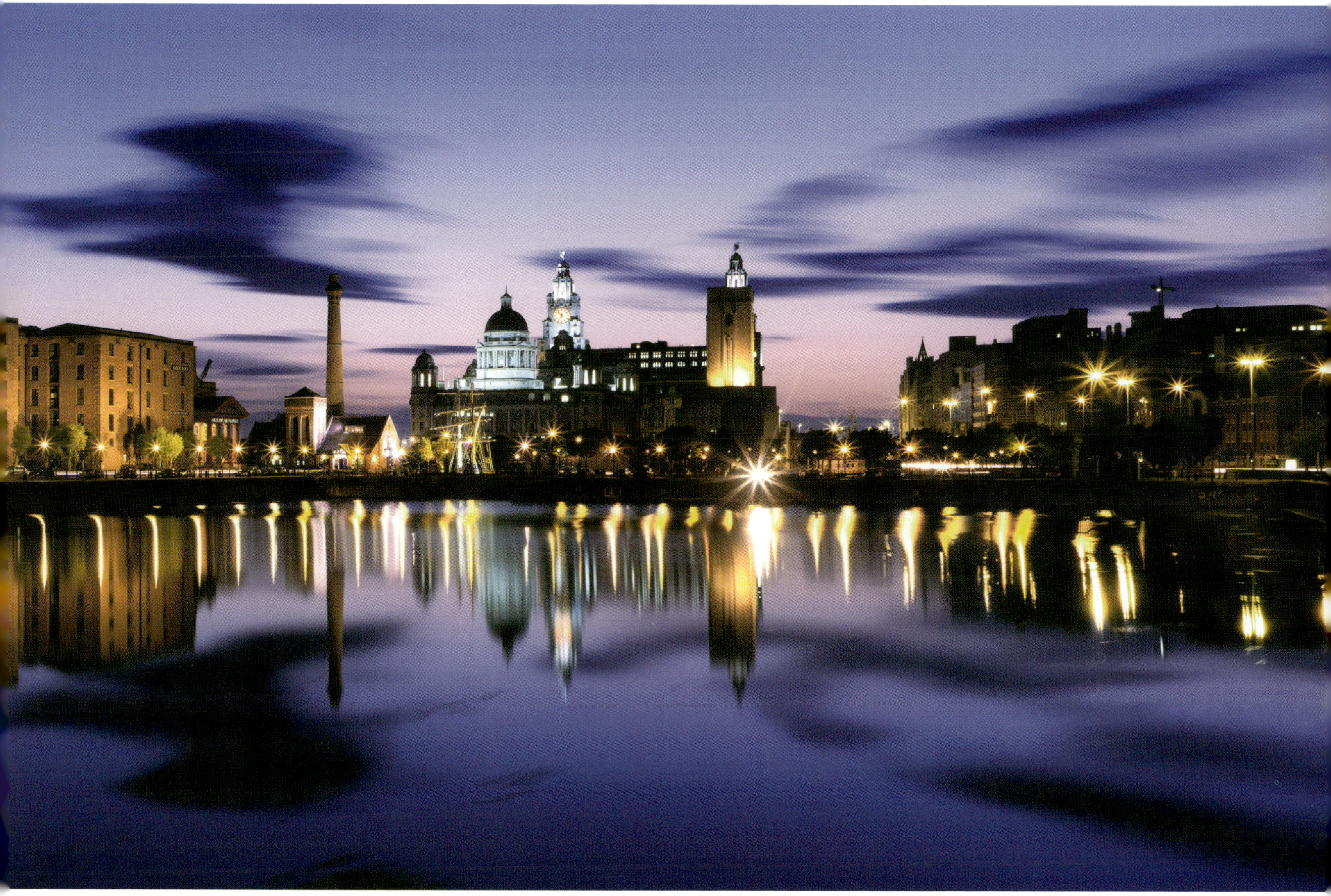

The Albert Dock and the Pier Head
The Albert Dock and the Pier Head as seen from Salthouse Dock.

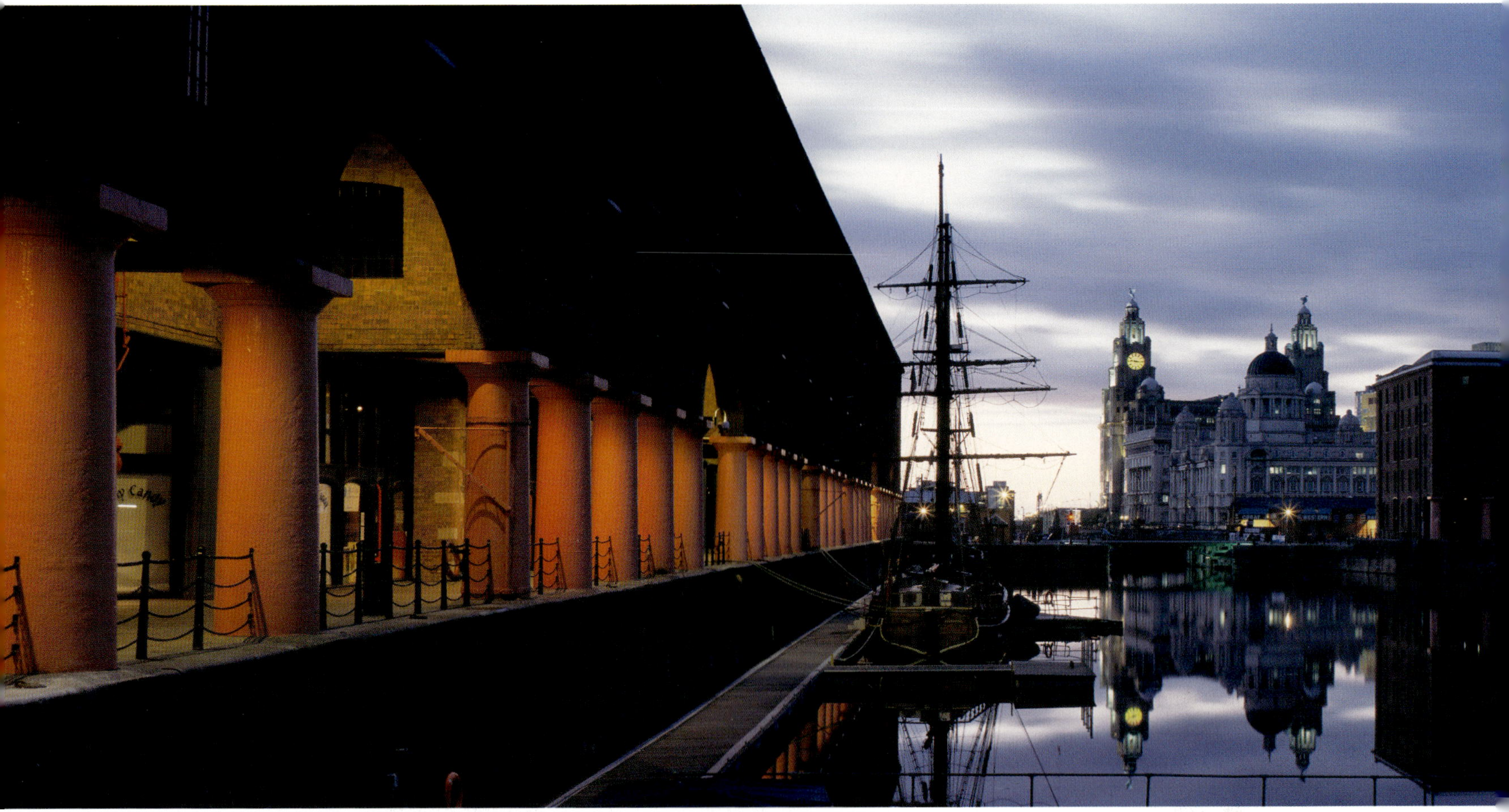

The Albert Dock

Now a major tourist attraction, the Albert Dock houses the Tate Liverpool and the Liverpool Maritime Museum, among many other shops and businesses. Modern apartments and a hotel feature on the upper floors. The sailing ship moored in the dock is one of a fleet used for adventure holidays for young people. The ships also feature regularly in period dramas on film and TV.

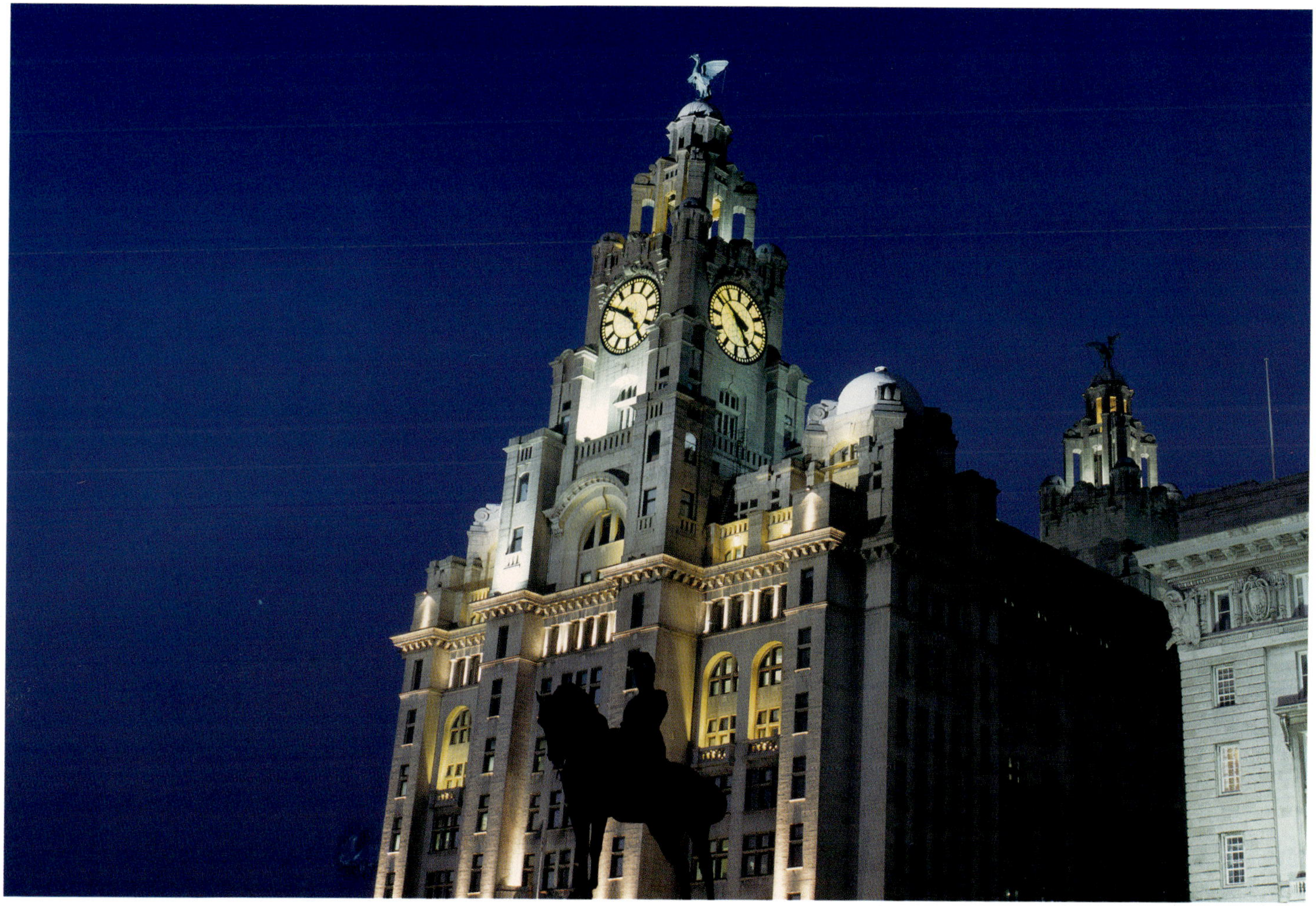

The Royal Liver Building

Designed by architect Walter A.Thomas and completed in 1911, the Royal Liver Building is famous the world over as the image of Liverpool. It has a cladding of grey-black granite, but was actually the first large-scale reinforced concrete building in the world. The success of the building method led to the construction of skyscrapers all over the world. The statue in silhouette is of King Edward VII.

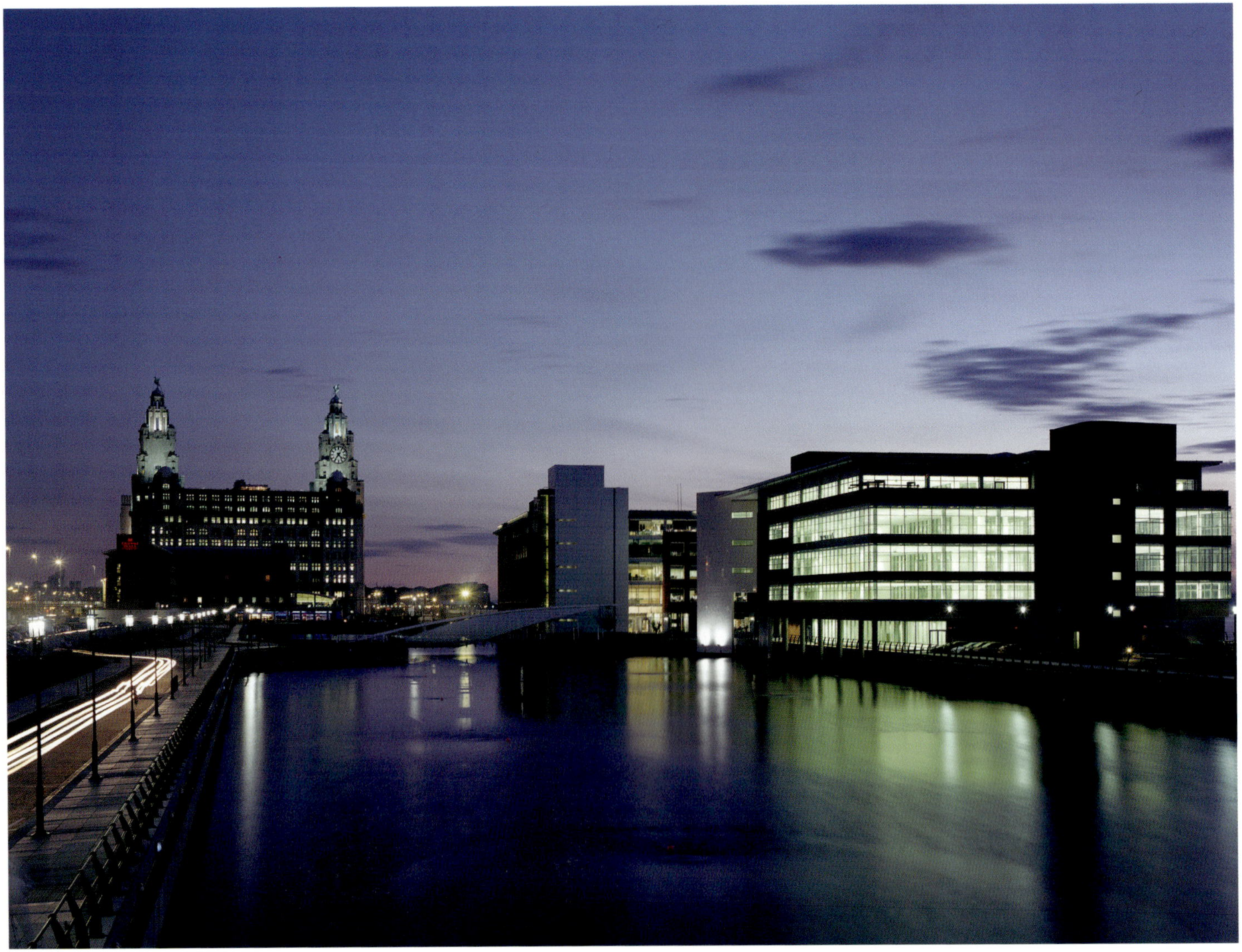

Prince's Dock

Looking back towards the Pier Head, with the new office buildings of Prince's Parade on the right. The Dockland area is one of the most successful regeneration programmes in Liverpool, and further offices are to be built on the left hand side of the dock.

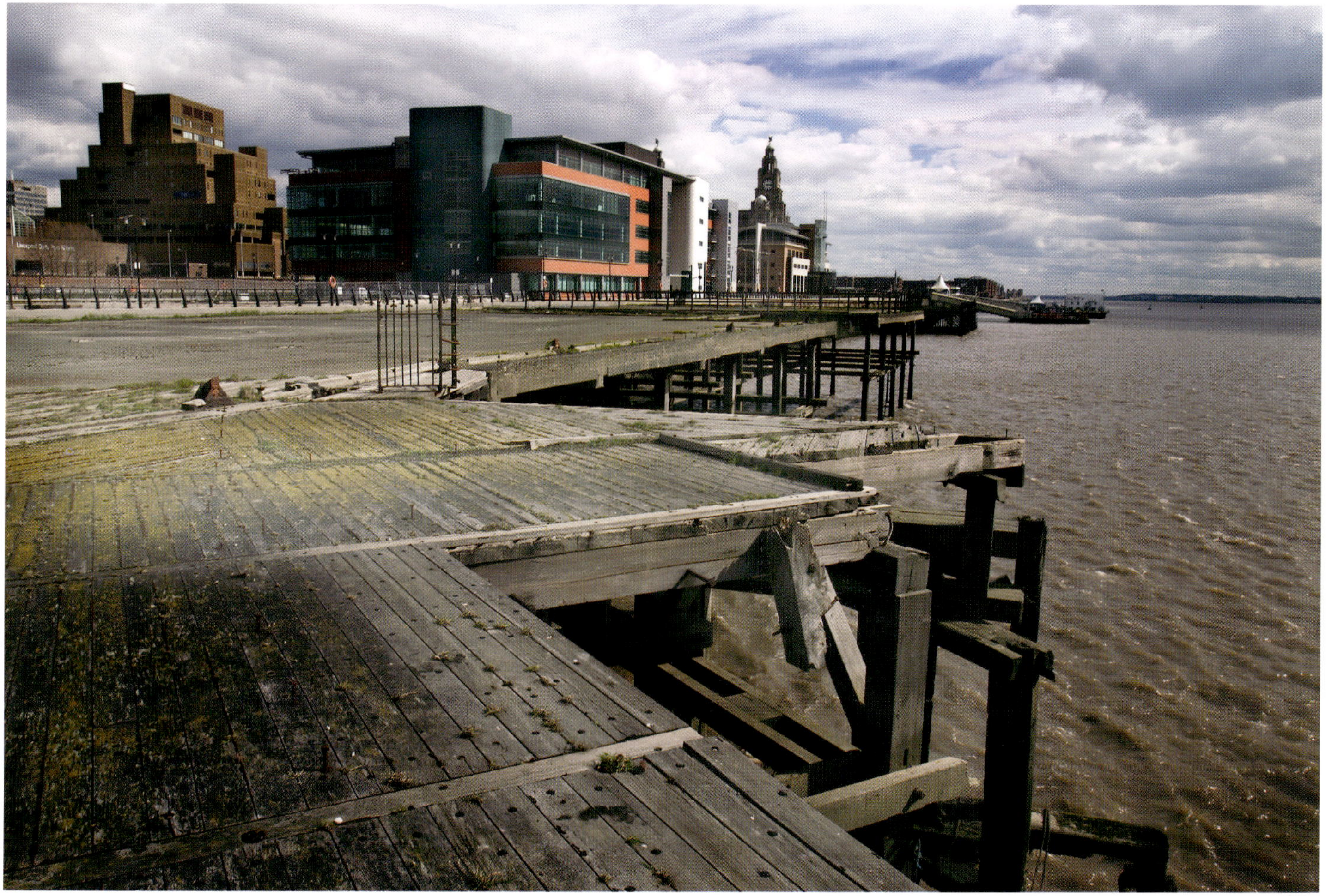

Where tranatlantic liners berthed
The remains of the Prince's Landing Stage, which is soon to be redeveloped into a new cruise line terminal. The Prince's Landing Stage stretched for over 2500ft and berthed transatlantic liners and larger vessels. Further south adjacent to the pier head, the George's Landing Stage is where the ferries tied up.

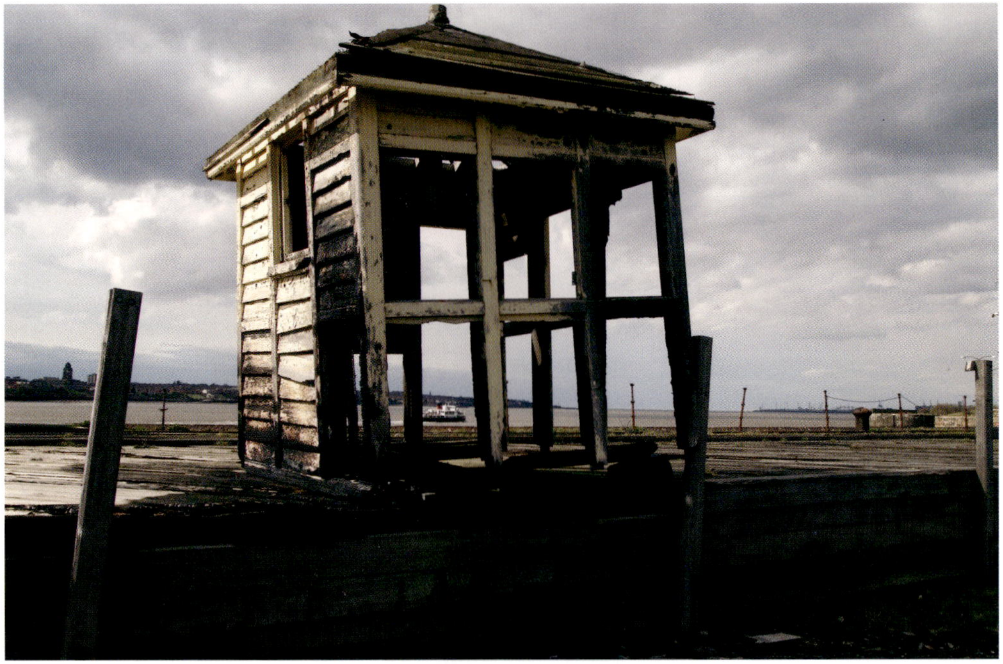

Ticket collector's kiosk, Prince's Landing Stage
Although the kiosk has fallen into disrepair and been damaged by fire, it is still possible to visualise the many people who queued to board the ferries and ships of the 1950s and 1960s.

All aboard!
The last of the gangways left abandoned on the Prince's Landing Stage. Built mainly of wood, it still has its original rollers attached.

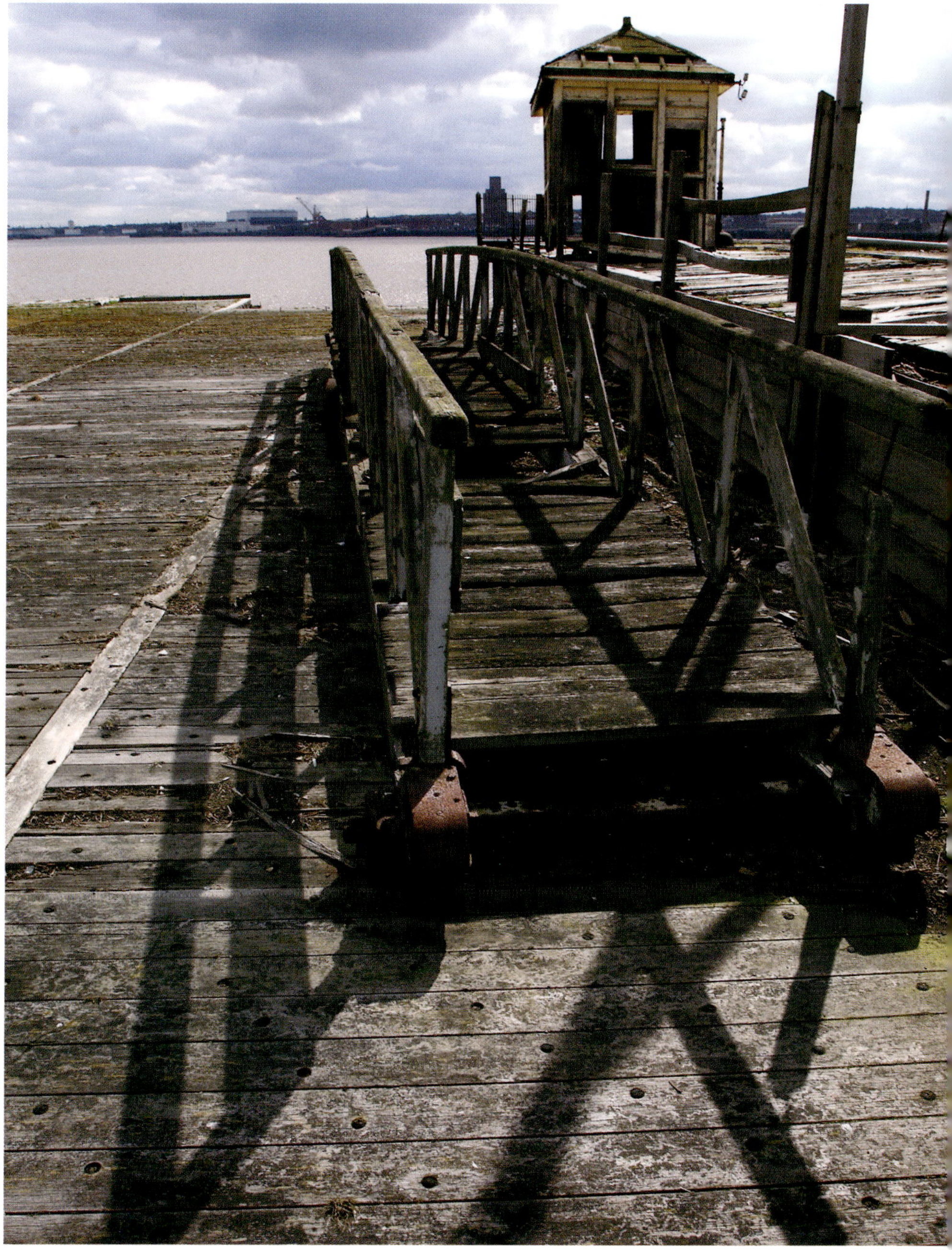

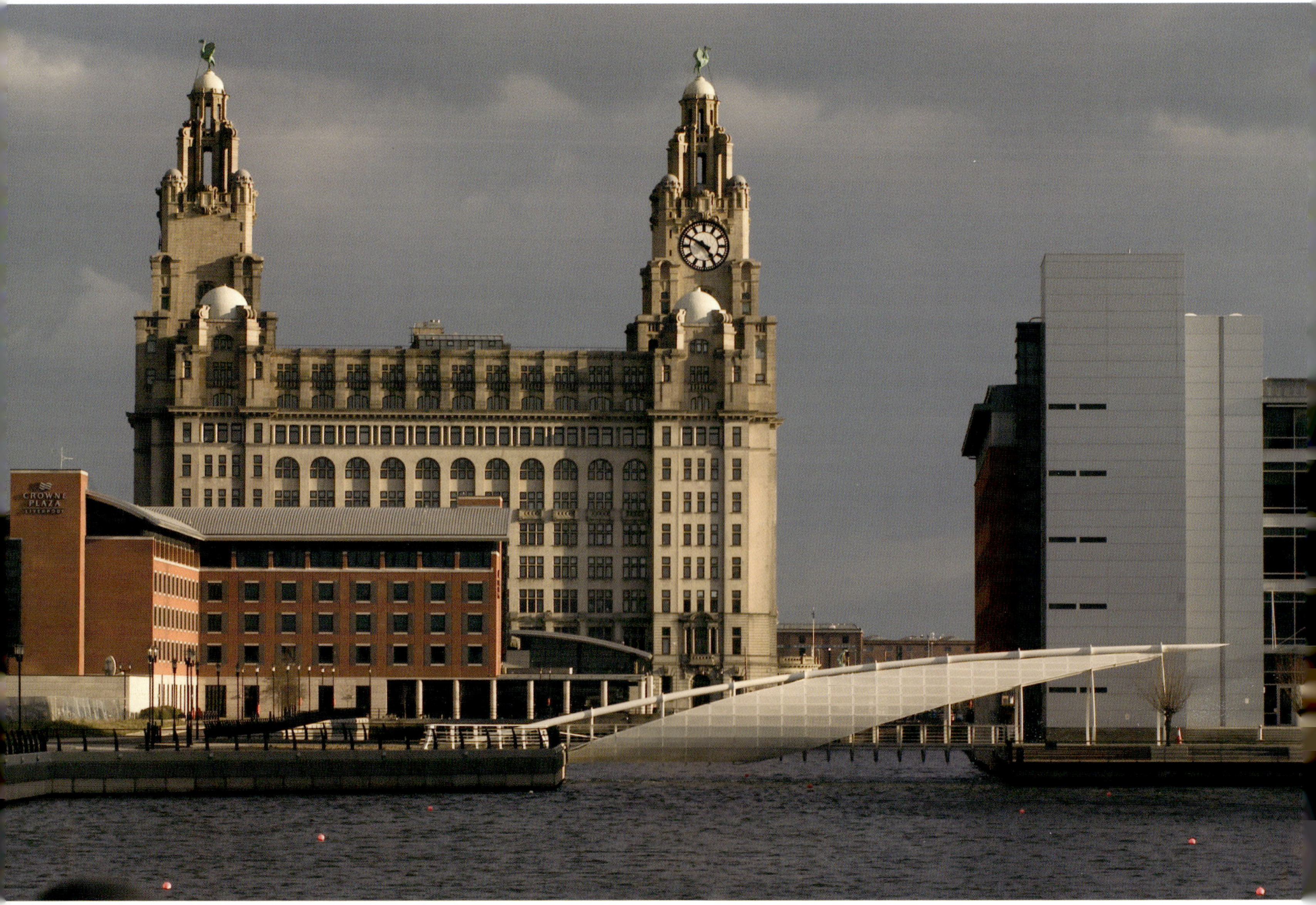

The Crown Plaza Hotel

Not a small building in any respect, the Crown Plaza Hotel is dwarfed by the sheer size of the Royal Liver Building.

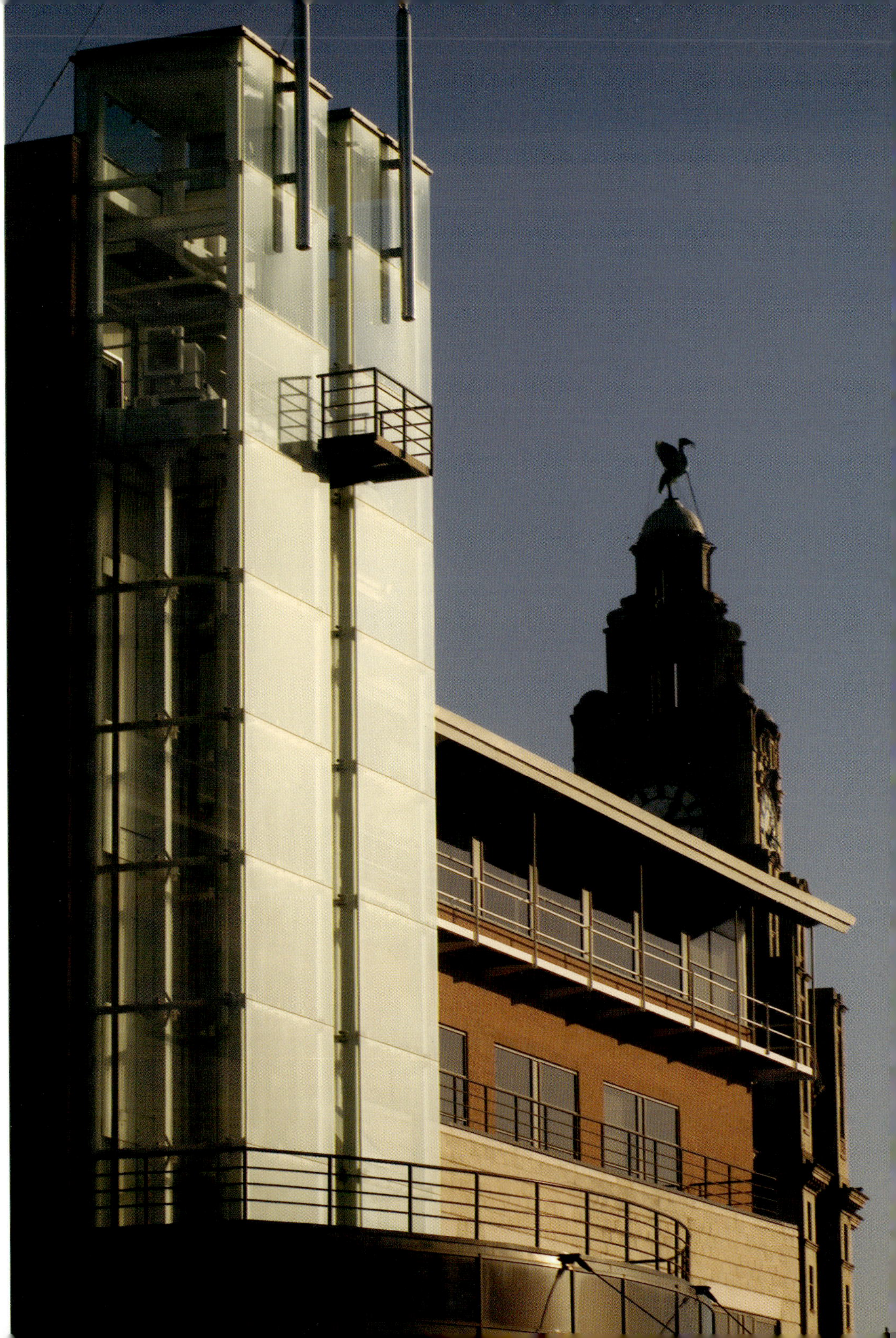

No 8, Prince's Quay
Modern offices on Prince's Parade, built in 2002, with the Royal Liver Building in the background.

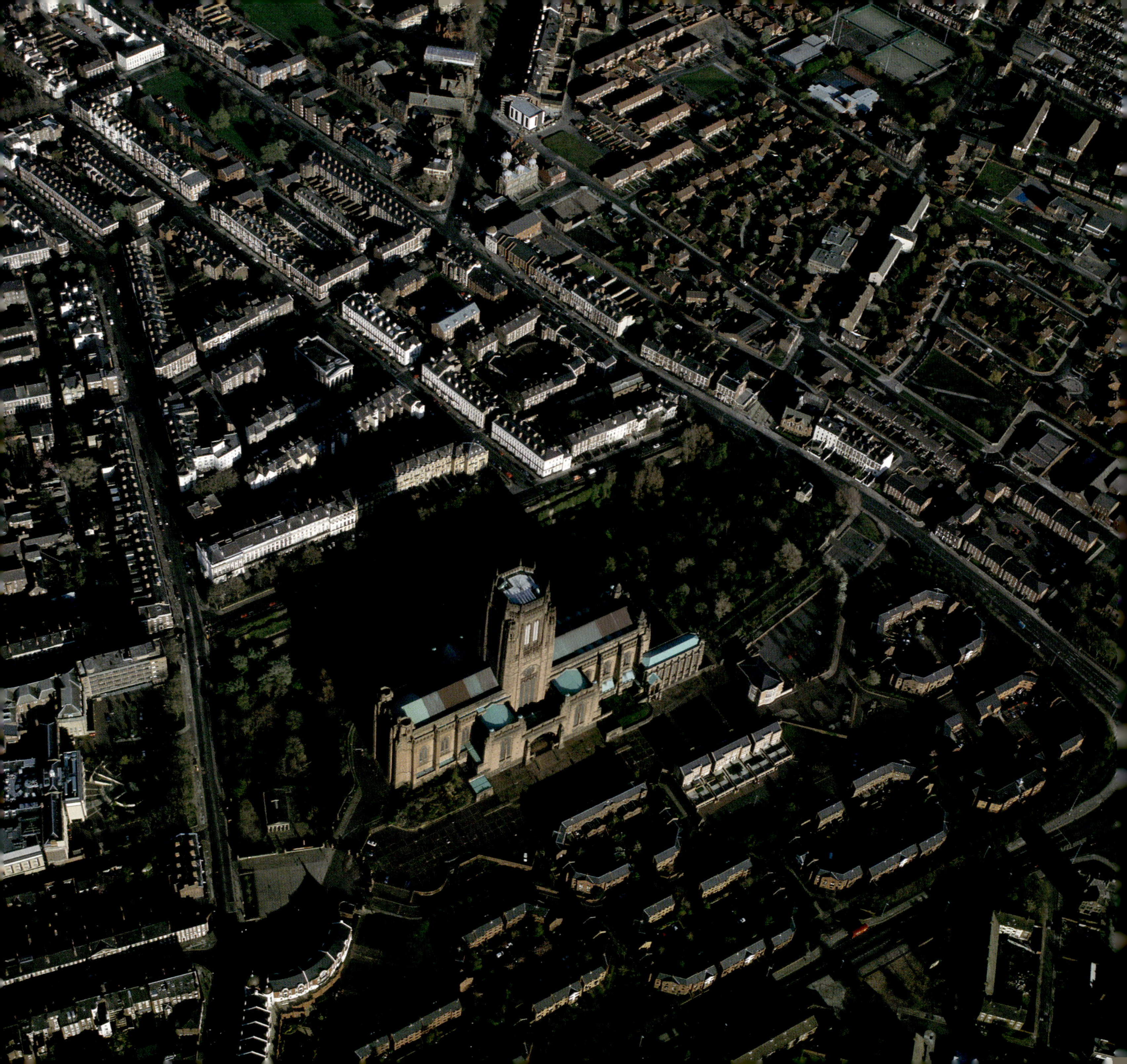

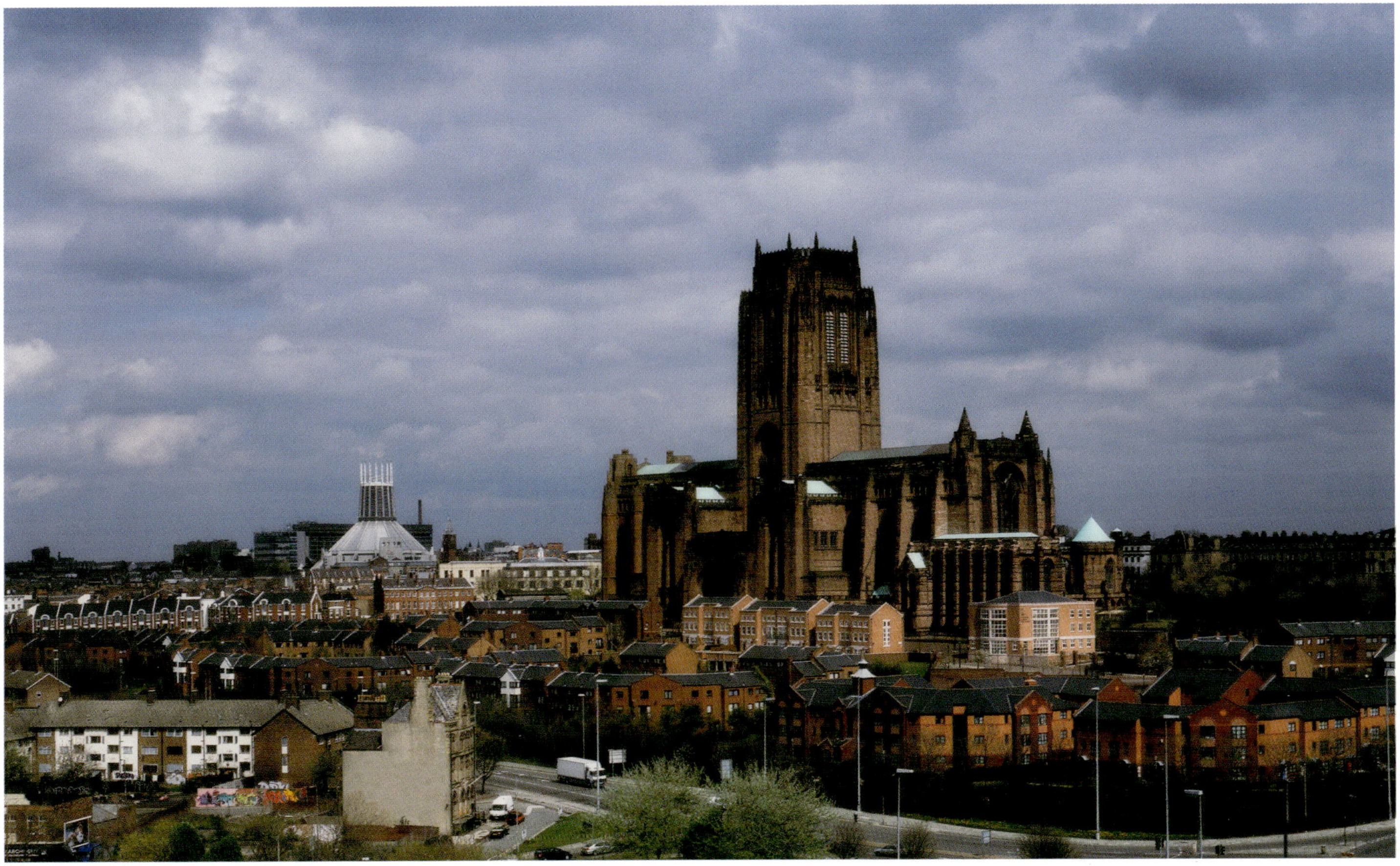

A City of two cathedrals
The Anglican and Roman Catholic cathedrals.

Serving four faiths *(left)*
This aerial view shows how the largest Anglican cathedral in the world stands on top of a sandstone ridge. The shadow of the huge tower casts onto Gambier Terrace, while a new complex of accommodation and educational buildings stand to the seaward side. This photograph reflects the multicultural diversity of the city, as places of worship serving four faiths are shown in this one image.

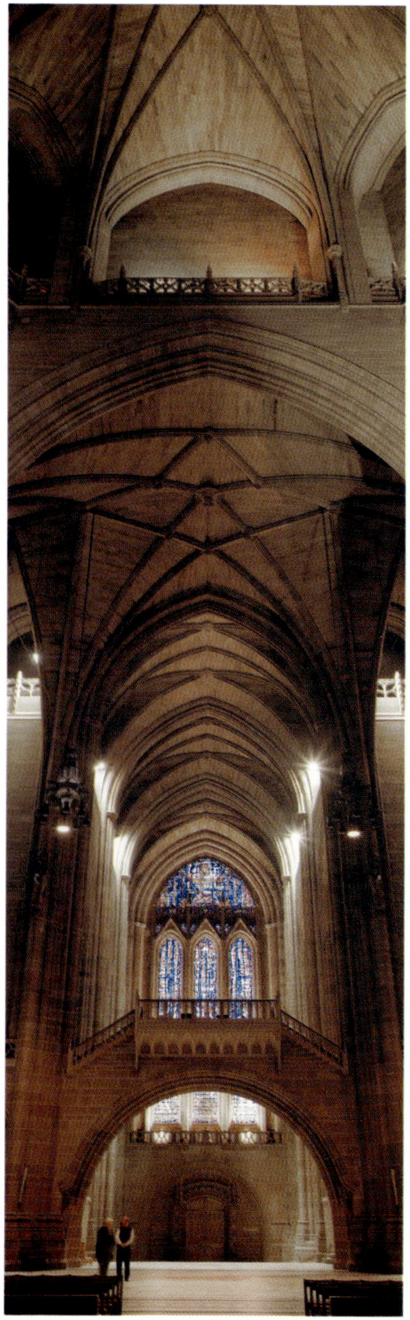

Liverpool Anglican Cathedral
This interior shows the nave bridge looking towards the west window. It also shows the height that the 35 tons of bells in the tower had to be hauled by hand. A team of twelve men worked in ten-minute shifts for the ten hours it took to lift the bells. The 9-foot-high largest bell is part of the highest peal of bells in the world.

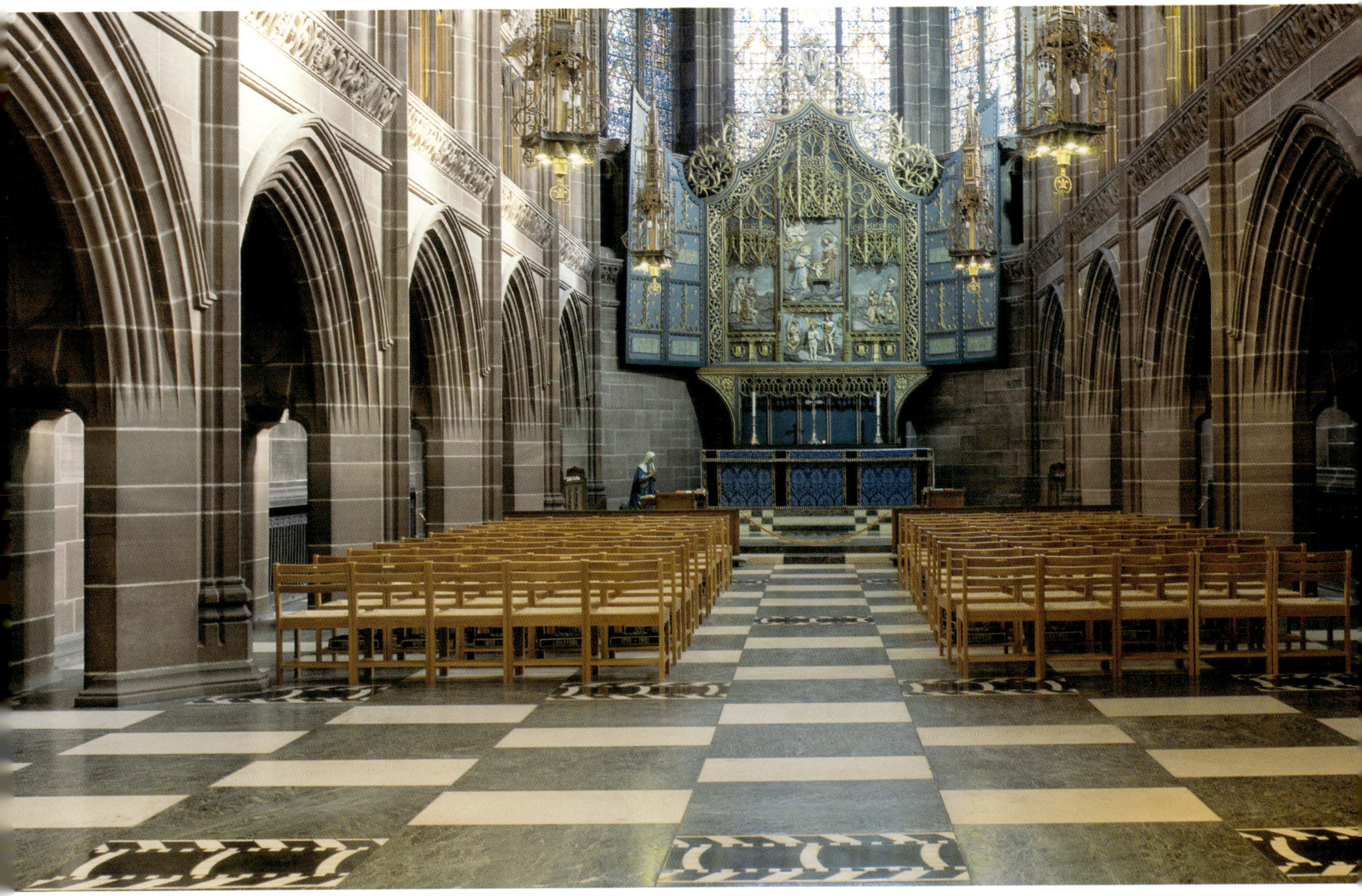

The Lady Chapel

The Lady Chapel is situated at the south-west corner of the Liverpool Anglican Cathedral. Although dwarfed by the main building, it is still larger than most parish churches. This was the first part of the cathedral to be completed and was consecrated for worship in June 1910. The original windows were blown out in the Blitz.

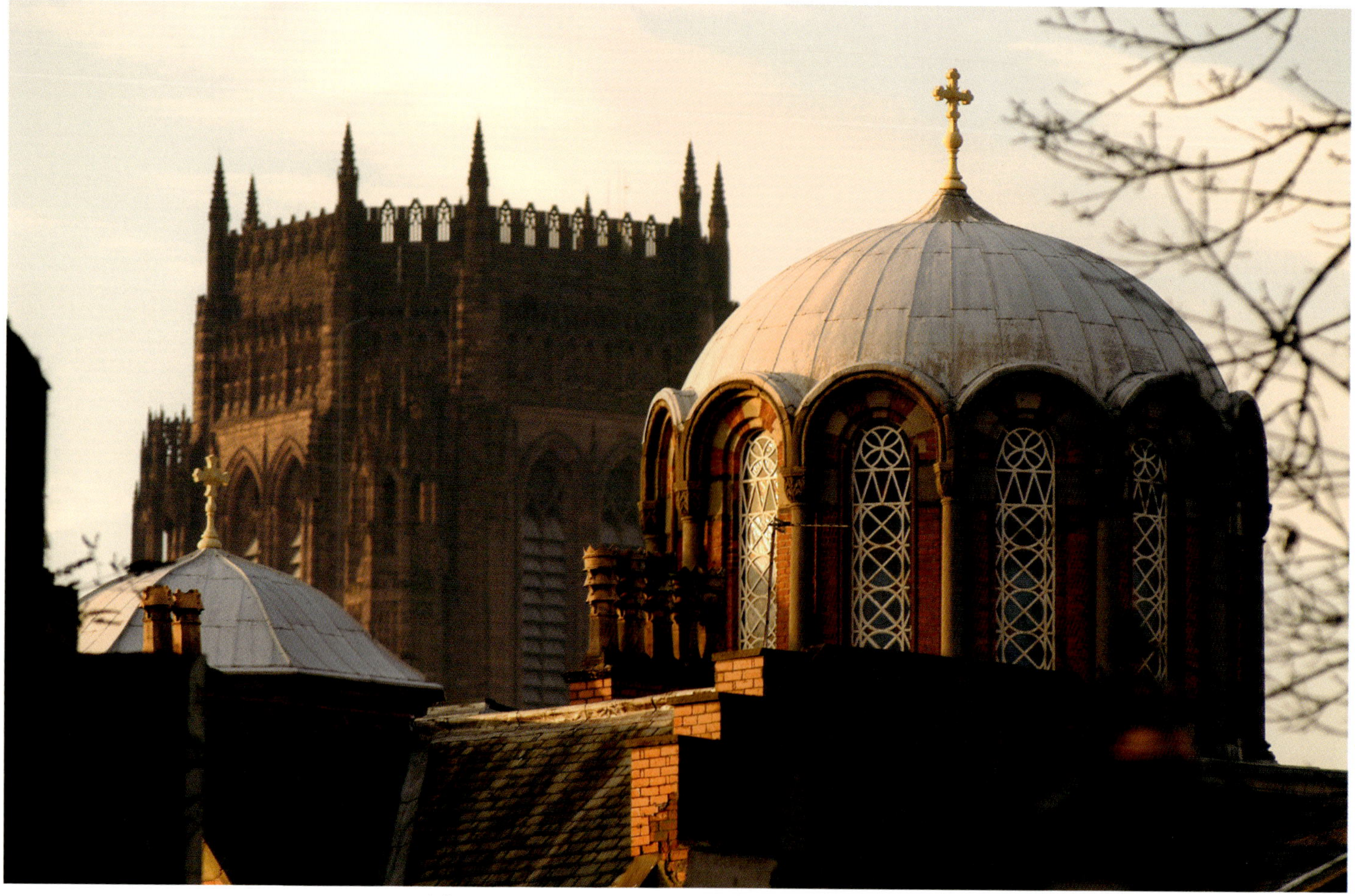

The Greek Orthodox Church of St Nikolaos
The dome of the Greek Orthodox Church on Prince's Road, with the towering Anglican cathedral in the background.

Liverpool Anglican Cathedral
Dame Elizabeth Frink sculpted the bronze 'Risen Christ' which stands above the west door. She had never visited the cathedral at the time of receiving the commission. When unveiled, the statue received a mixed reaction and with typical scouse humour was named 'Frinkenstein'.

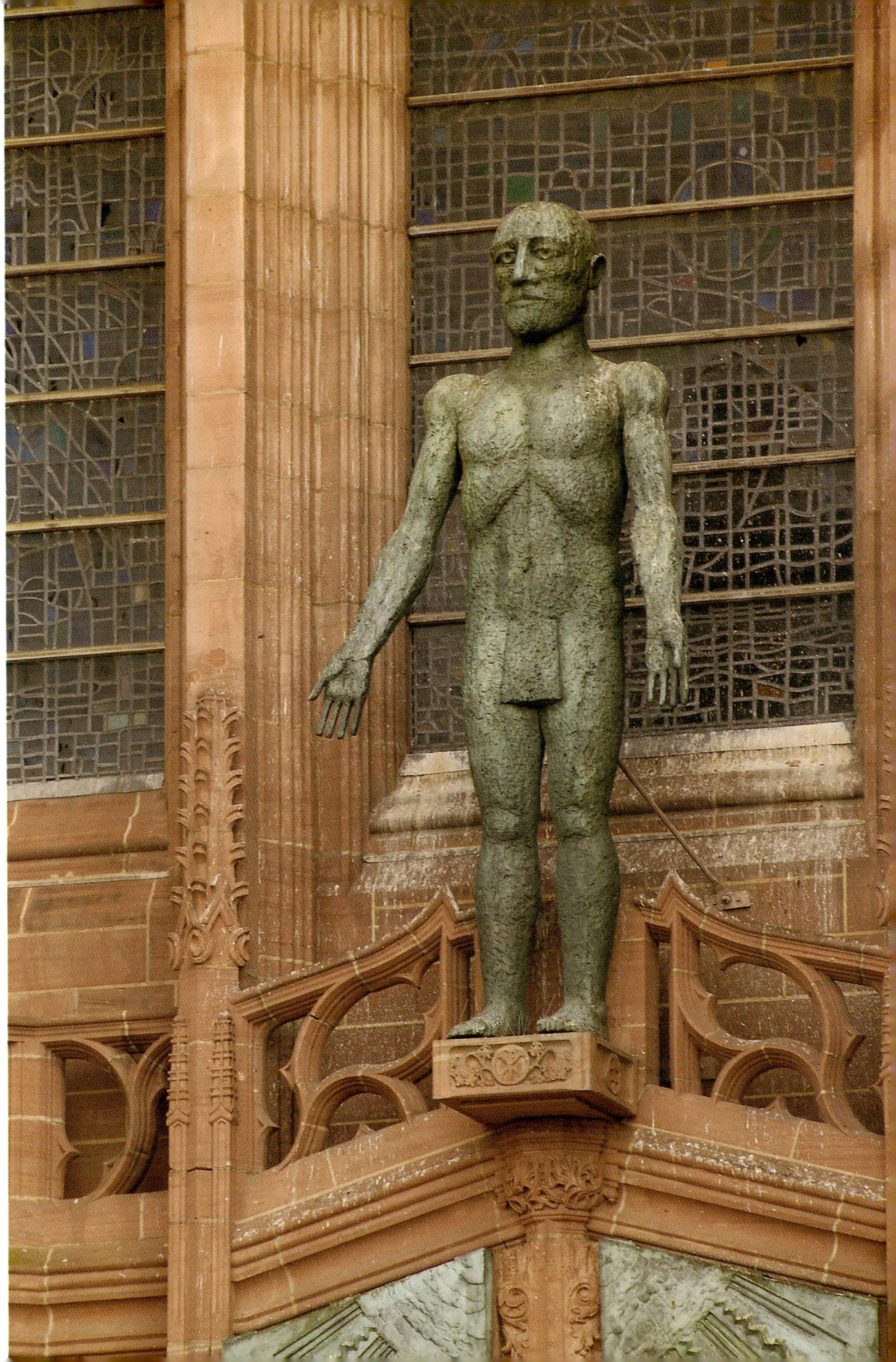

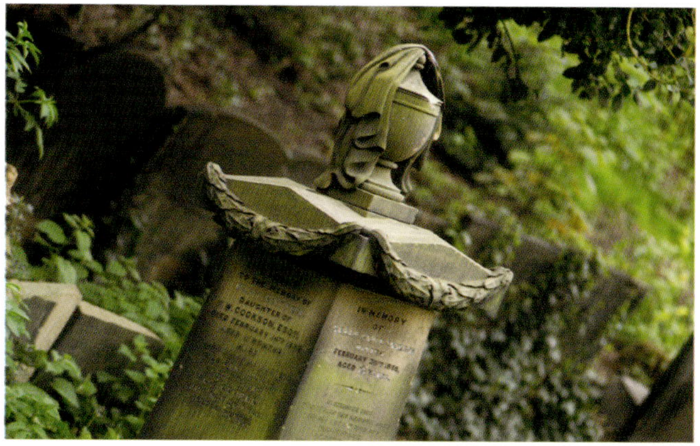

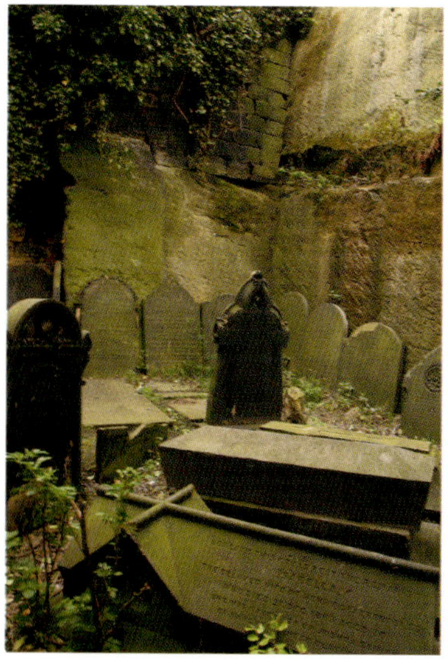

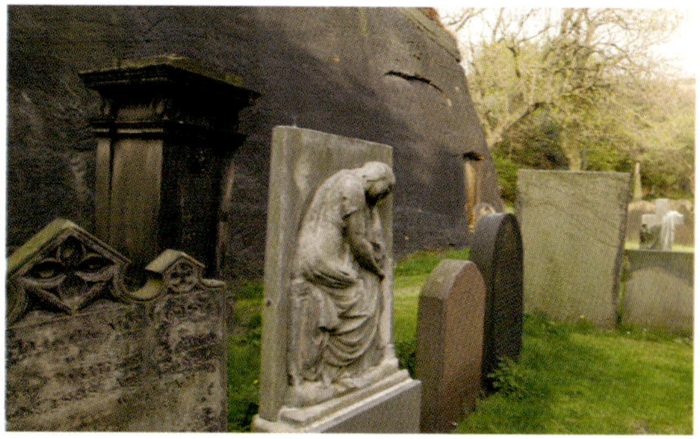

St James's Cemetery

The foundation stone to St James's Cemetery was laid in 1827, and the first burial took place in 1829. It was not long before the cemetery received one of its most celebrated residents, the Right Honourable William Huskisson M.P (1770 – 1830), who has the dubious distinction of being the first person to be killed by a train. He was struck by Stephenson's 'Rocket' on 15 September, 1830.

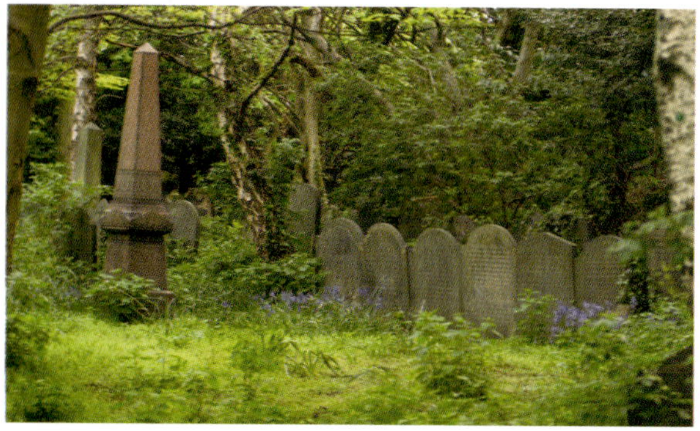

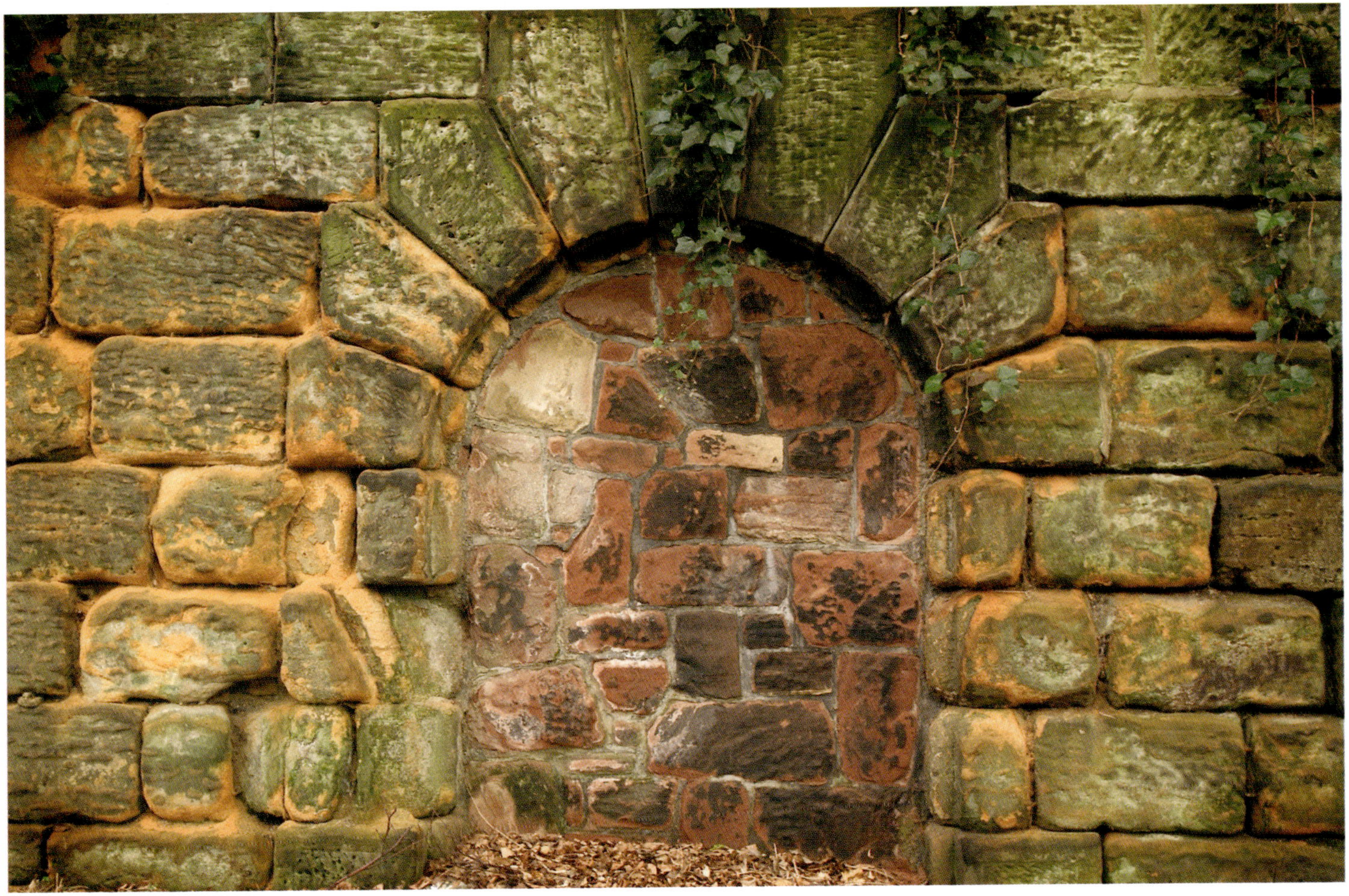

St James's Cemetery

This photograph in St James's Cemetery shows one of the entrances to the catacombs, which are now sealed off. One hundred and seven years after opening in 1829, the main cemetery was full after over 57,000 burials had taken place.

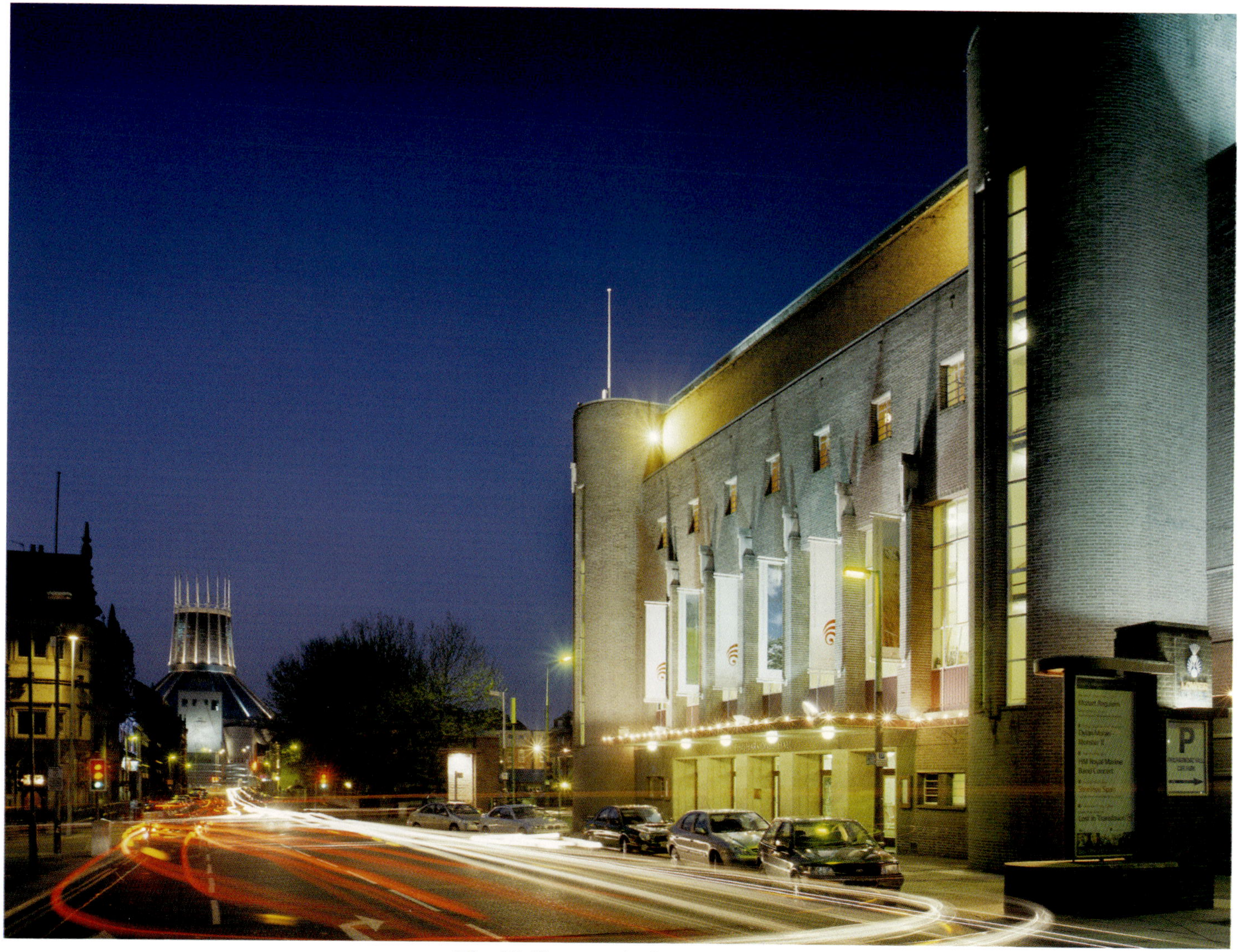

The Philharmonic Concert Hall

The home of the Royal Liverpool Philharmonic Orchestra was built between 1933 and 1939 (architect: Herbert J. Rowse), after the original was burnt down in 1933. It was extended and refurbished in 1994/5. The 'Phil' – as it it affectionately known – is approximately half-way between Liverpool's two cathedrals, and the Metropolitan Cathedral of Christ the King can be seen at the far end of Hope Street.

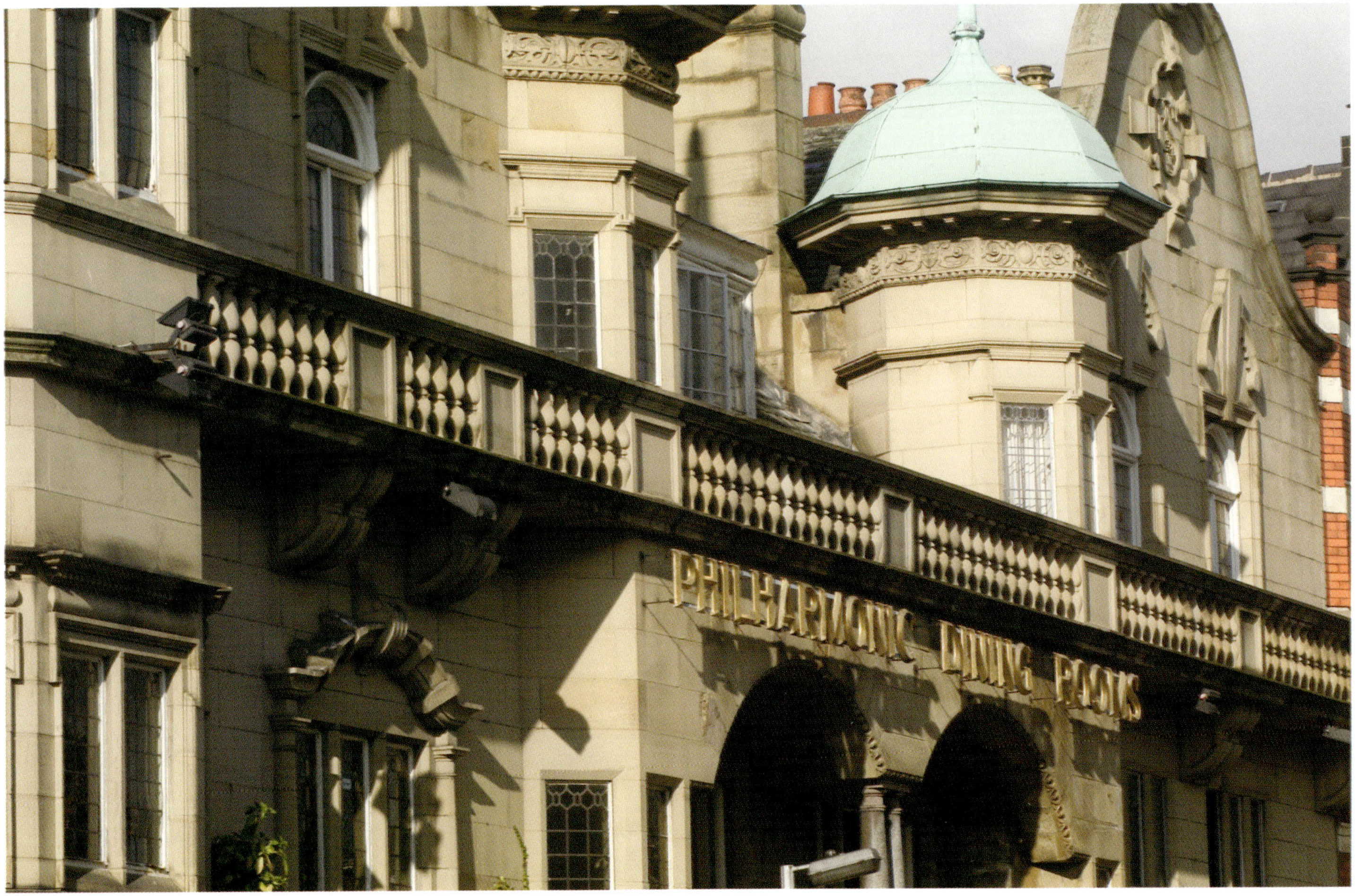

The Philharmonic Dining Rooms

Situated on Hope Street just across the junction from the Royal Philharmonic Hall, the Dining Rooms is now a bar featuring the most famous mens' toilets in the city. They are well-known for their ornate marble architecture, and are one of the few mens' conveniences which can be visited by ladies (usually tourists).

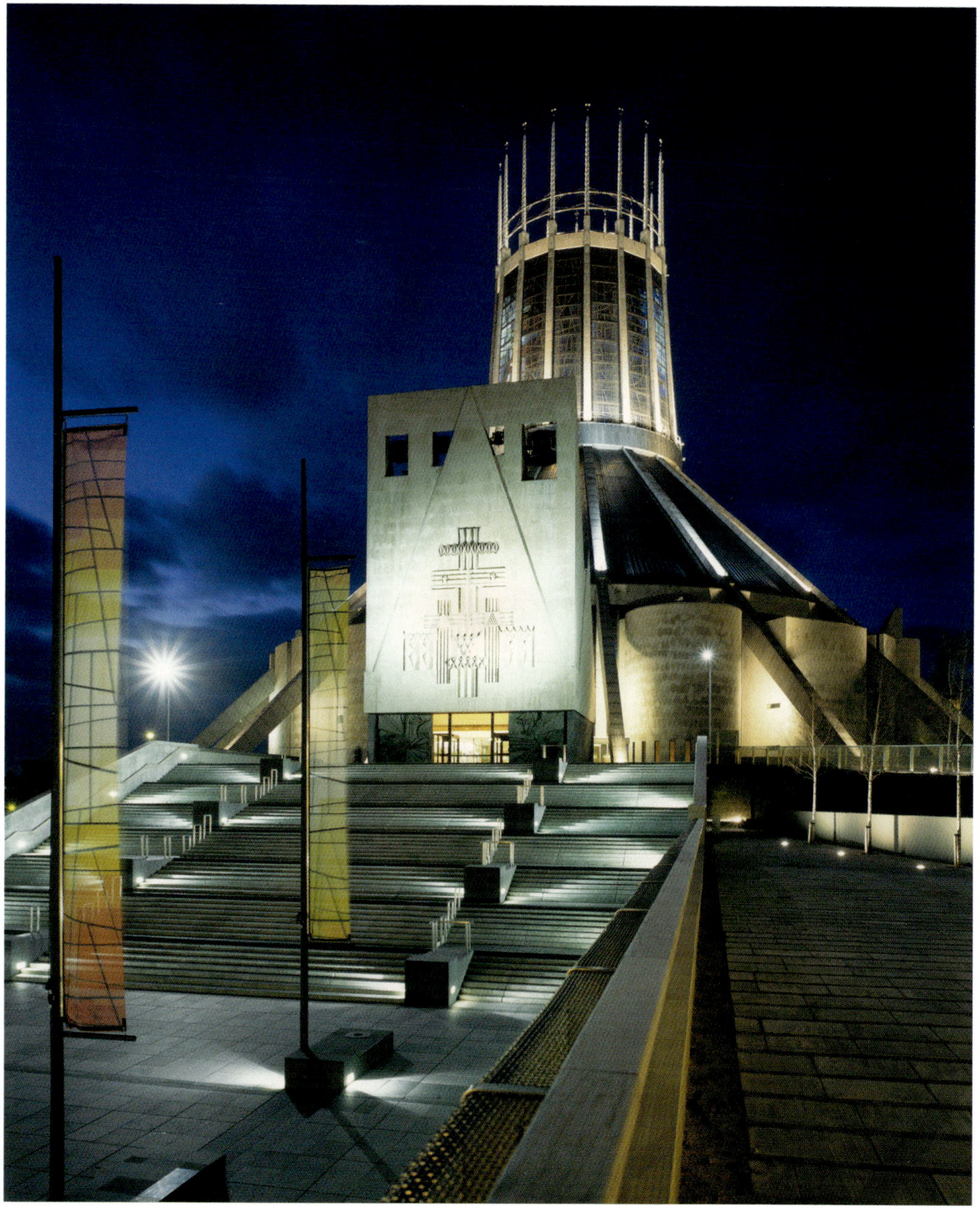

Metropolitan Cathedral of Christ the King

Opened in 1967, this is the second largest Roman Catholic cathedral in the world. The crypt architect was Sir Edwin Lutyens and the architect of the main cathedral was Sir Fredrick Gibberd. It was built on the site of Europe's largest workhouse on Brownlow Hill. The building took just five years to complete at a cost of £1.9 million. The use of new materials and techniques in construction quickly led to leaks and large areas of the original mosaic of white cladding became detached. Impossible to repair, it has now been completely replaced with an off-white glass-reinforced plastic. The roof, originally covered in aluminium, has been replaced with stainless steel.

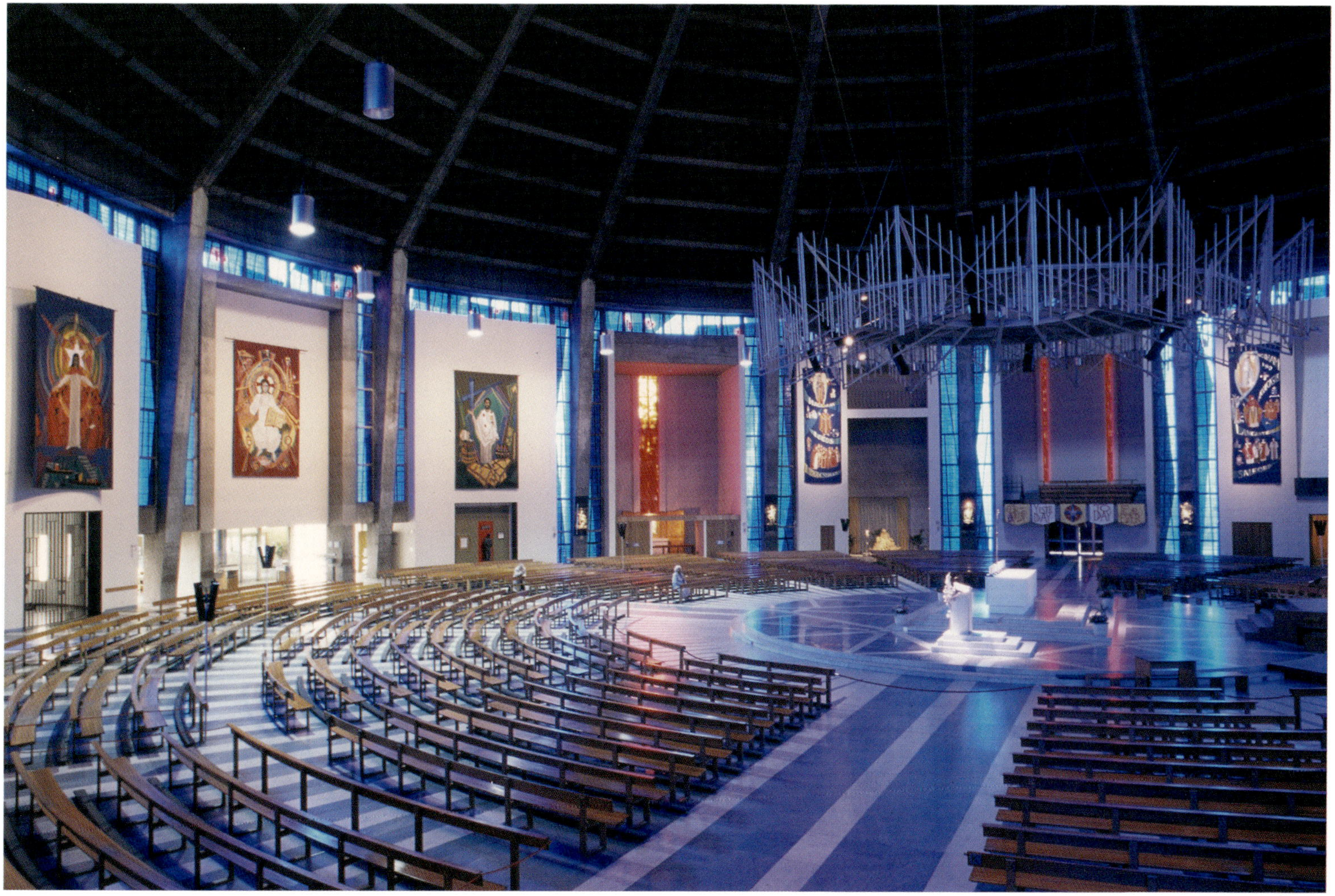

Metropolitan Cathedral of Christ the King

One of the major factors which influenced the design of the Roman Catholic cathedral was that it should be able to seat 3000 (later reduced to 2000) worshippers, all within sight of the altar. The competition for the commission was won by Frederick Gibberd, who incorporated a central altar into a circular plan. The cathedral is 195ft in diameter and surrounded by 13 internal chapels.

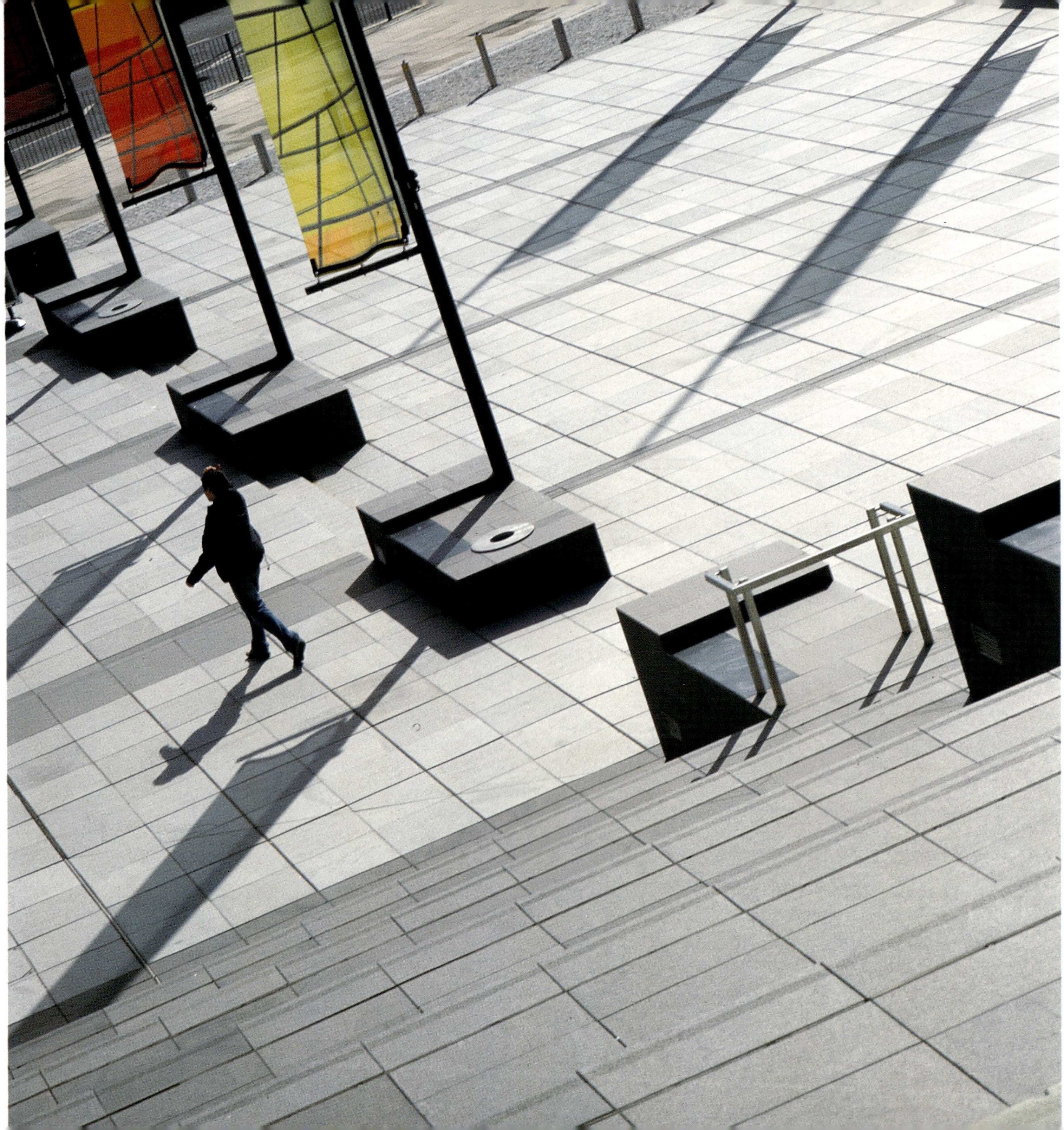

Metropolitan Cathedral of Christ the King *(left)*
The approach steps to Liverpool's futuristic Roman Catholic cathedral were completed in 2003.

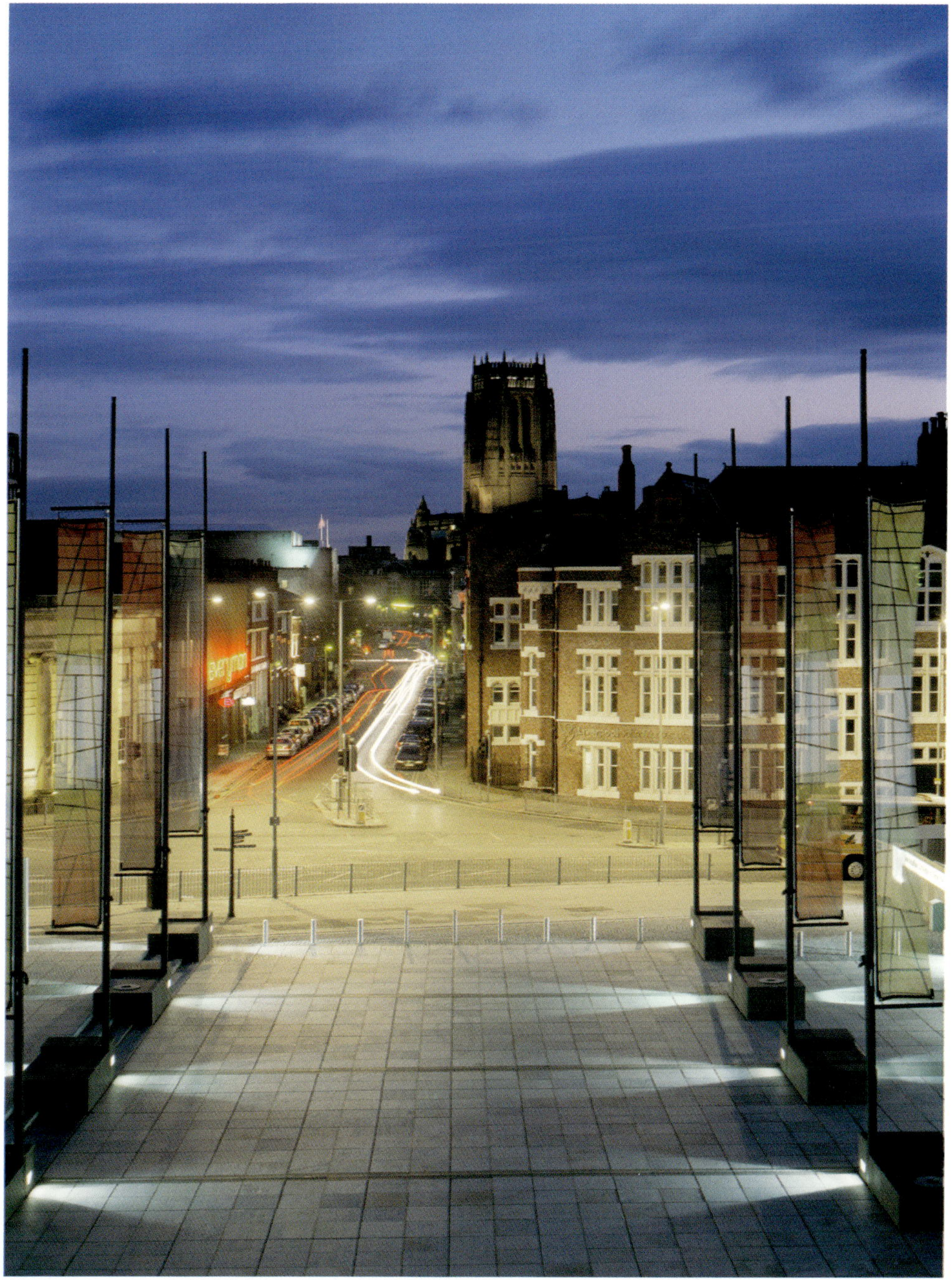

Hope Street
Looking down Hope Street from the entrance of the Metropolitan Cathedral of Christ the King to the Anglican cathedral. The Everyman Theatre is situated just at the start of Hope Street on the left.

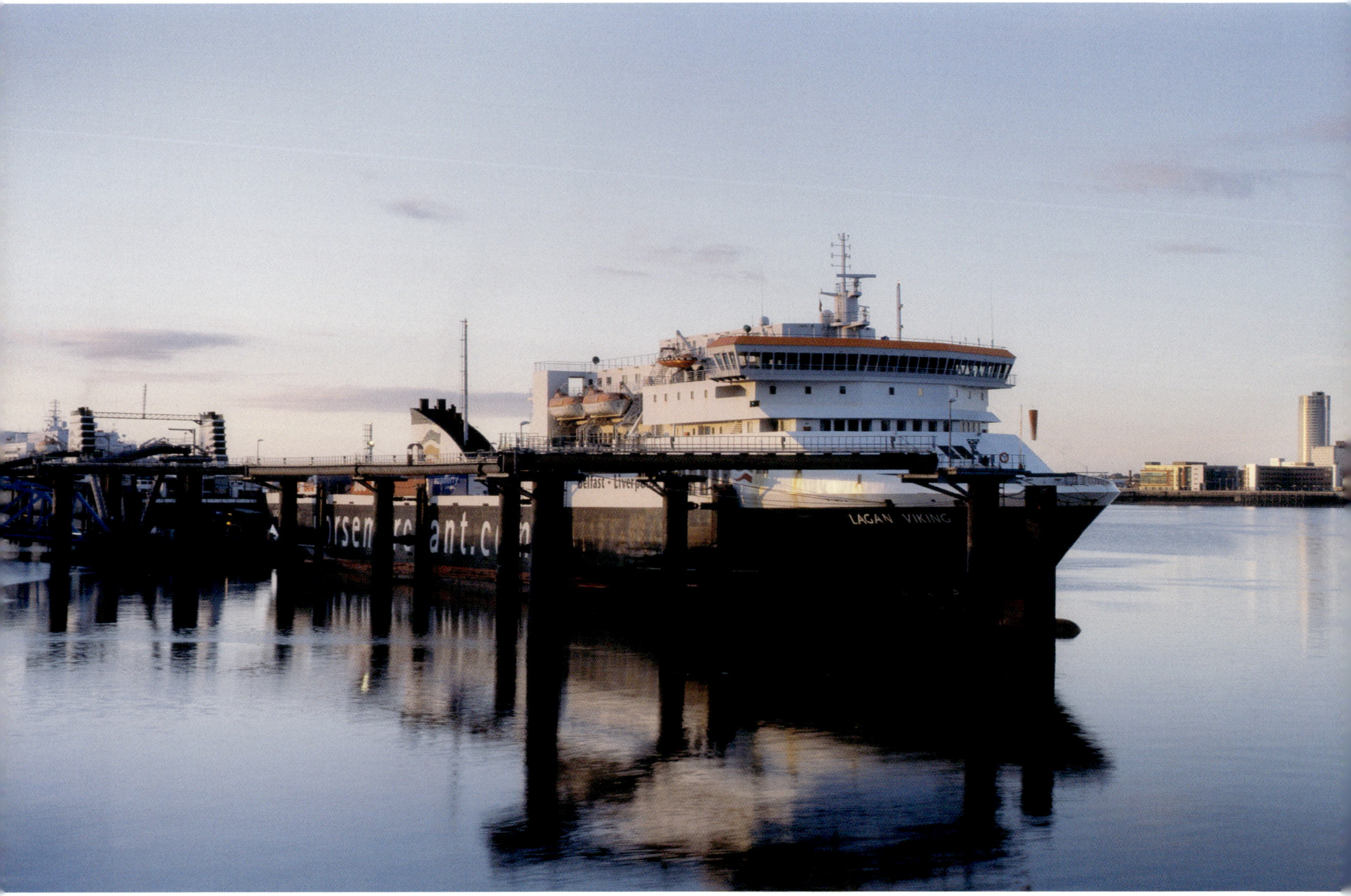
LAGAN VIKING

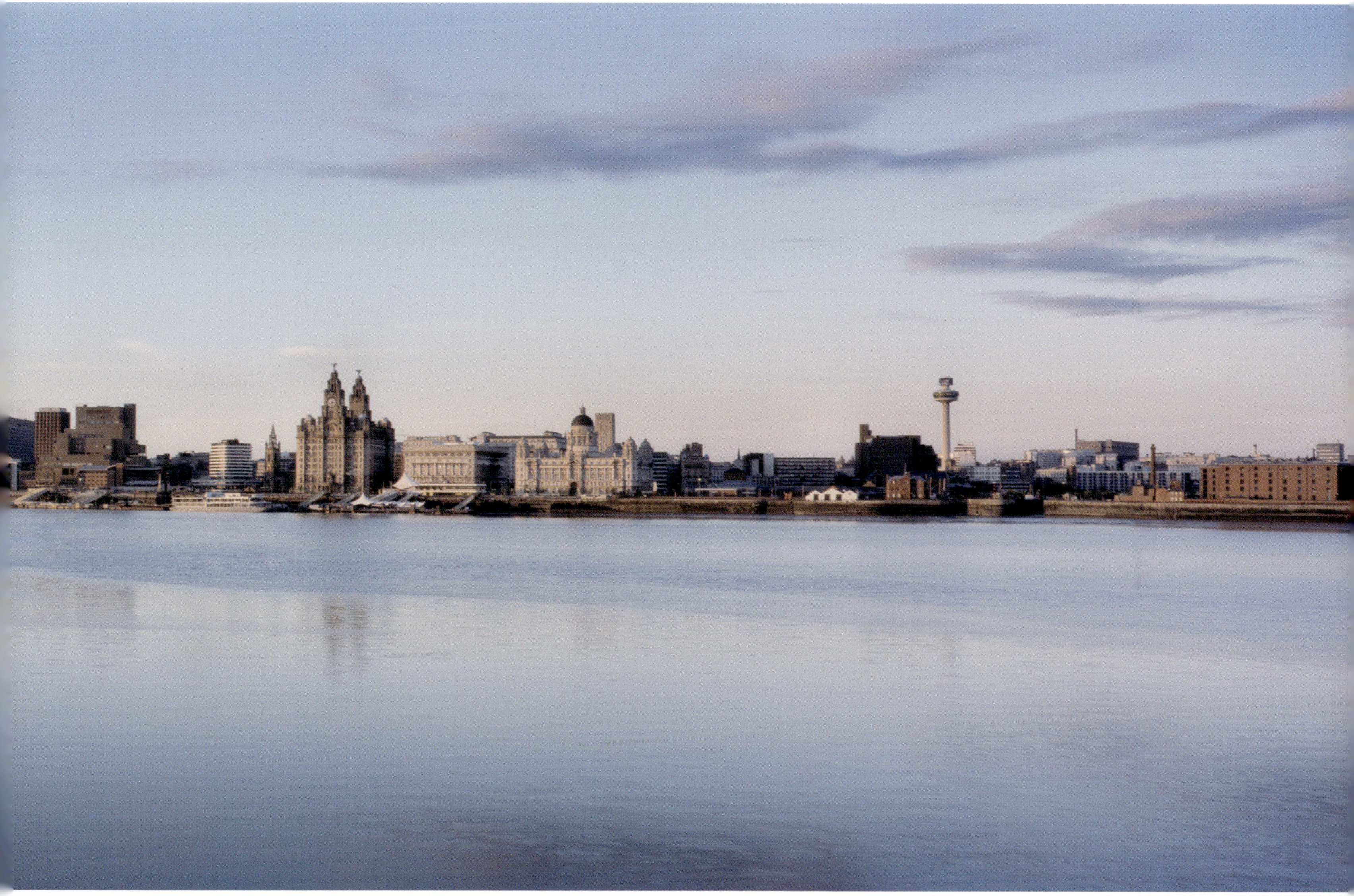

Twelve Quays

Taken on a calm spring evening, this picture shows the new Twelve Quays ferry terminal, looking back towards the Liverpool waterfront. The terminal is a 'RoRo' (roll-on, roll-off) design, and serves Belfast and Dublin. It has the capacity to load two vessels at the same time.

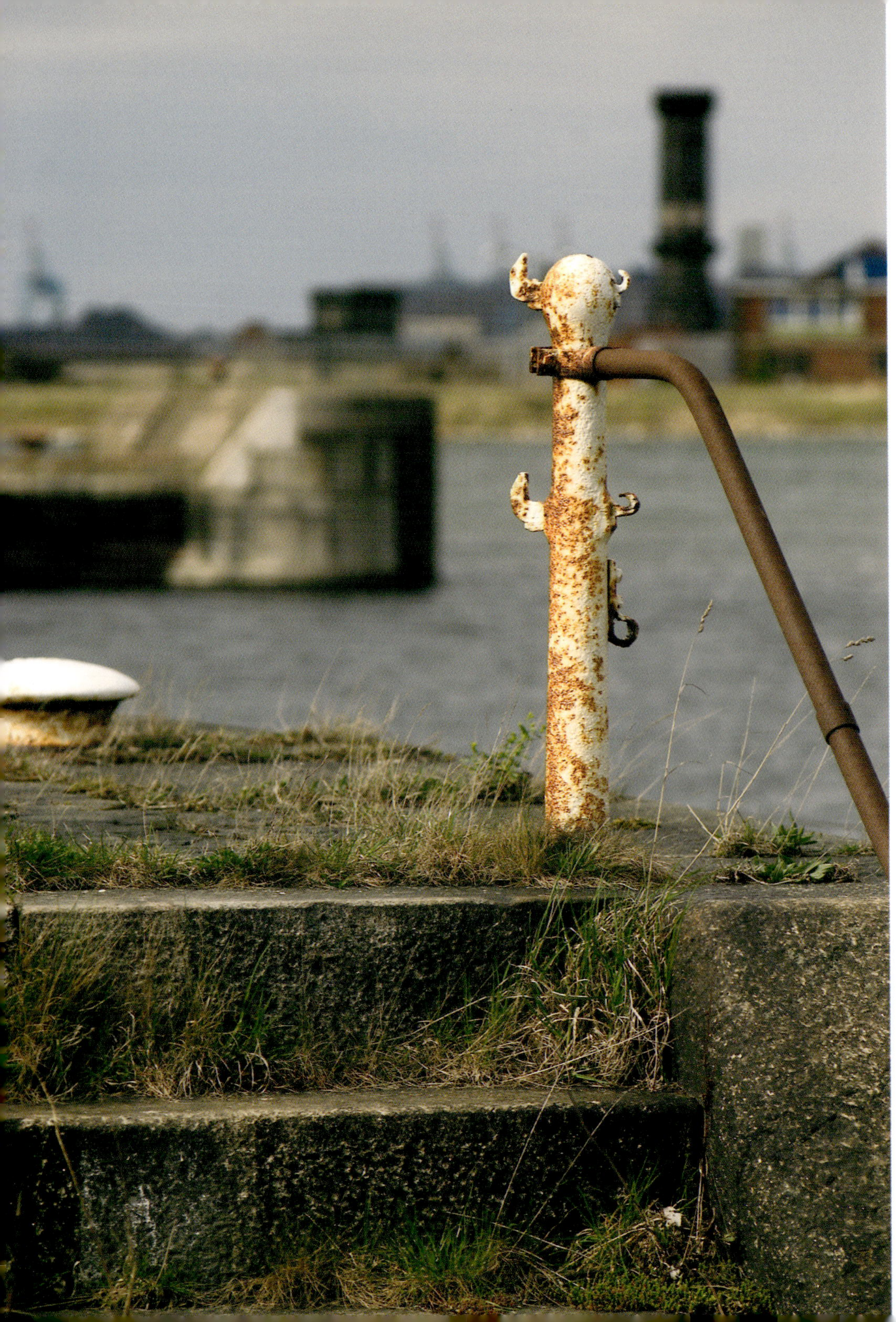

Giving a hand
One of the few remaining handrails at the now-abandoned Prince's Half Tide Dock, with the Victoria Tower by Jesse Hartley at Salisbury Dock in the background.

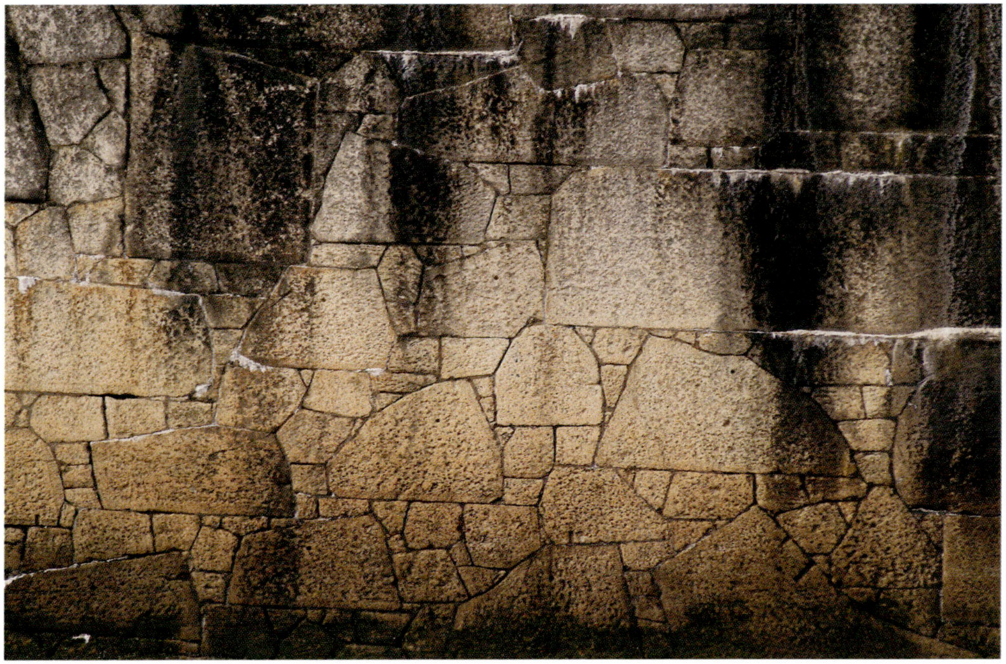

Continuous-face dock walls

Up until the building of the dock at Seaforth, the dock walls were constructed using granite facings, to designs by Jesse Hartley from the mid 1800s. These walls were exceptionally precise, with irregular pieces of rubble being used and set in the thinnest of limestone mortar. This method of construction using 'Hartley granite' was no more expensive than that used with the previous sandstone facings.

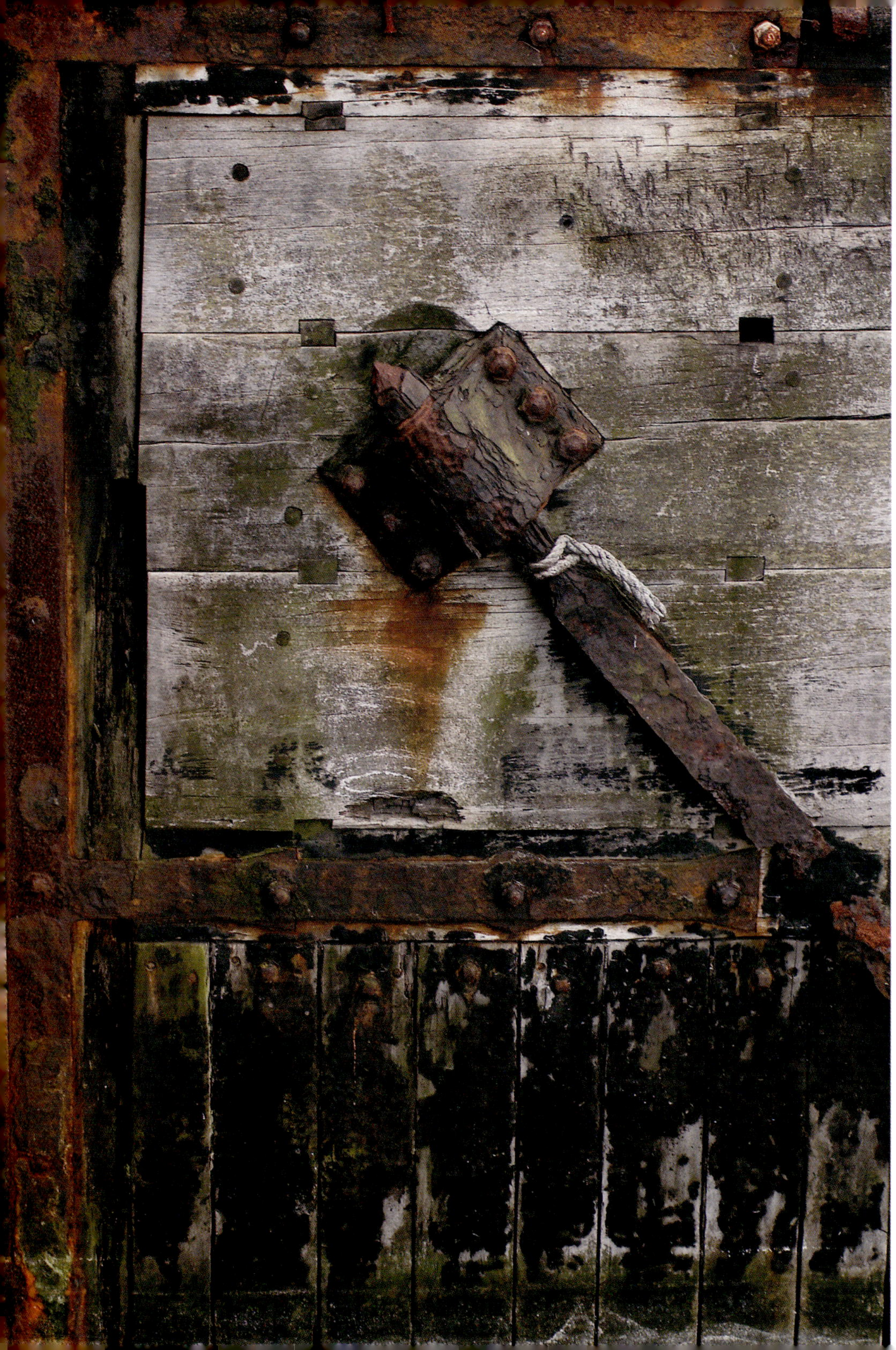

Dock gate

One of the old dock gates leading into the Prince's Half Tide Dock. Installed probably in the mid 1800s and now unused, it is still in remarkable condition, despite the elements it has been exposed to over the years.

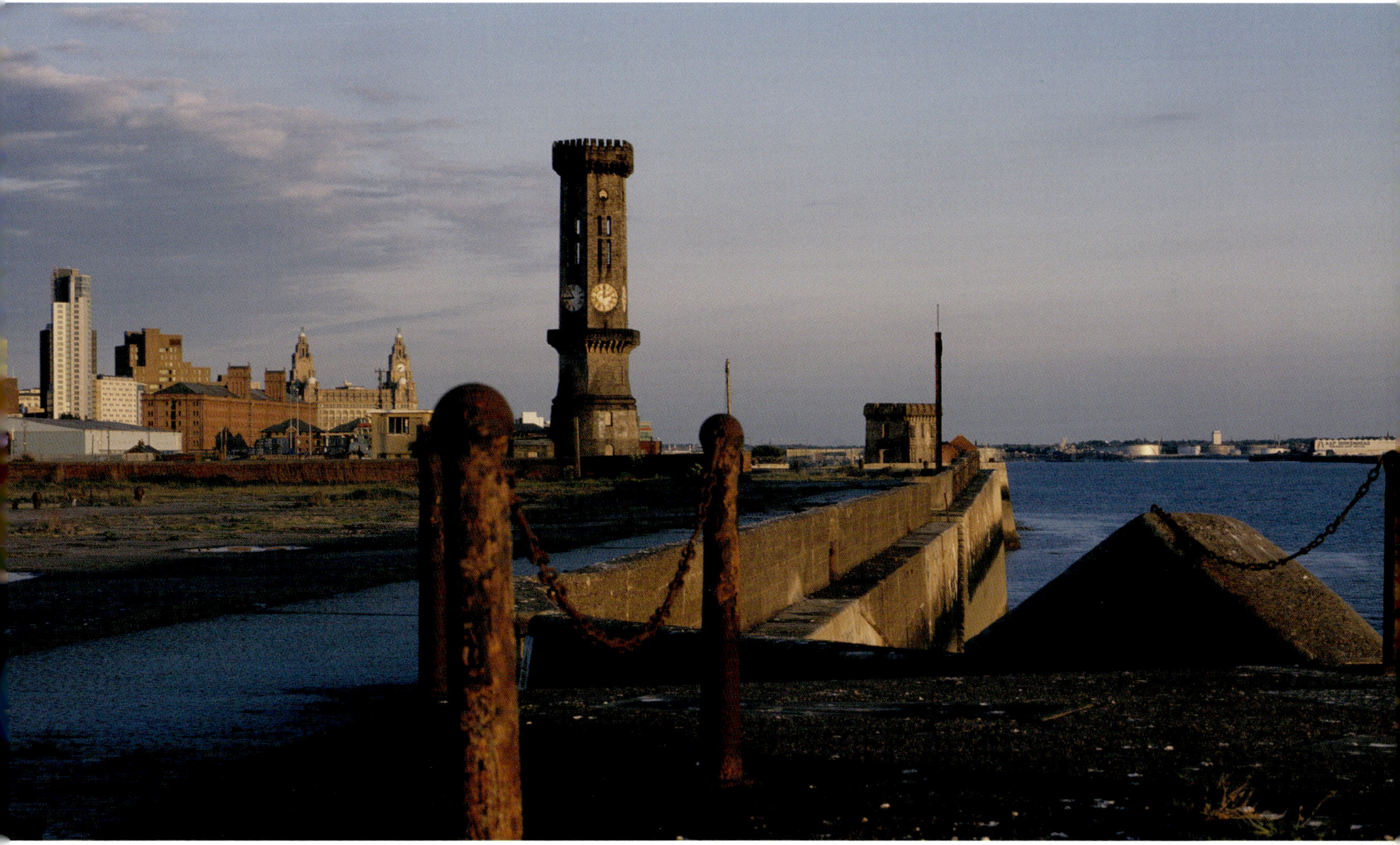

Victoria Tower

Built to commemorate the opening of the Salisbury Dock, the tower was built between 1845 and 1849, and is hexagonal in shape with a clock face on each of its sides. A bell was positioned high in the tower to ring out the high tide and warnings. The architect was Jesse Hartley.

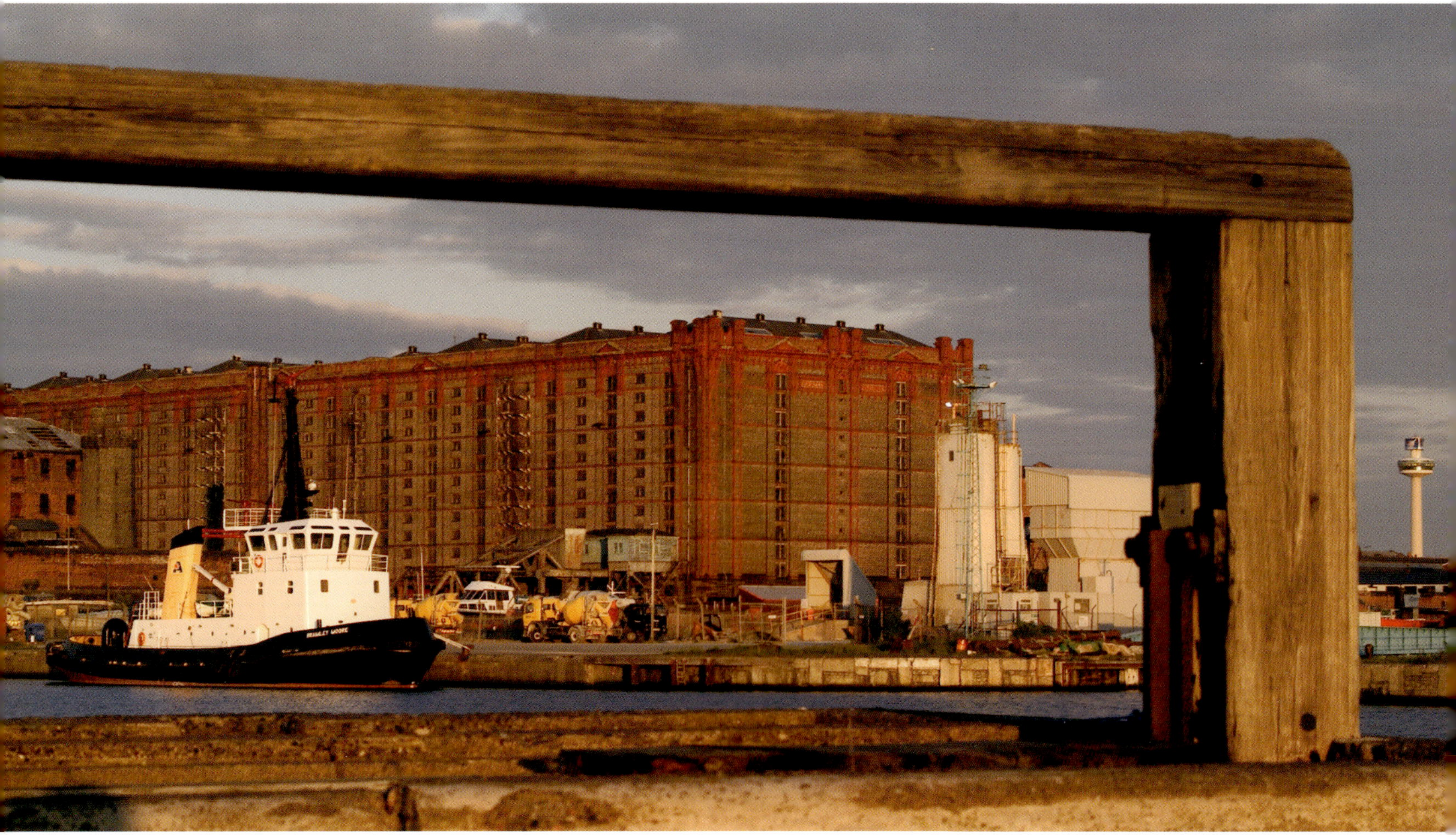

Stanley Dock

Built in 1900 as a tobacco bonded warehouse, this building is said to be the largest brick-built warehouse in the world. A total of around 27million bricks were used in its construction.

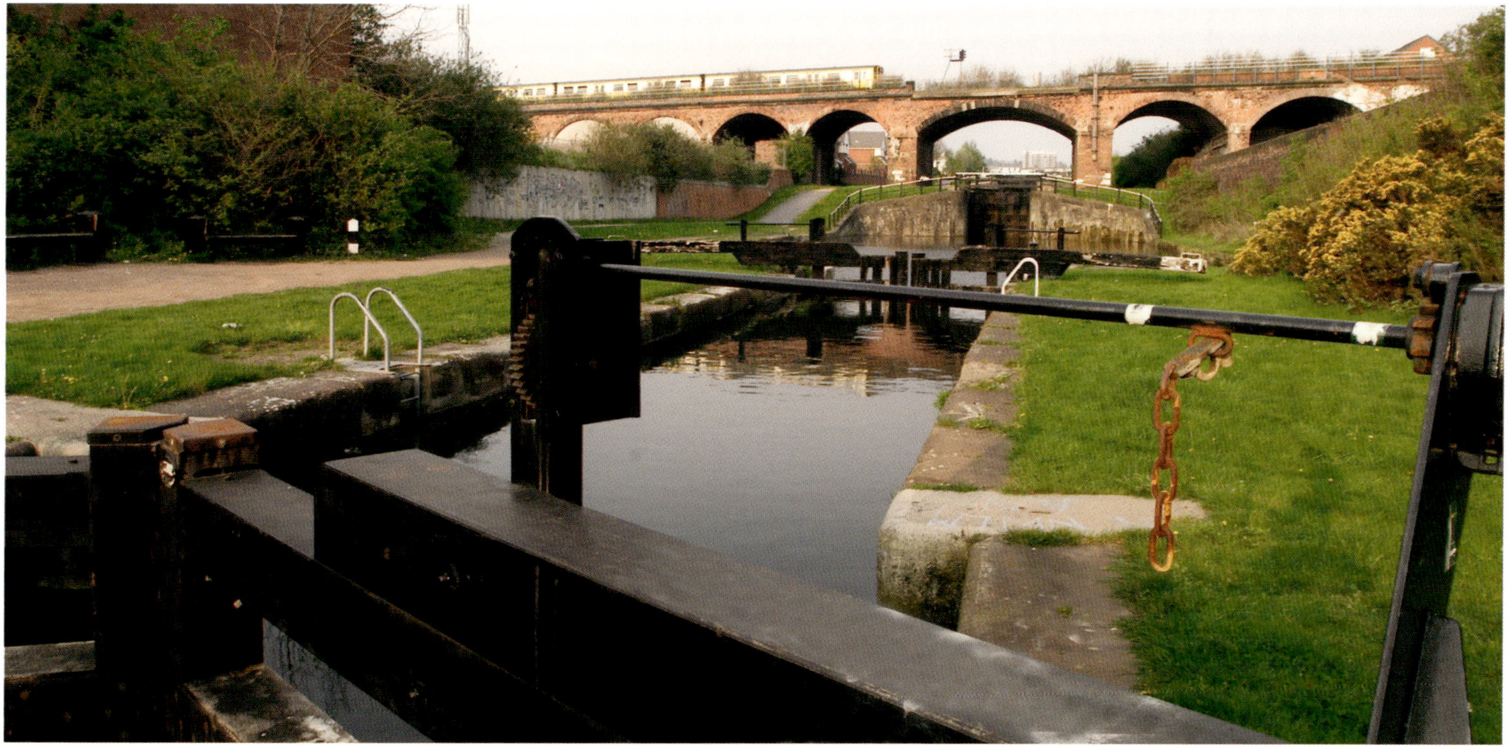

Leeds-Liverpool Canal
A four-tier lock system links the Leeds-Liverpool Canal to the Stanley Dock and beyond that, to the River Mersey.

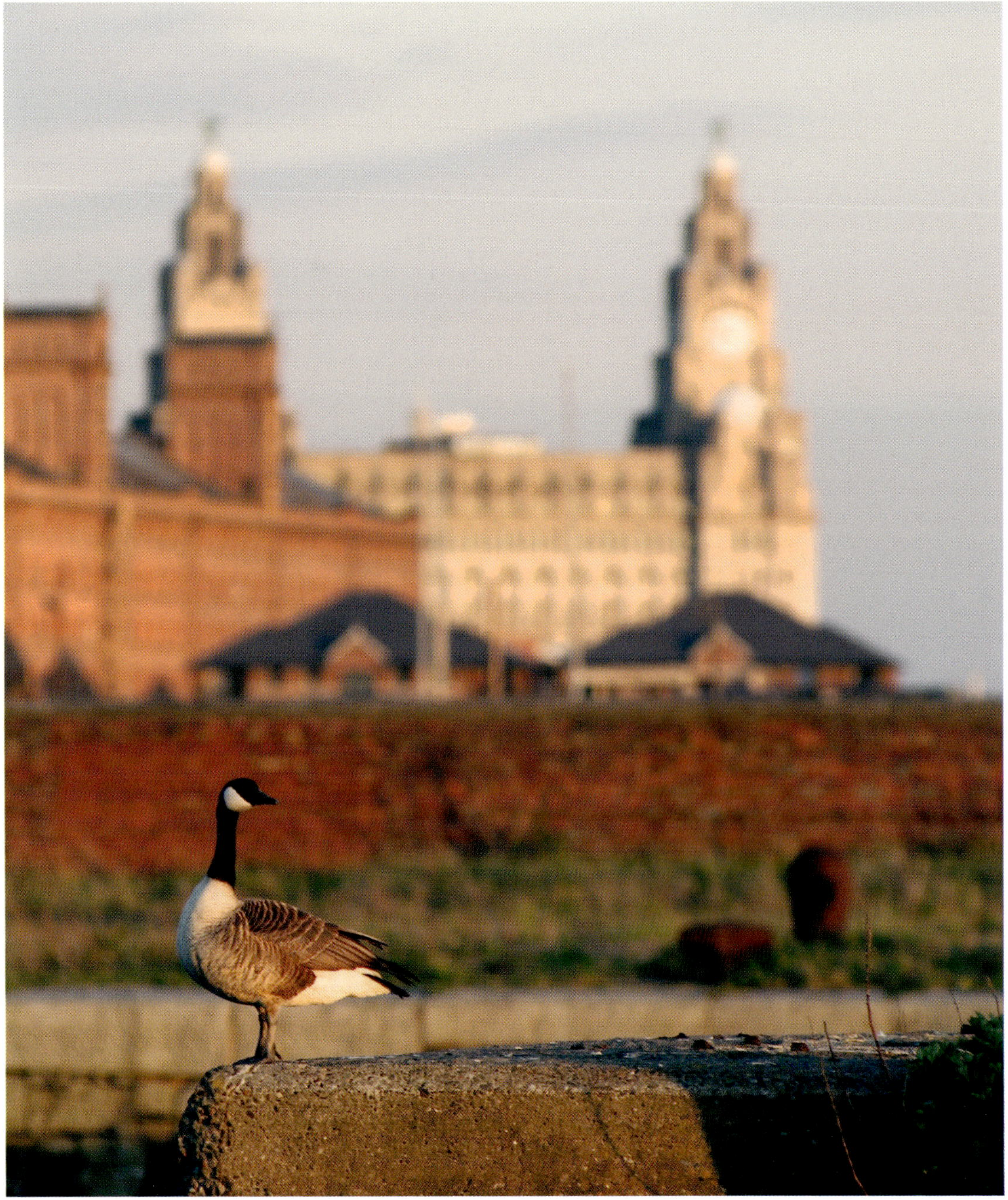

Canada goose
Relatively quiet and serene, Nelson Dock is an ideal place for wildlife and Canada geese are frequent visitors. Canada Dock, further into the North Docks, would have been a more appropriate calling point for these birds, but it is a much busier place and therefore not so attractive.

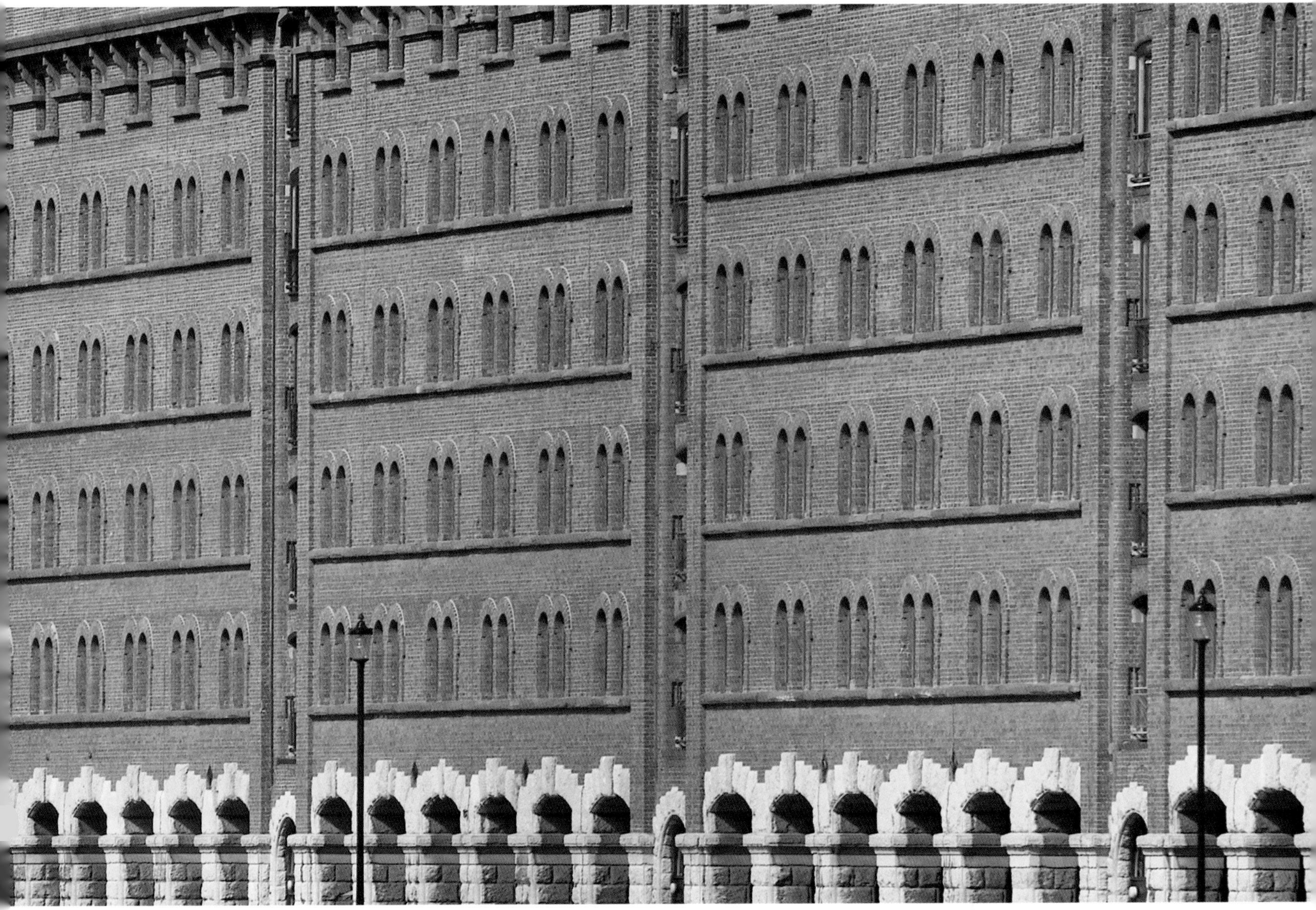

Waterloo Warehouse

Built in 1867 as a grain warehouse, this impressive building has now been converted to luxury apartments. It was an extension of the Albert Dock.

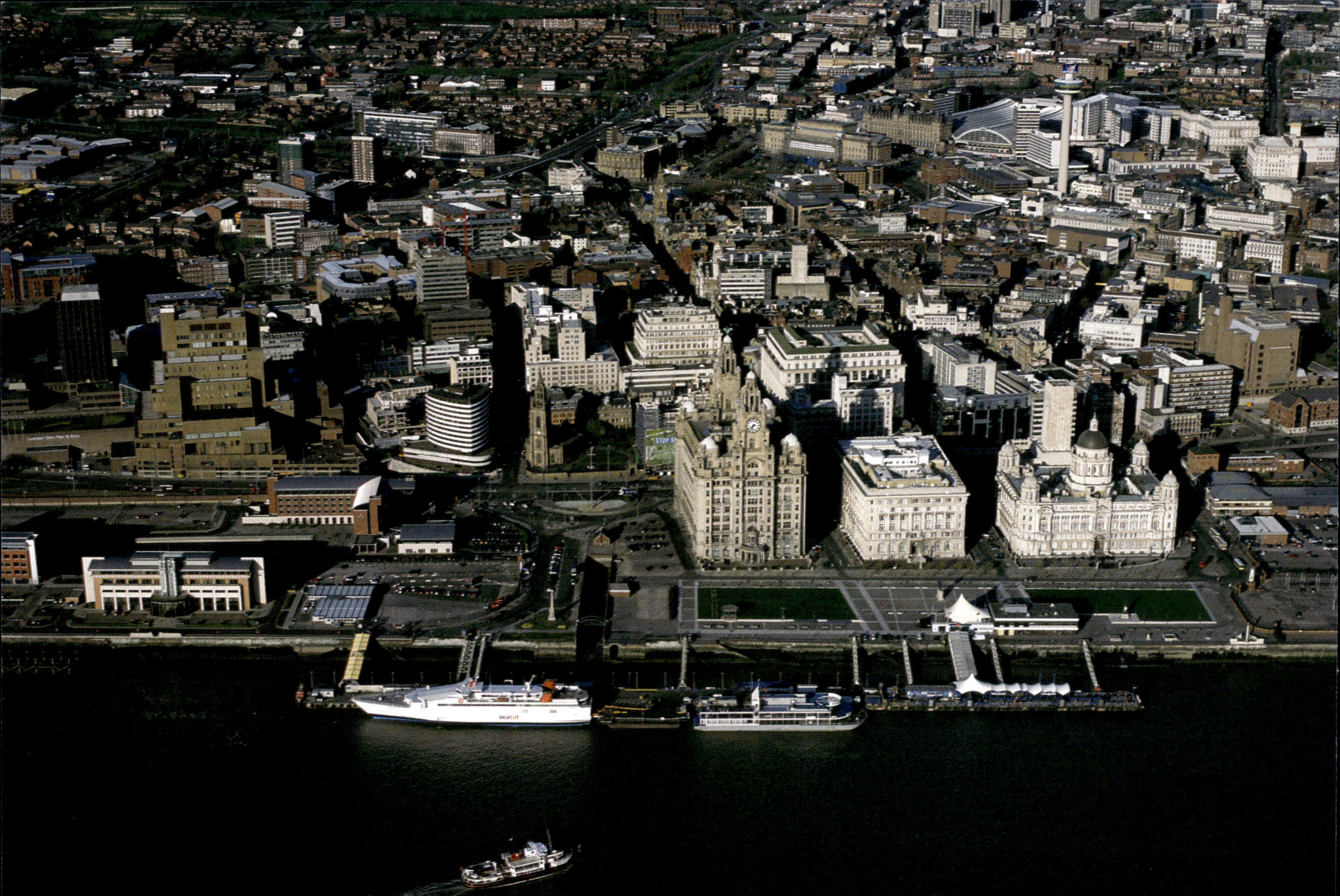
seacat

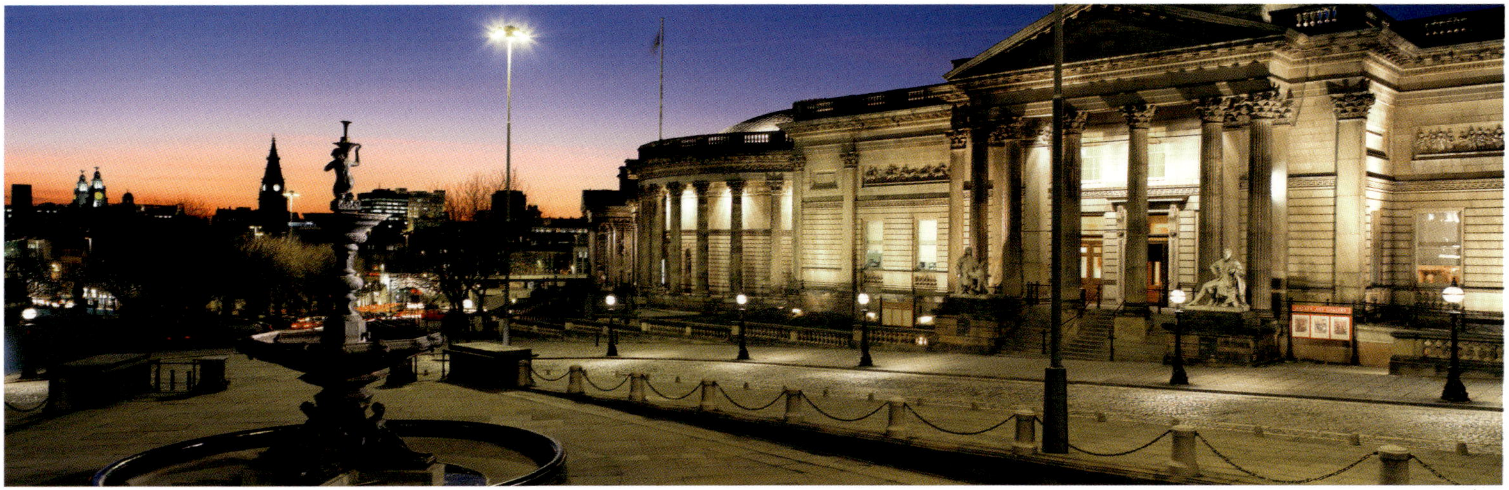

The Walker Art Gallery

The famous Walker Art Gallery was built between 1873 to 1877, and the architects were Sherlock and Vale. Also seen is the Steble Fountain (near left foreground), the Municipal Buildings, and in the distance, the Royal Liver Buildings, which once again dominate the skyline of Liverpool.

Aerial view of the Mersey Ferry *(left)*

The ferry boats always dock facing the flow of the tide. Here *Royal Daffodil* makes its approach and an opportunist jet skier riding the wake turns his sweep into a question mark.

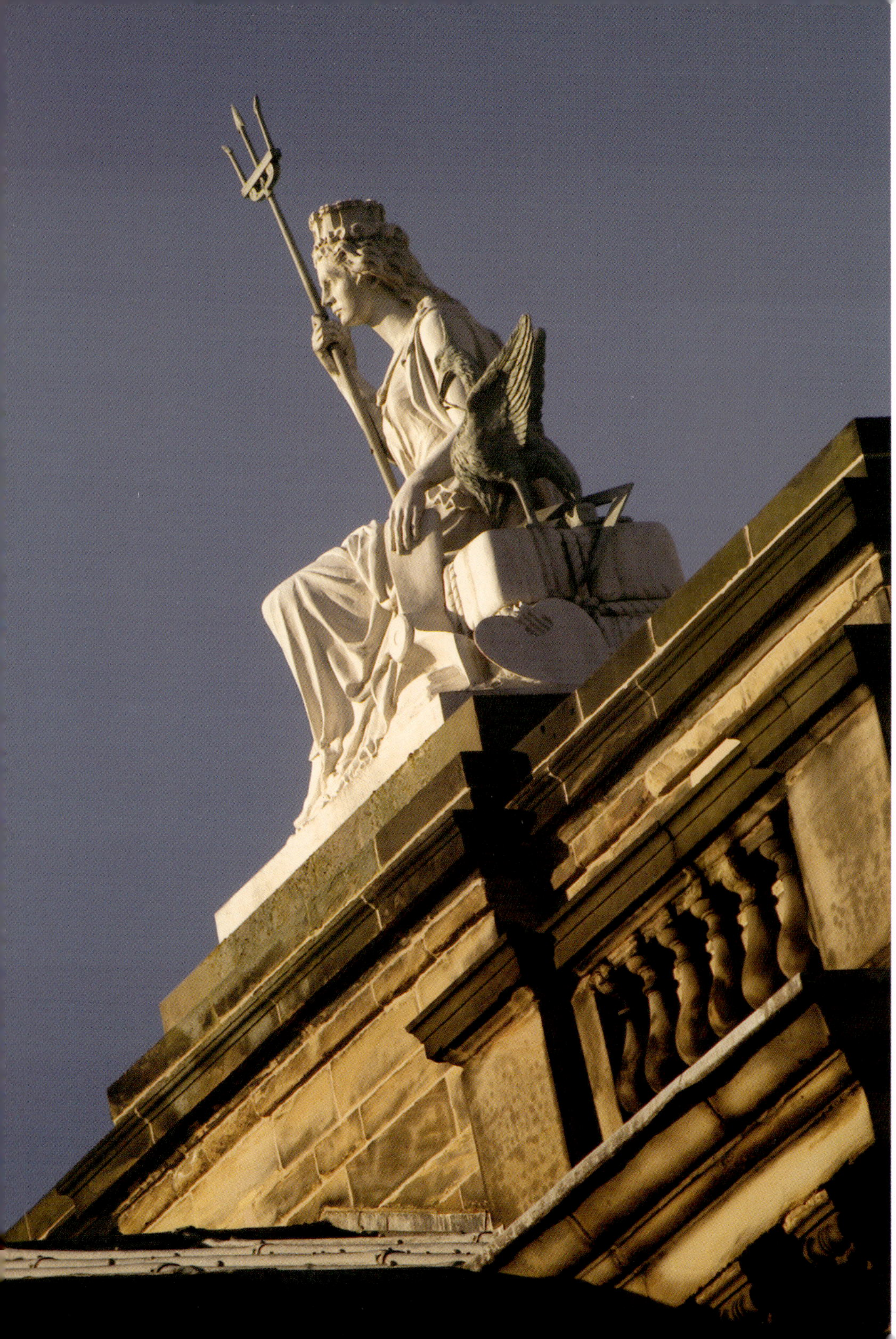

New Liverpool

This statue representing the new Liverpool is situated on the roof of the Walker Art Gallery. The old statue dating from 1877 was removed in 1993 due to its poor condition. Now displayed at the Conservation Centre on Victoria Street, it has been left in its deteriorated state to show the ravages of atmospheric pollution. This new statue was rough-hewn from a 42-ton block of marble in China, and then finished by Chinese craftsmen on site. Installed in 1998, she is attended by a Liver Bird.

Raphael

One of a pair of statues situated at the entrance of the Walker Art Gallery; the other is Michelangelo. Raphael was installed in 1877, and unfortunately he is now showing signs of deterioration due to previous decades of pollution.

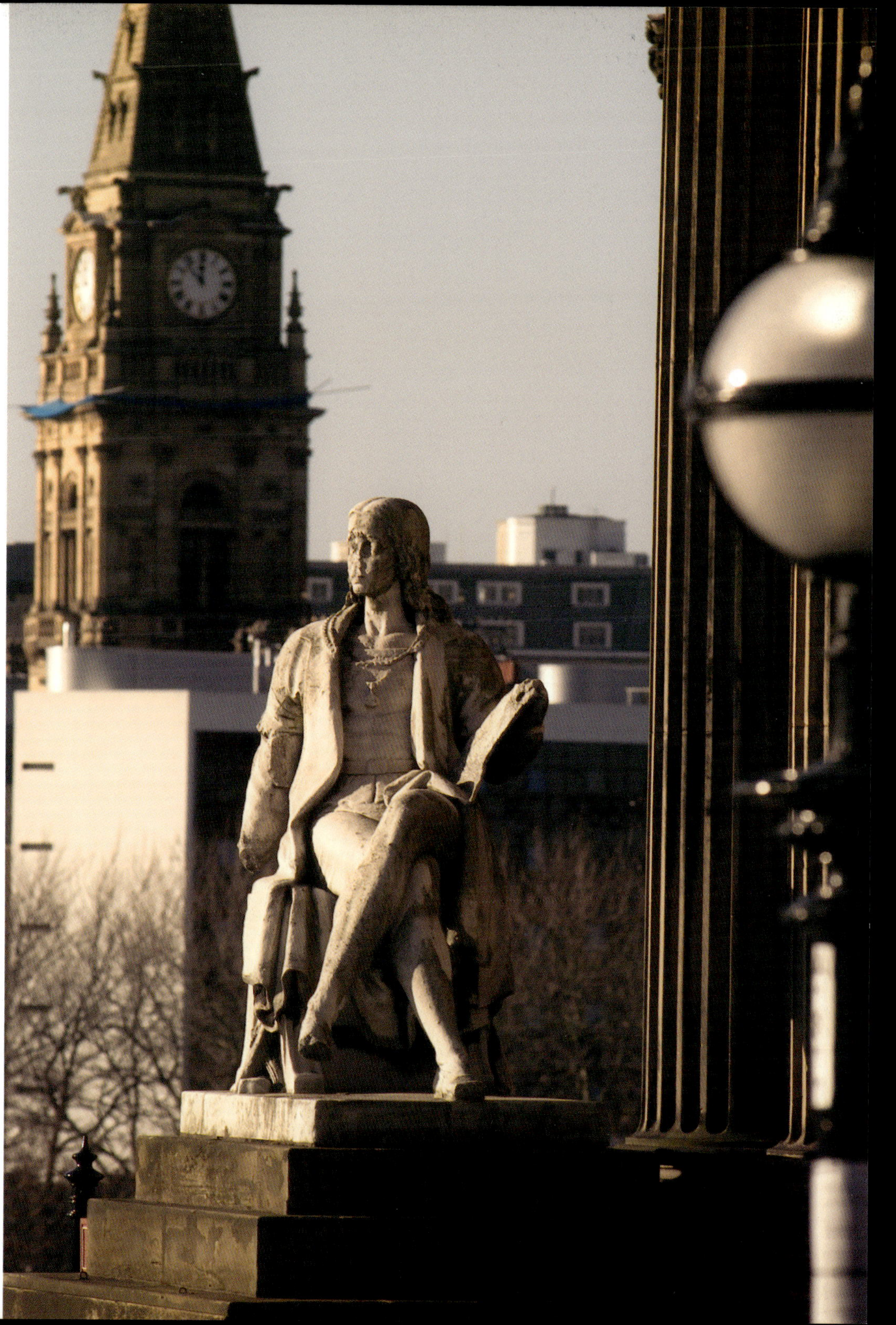

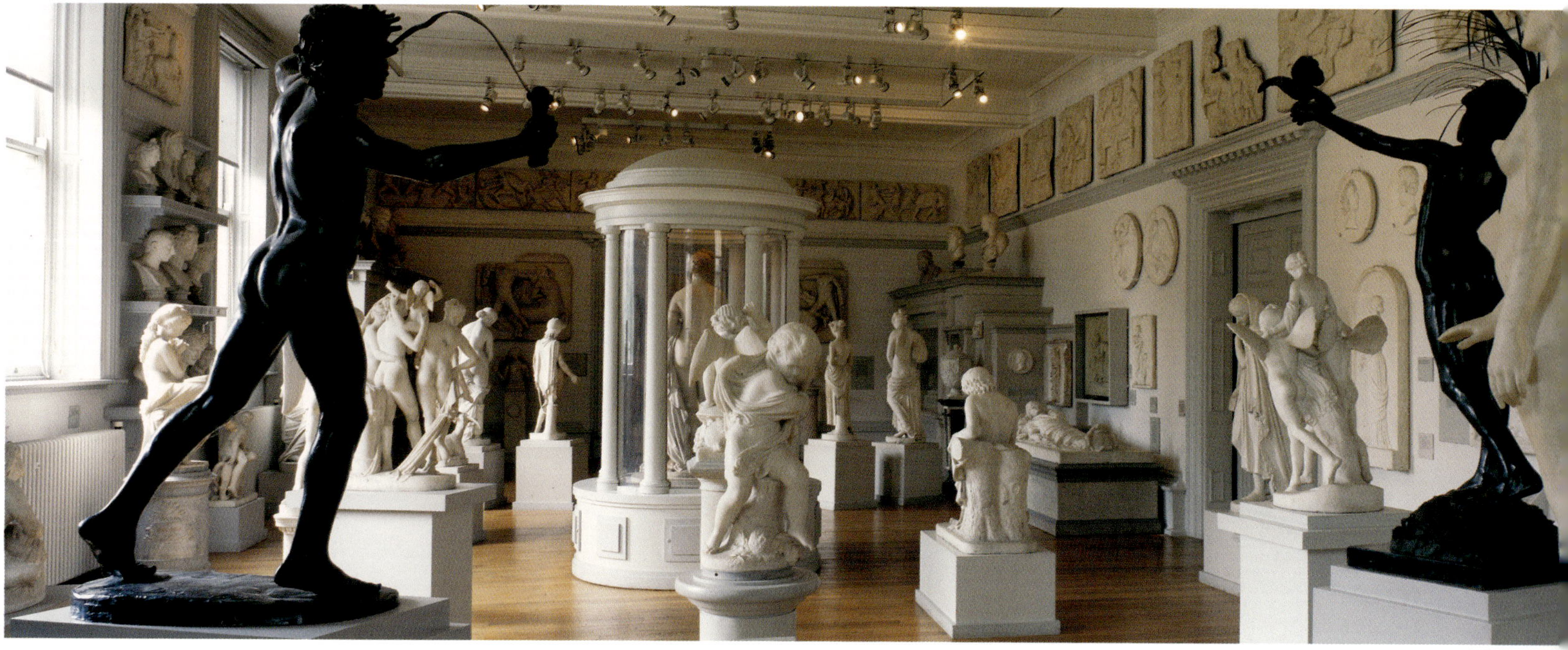

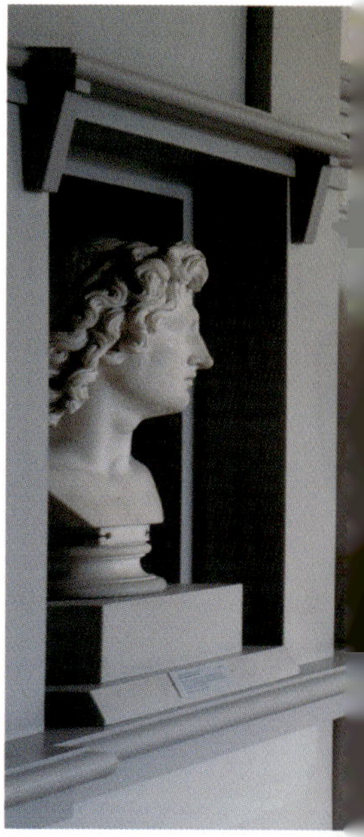

The Walker Art Gallery interior
The spectacular marble statue section within the Walker Art Galley.

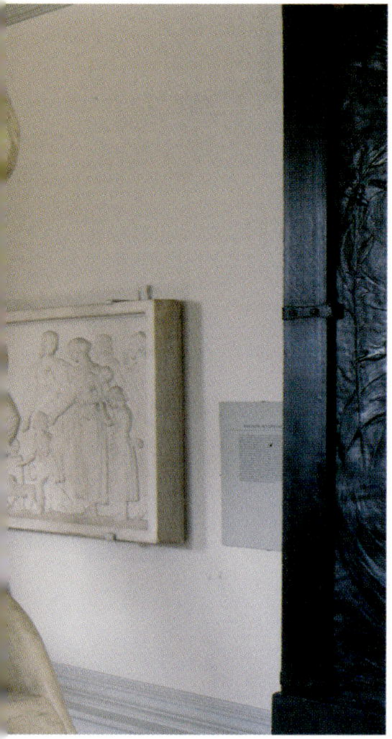

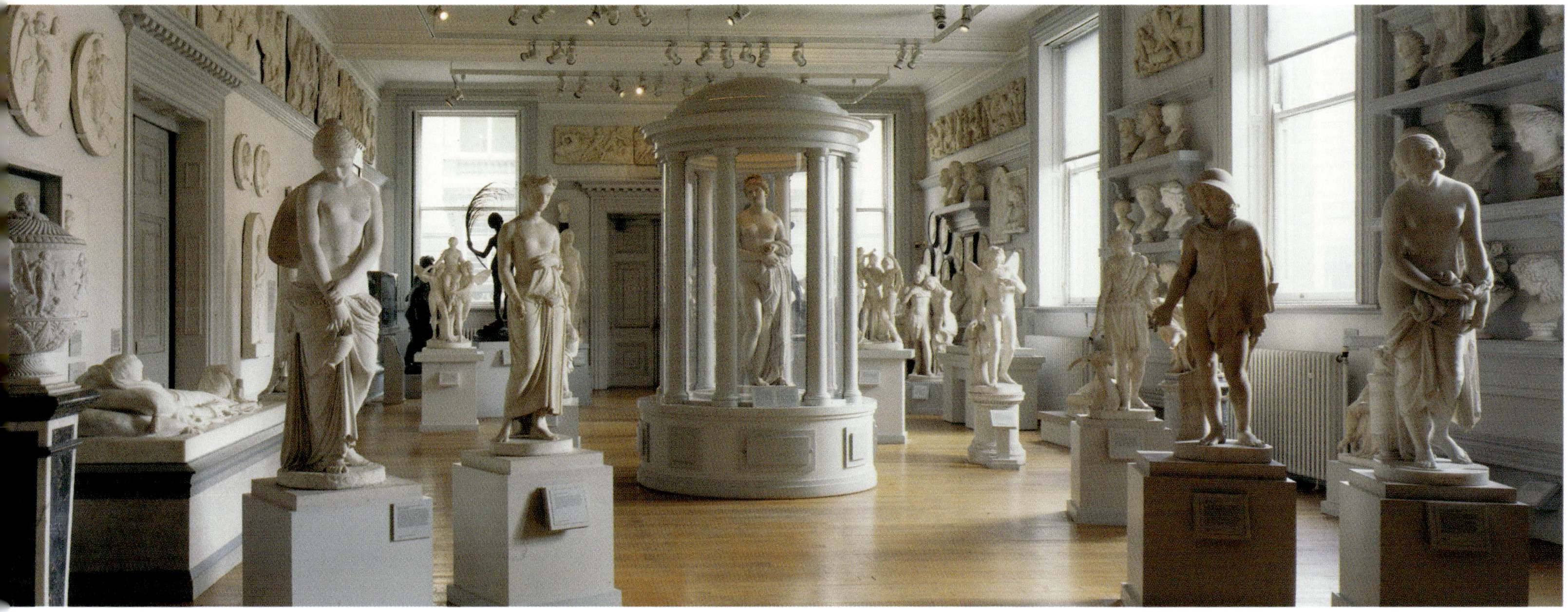

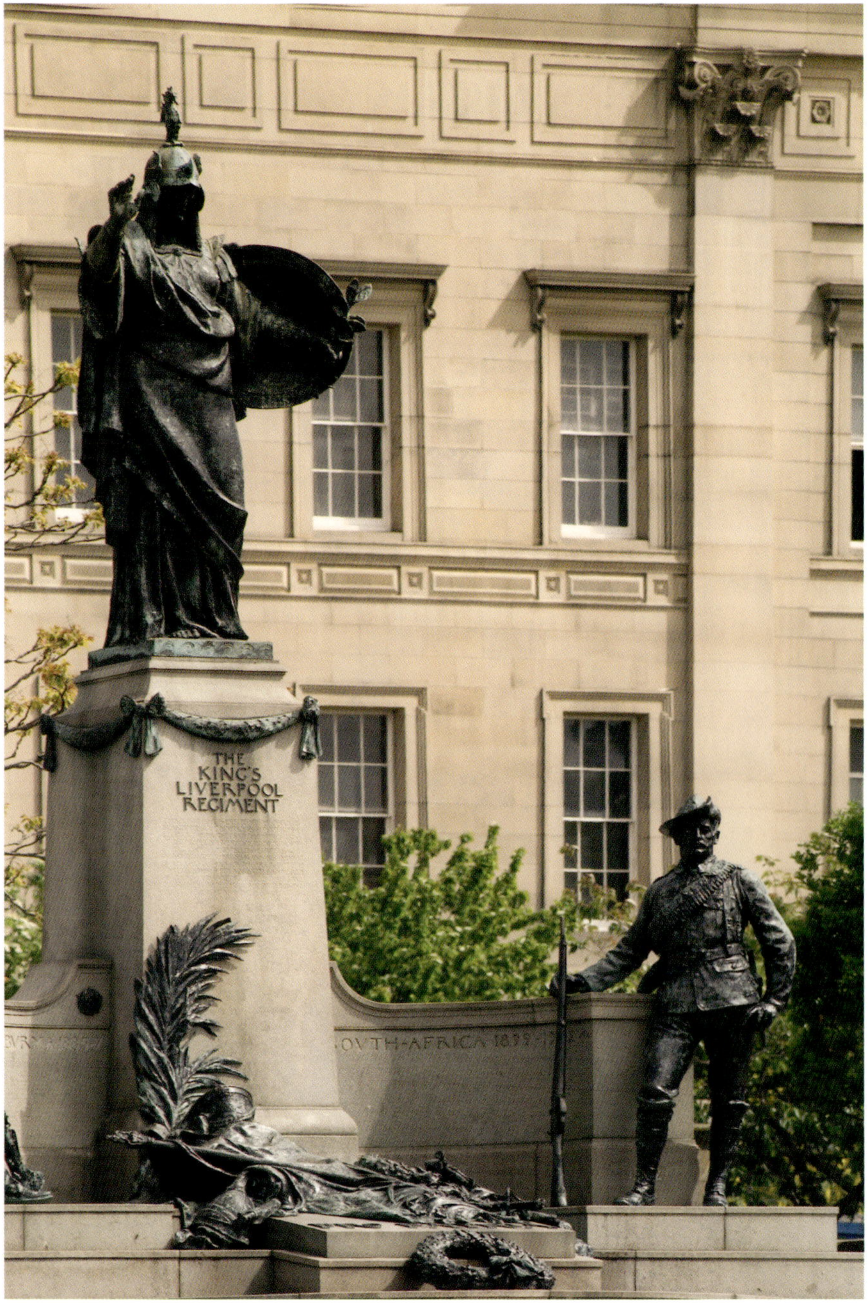

St John's Gardens
Placed behind St George's Hall in the gardens is this memorial to the King's Liverpool Regiment by Sir William Goscombe John. Unveiled by Field Marshal Sir George White VC in September 1905, the cost of the memorial was £3000.

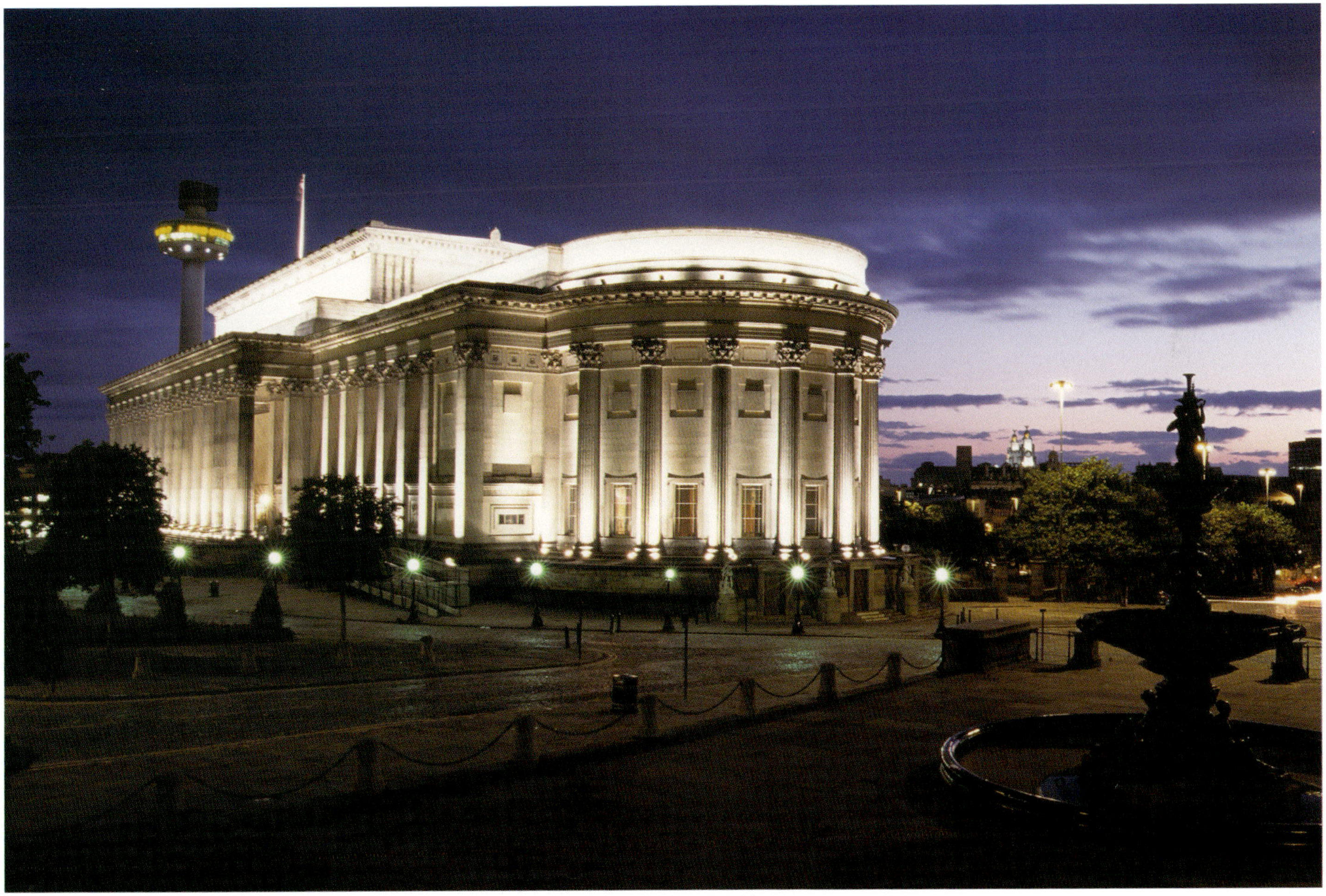

St George's Hall

Once described as one of greatest buildings in the world, St George's Hall was designed with a budget of £30,000 following a competition which was won by architect Harvey Lonsdale Elmes. It has a sophisticated heating system and a floor of Minton tiles. Some of these were also used in the Capitol Building in Washington DC. The Law Courts which are still in existence are often used to replicate the Old Bailey in London in film and TV drama series.

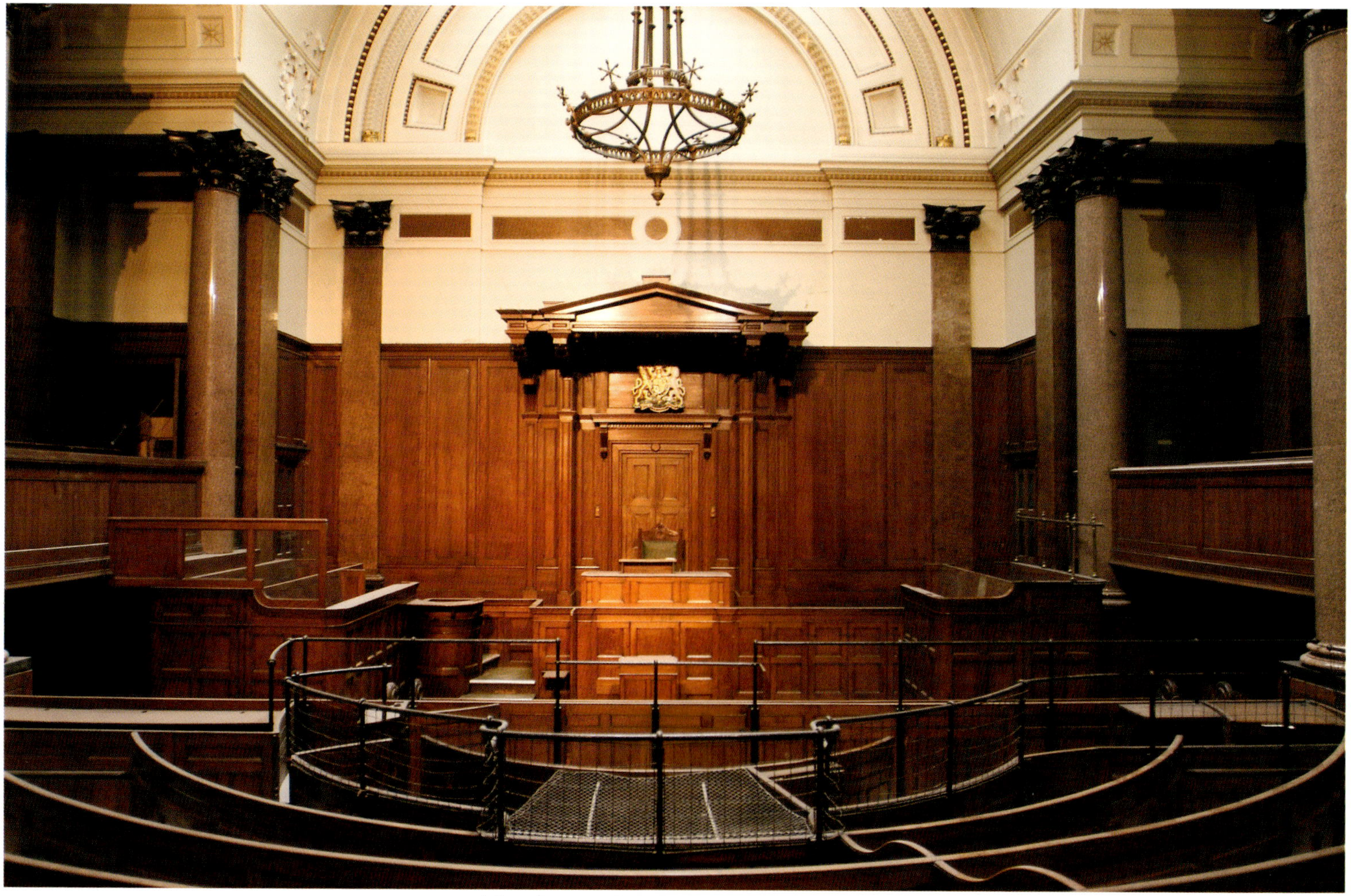

The Crown Court, St George's Hall.
This famous court has seen many infamous trials, notably the Florence Maybrick case of 1889, the 1931 Julia Wallace murder and the Cameo Cinema murders of 1949. However what is more interesting is that this sombre-looking court room was only a step away from the majesty of the Grand Hall and Victorian high society. Often cases were of only six minutes in duration and in effect there was a production line mentality to the court proceedings. It was last used in 1984.

St George's Plateau
The statue of Prime Minister
Benjamin Disraeli (1804-81) in
bronze by Charles Bell Birch was unveiled
in 1883 on the St George's Plateau.

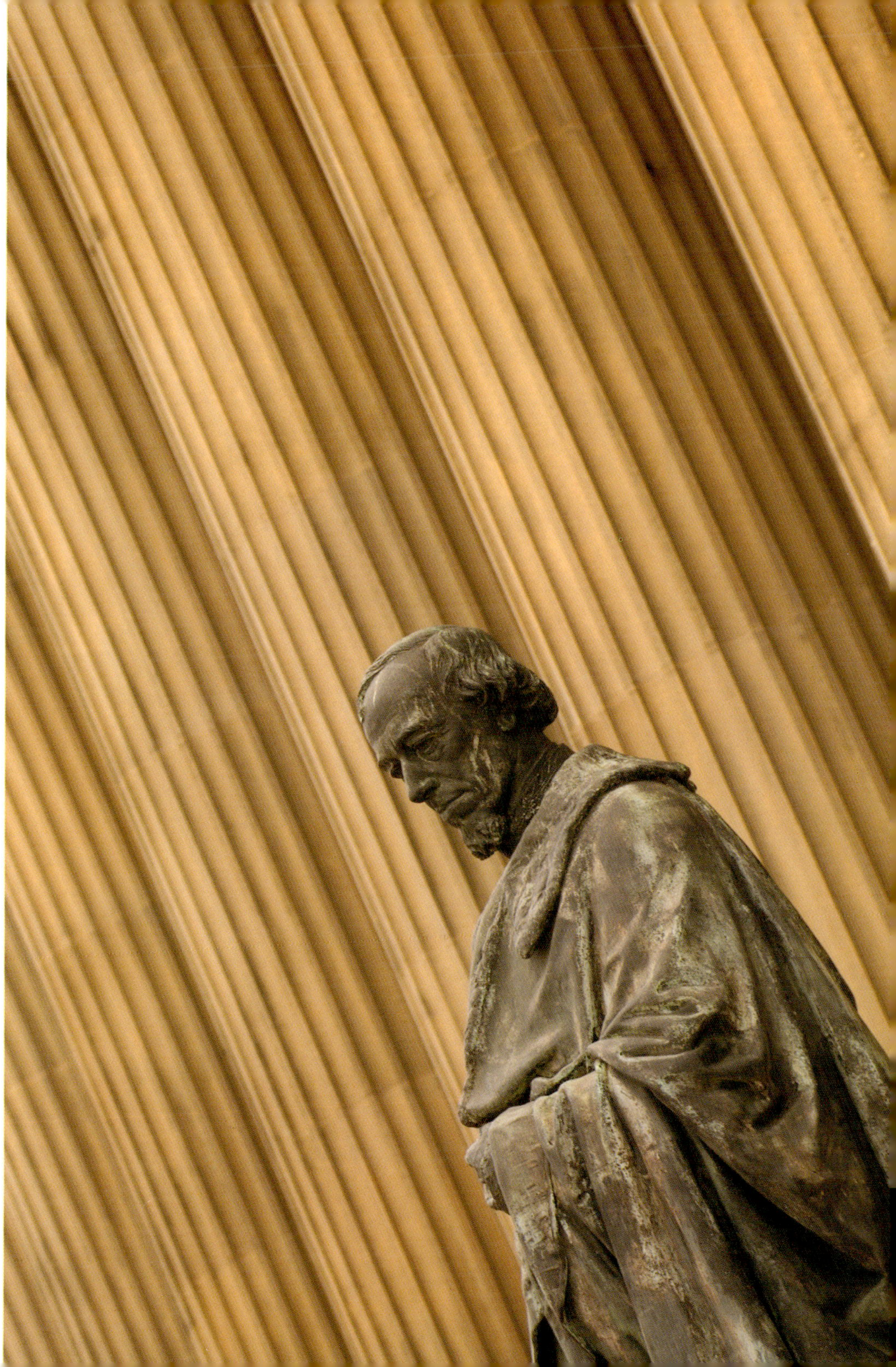

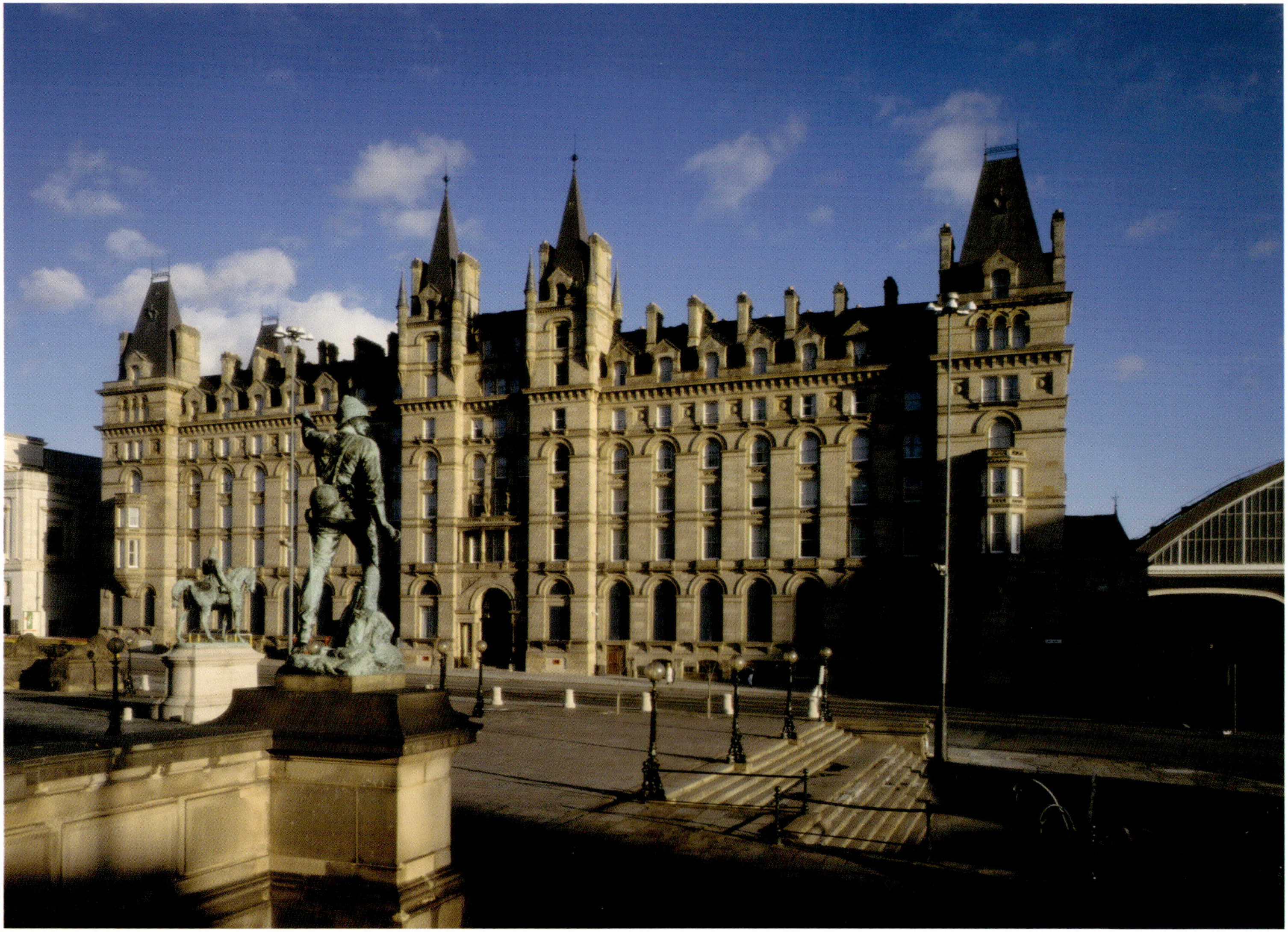

North Western Hotel

Opened in 1871 as a 330-room hotel serving Lime Street Station, the North Western was eventually changed for use as a railway office. In the 1990s, it was converted to student accommodation for Liverpool John Moores University. The building stands opposite St George's Hall.

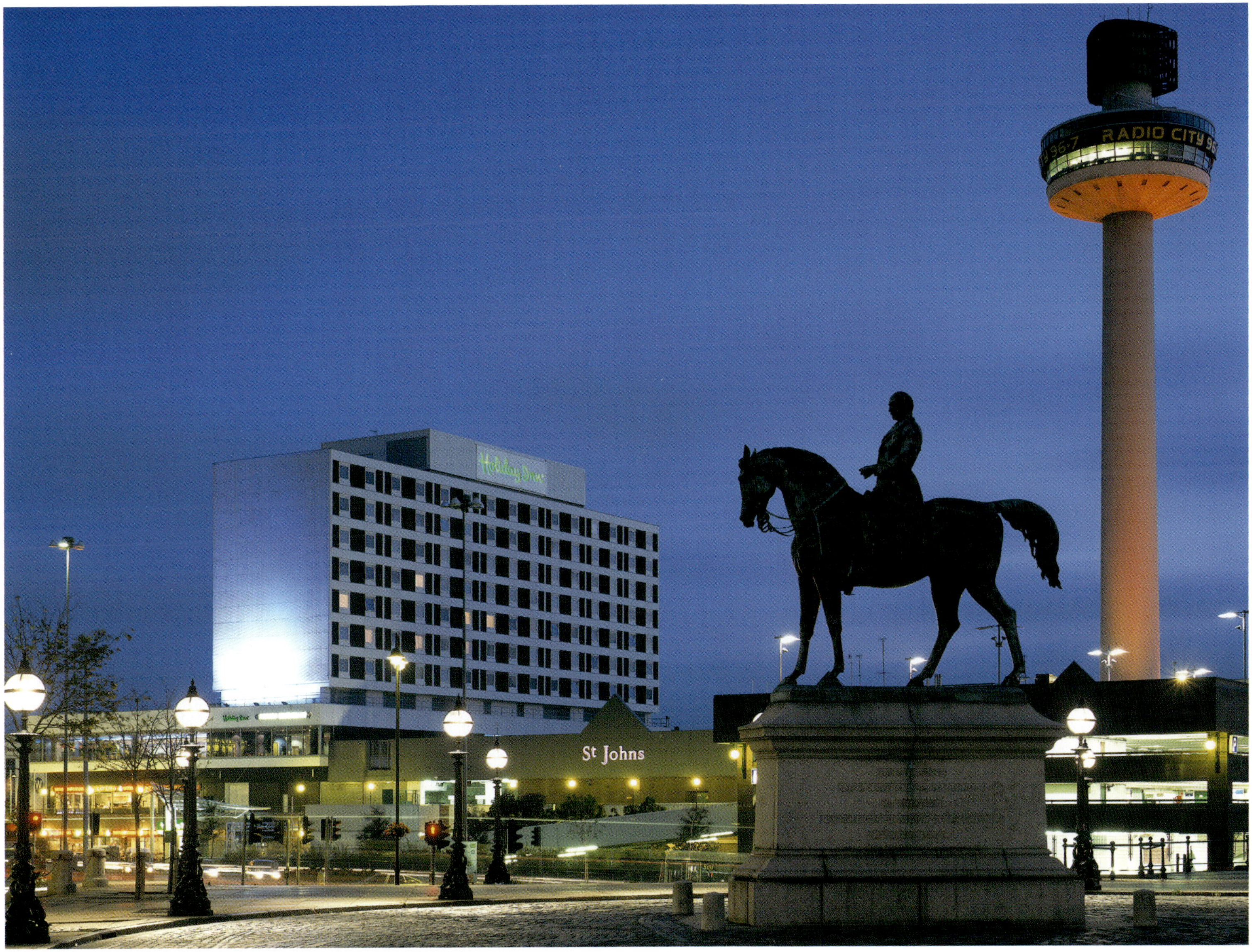

St George's Plateau

Looking towards the Holiday Inn Hotel and St John's Beacon. The Beacon is now home to Radio City, and these two modern structures contrast strongly with the statue of Prince Albert, which was erected in his honour after his death in 1861. The statue was unveiled in 1866, and a second statue of his wife, Queen Victoria, at the east end of the Plateau was unveiled in 1869.

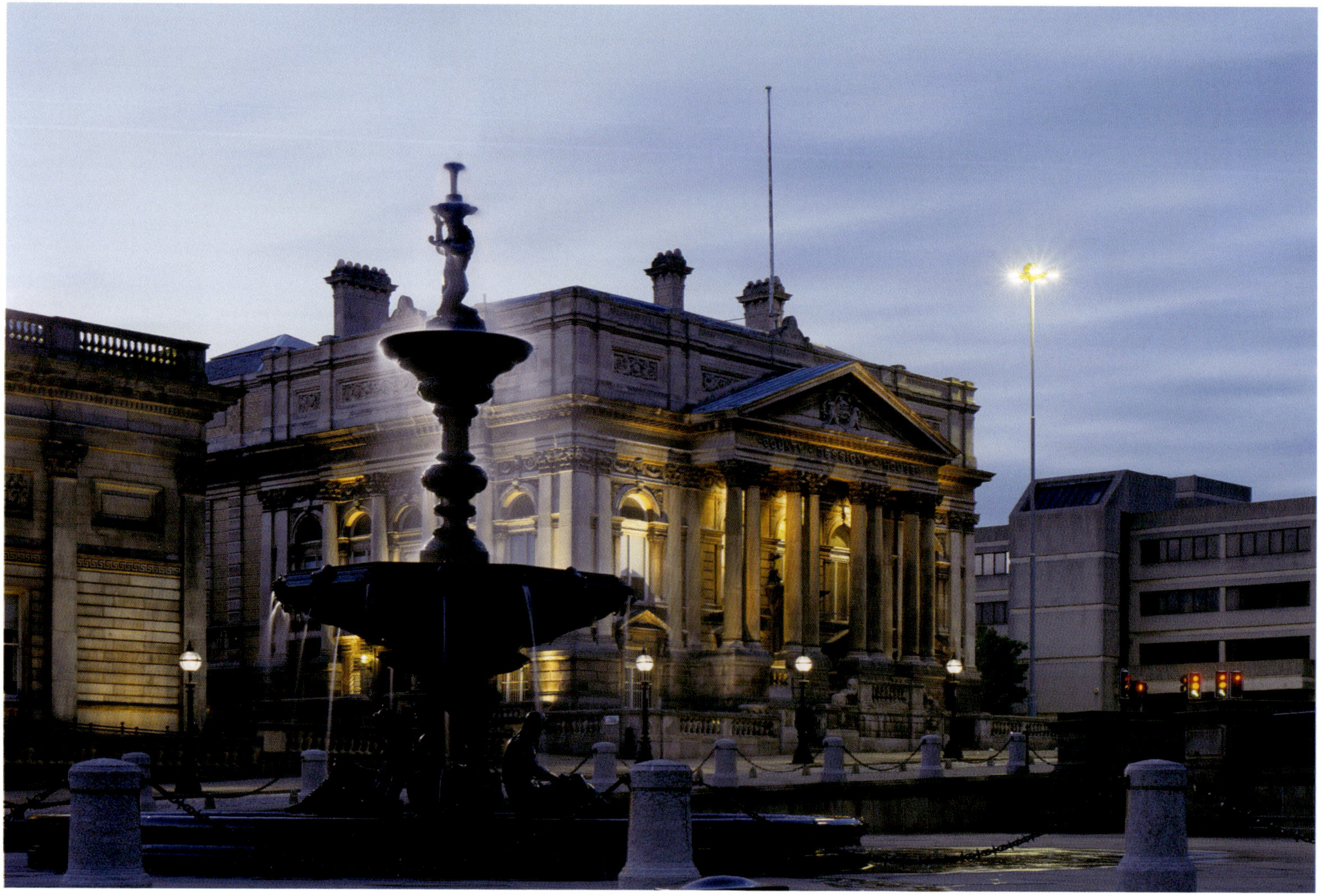

County Sessions House

Situated next door to the Walker Art Gallery, this building on William Brown Street was built in 1882-4 by F.G. Holme. The interior featured separate circulation for prisoners, public, solicitors and witnesses, barristers and magistrates. The Sessions House had two court rooms, with the cells in the basement.

The Steble Fountain

Presented to the town in 1877 by Lieut Col R.F. Steble, the Steble Fountain was restored in 1992 when the Tall Ships Race called at the city. This is one of two almost identical fountains designed by Paul Lienard: the other one is in Boston, Massachusetts.

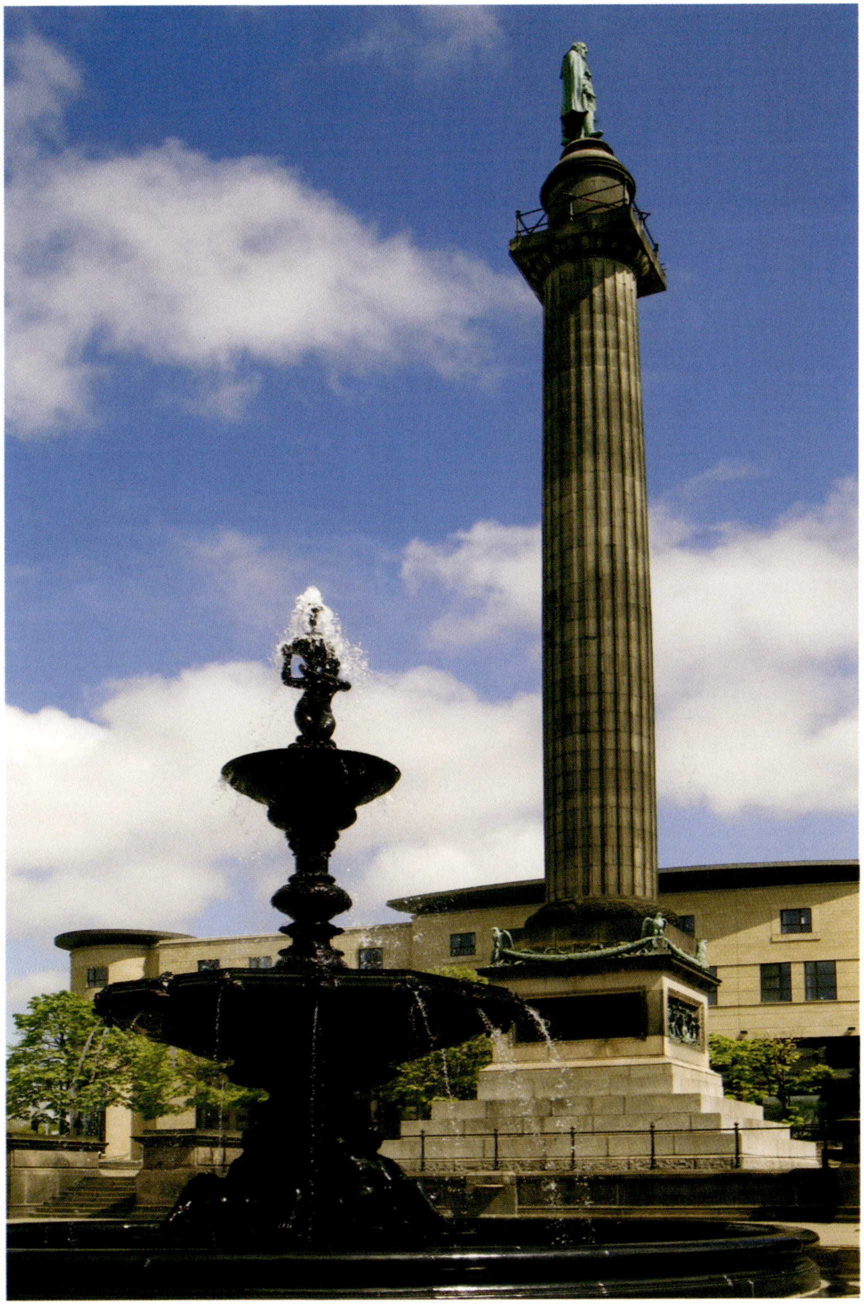

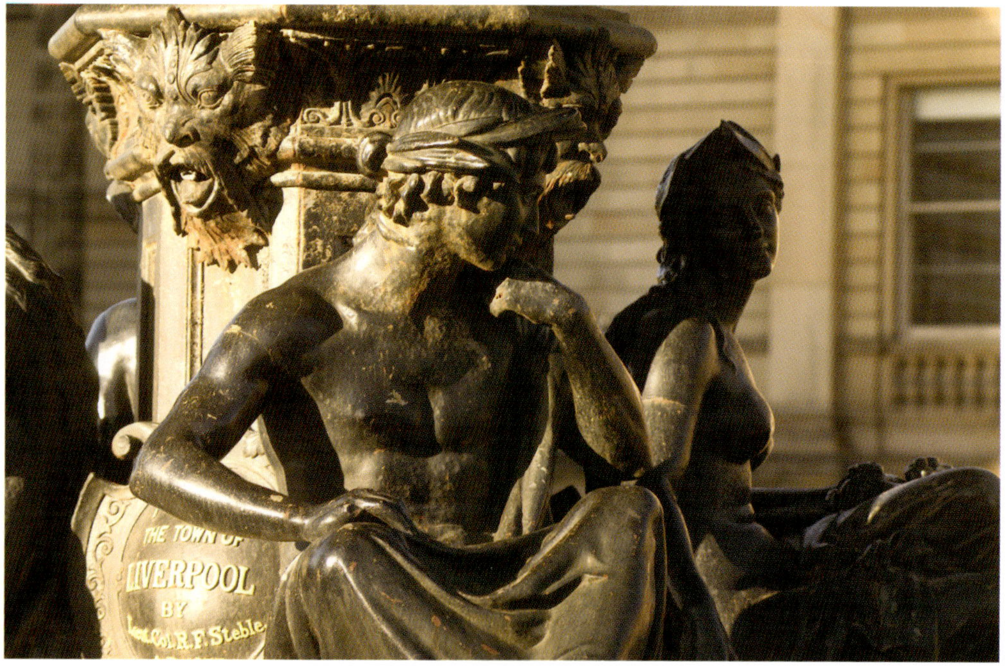

The Steble Fountain

St John's Beacon

Modern and classical architecture contrast starkly in height as this view from Everton Brow clearly demonstrates. St John's Beacon was erected in 1972 and is 450ft high, while the Wellington Column of 1863 is only 132ft in height.

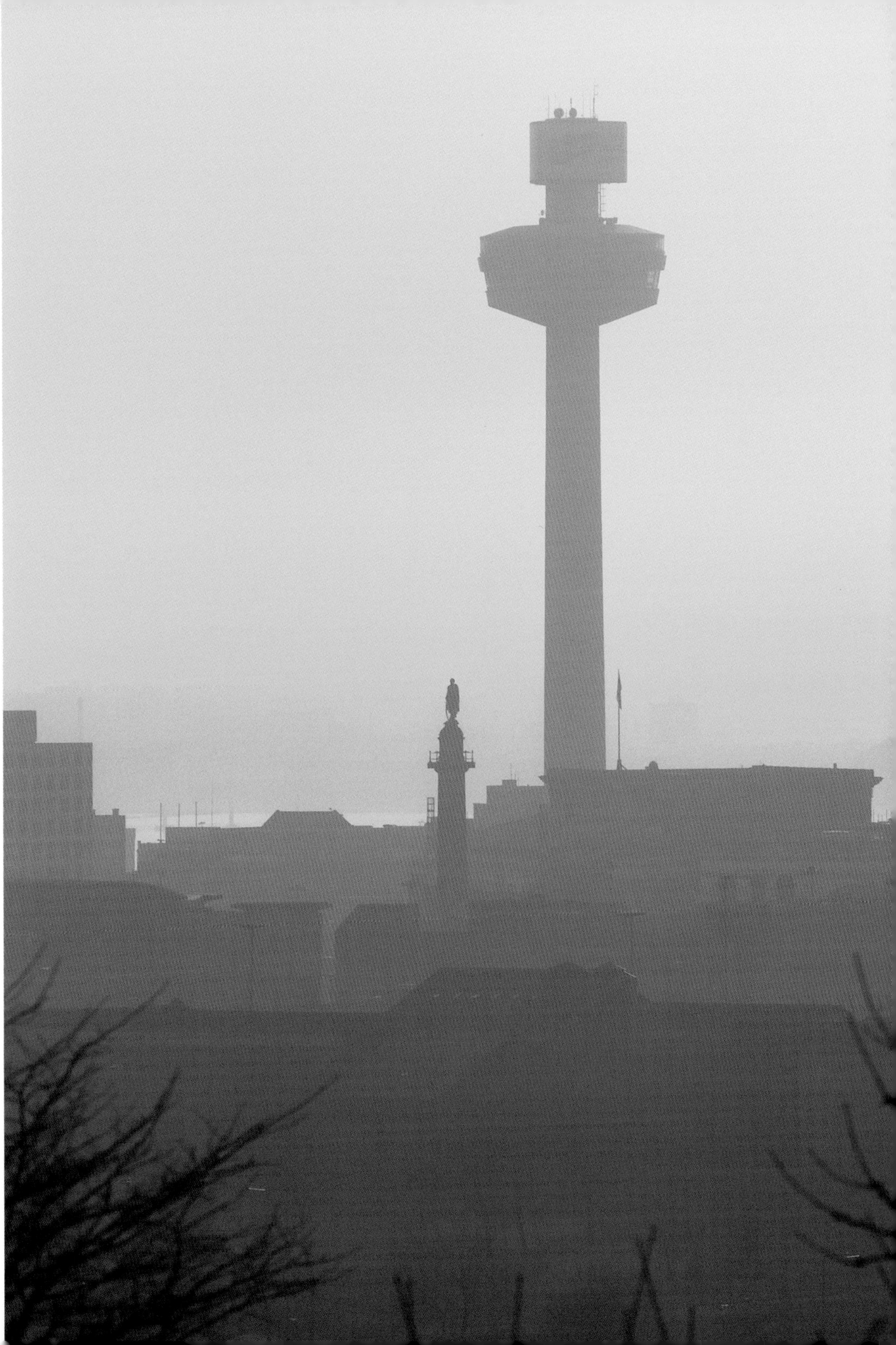

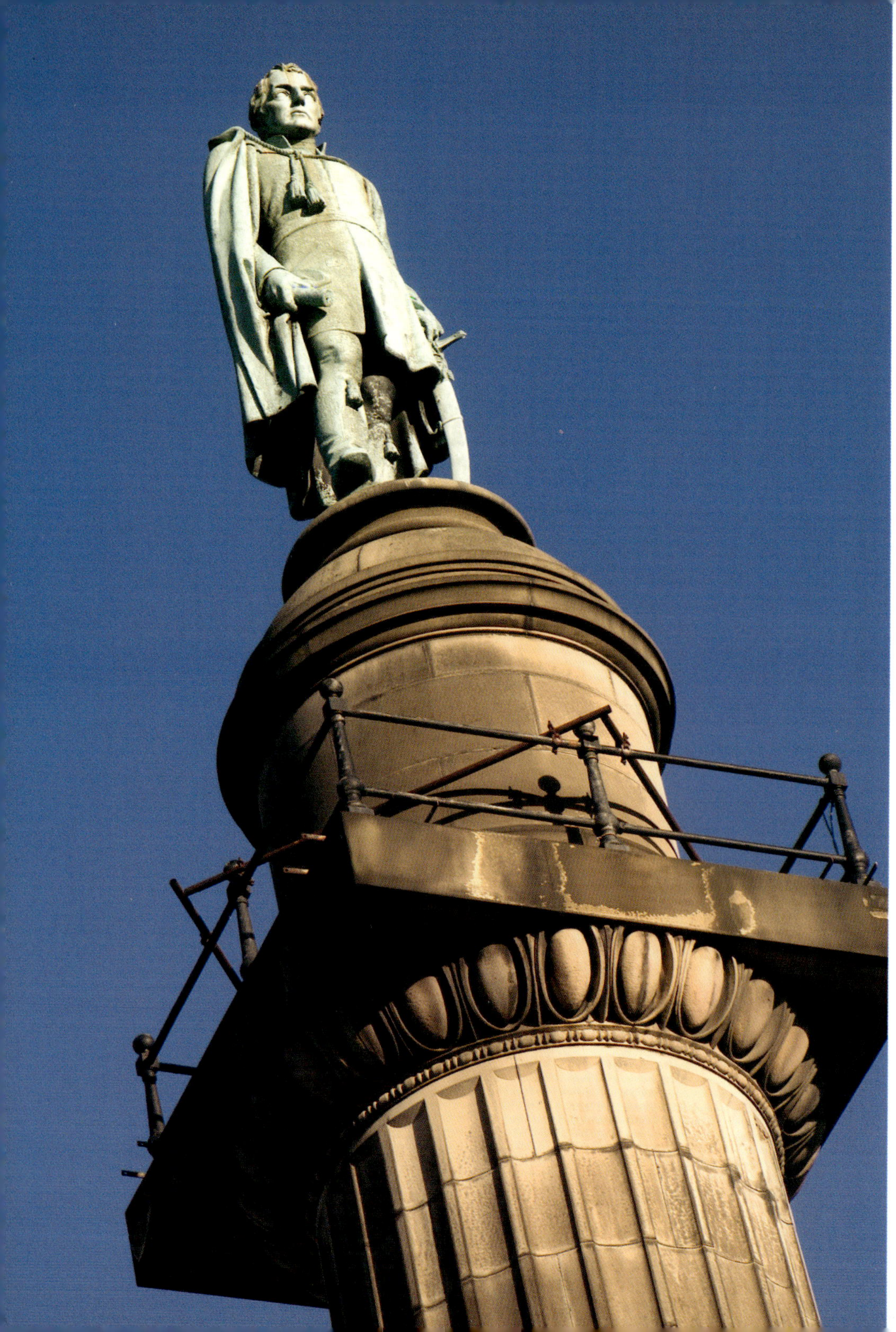

Wellington Column

The Wellington Column was erected in 1863, and it is possible to climb to the top via internal steps. The scaffolding poles seen securing the iron railing were fixed into place after VE day in 1945. Damage occurred from revellers hanging victory banners, and they remain as a memento of the occasion.

On a winter's evening
The Liver Birds on top of the Royal Liver Building. The domed building on the right is the top of the former Royal Insurance building on Dale Street/ North John Street.

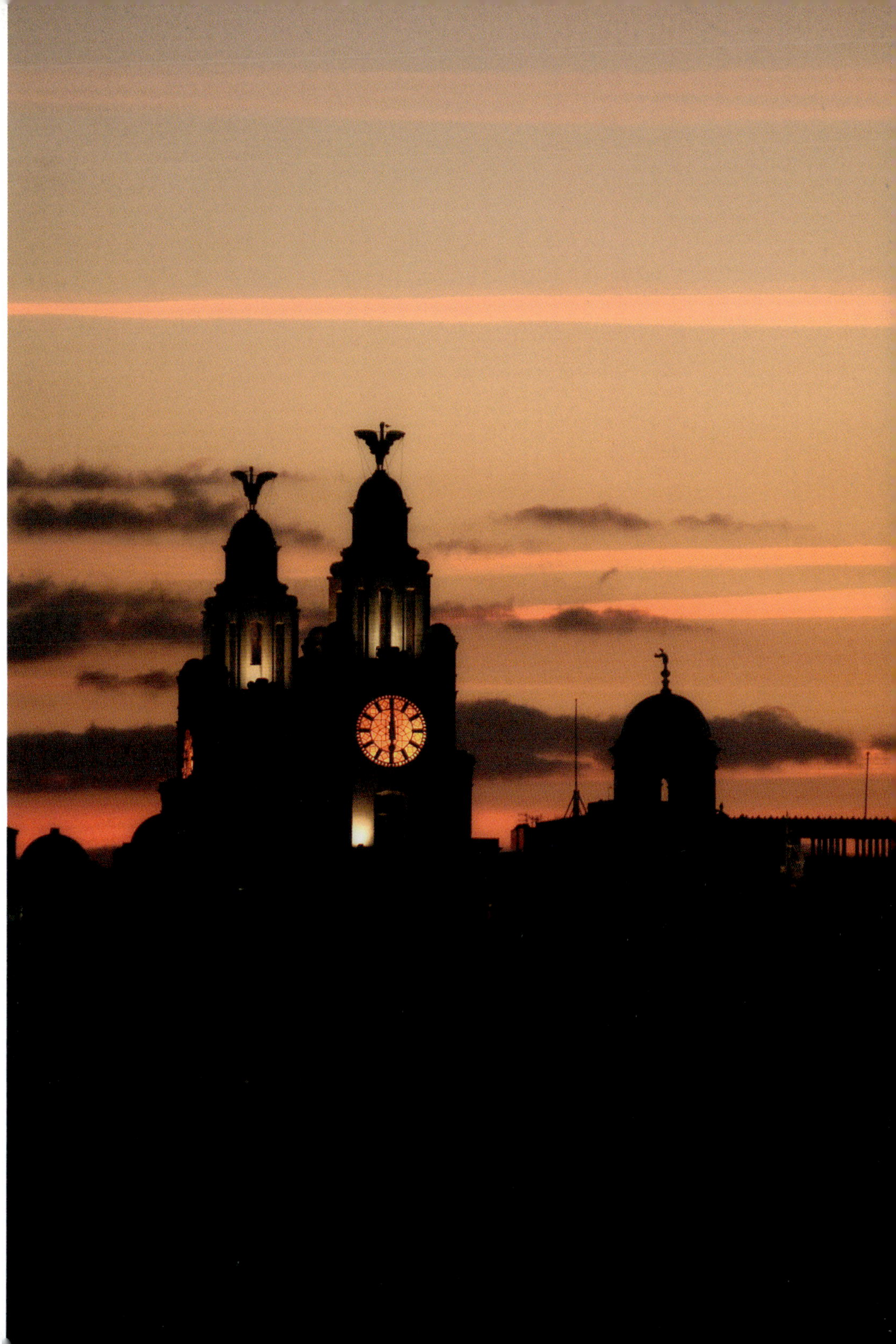

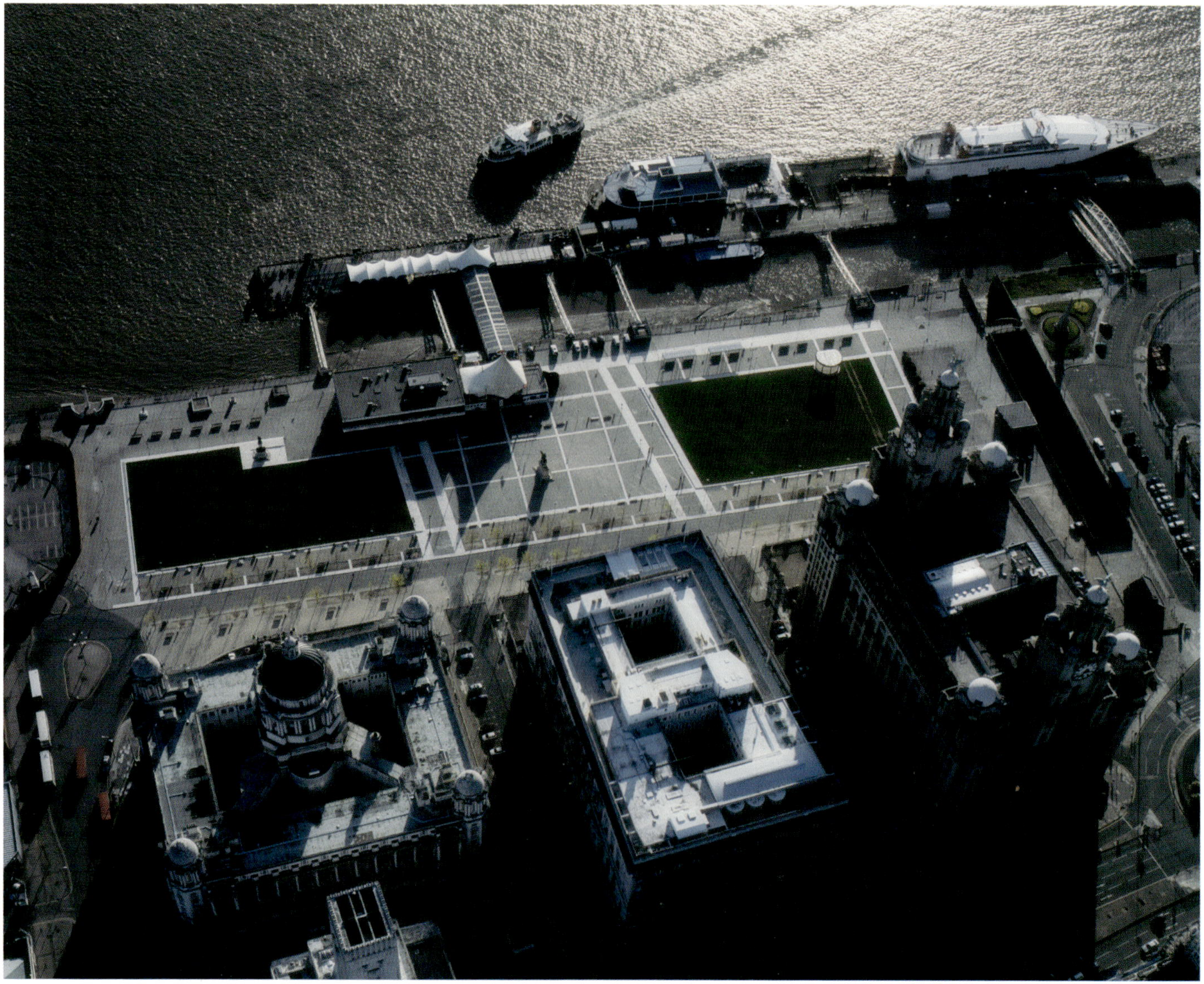

Aerial view of Pier Head

The majority of Liverpool people and visitors are unaware that the massive waterfront buildings have mini-cities on top of them. Overshadowed by its two mighty neighbours left and right, the Cunard Building is in the style of an Italian palazzo. From within these walls, the decisions to build the liners *Queen Mary I* and *Queen Elizabeth I* were made.

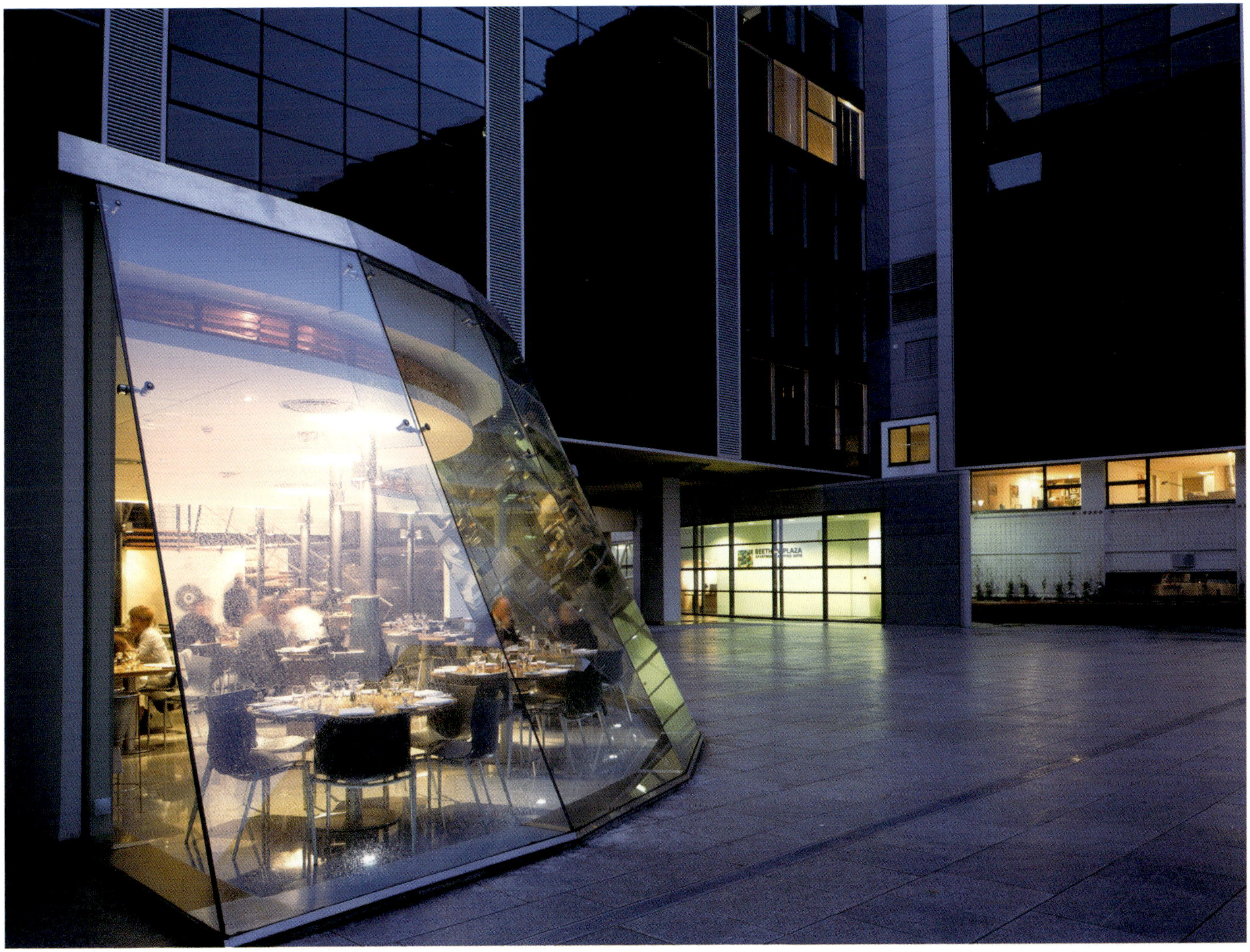

Beetham Plaza

Beetham Plaza is part of the new development of luxury apartments and offices fronting the Strand. Refurbished from the original office blocks of 1965-7, it was completed in 2000. 'Simply Heathcotes' restaurant forms an attractive addition.

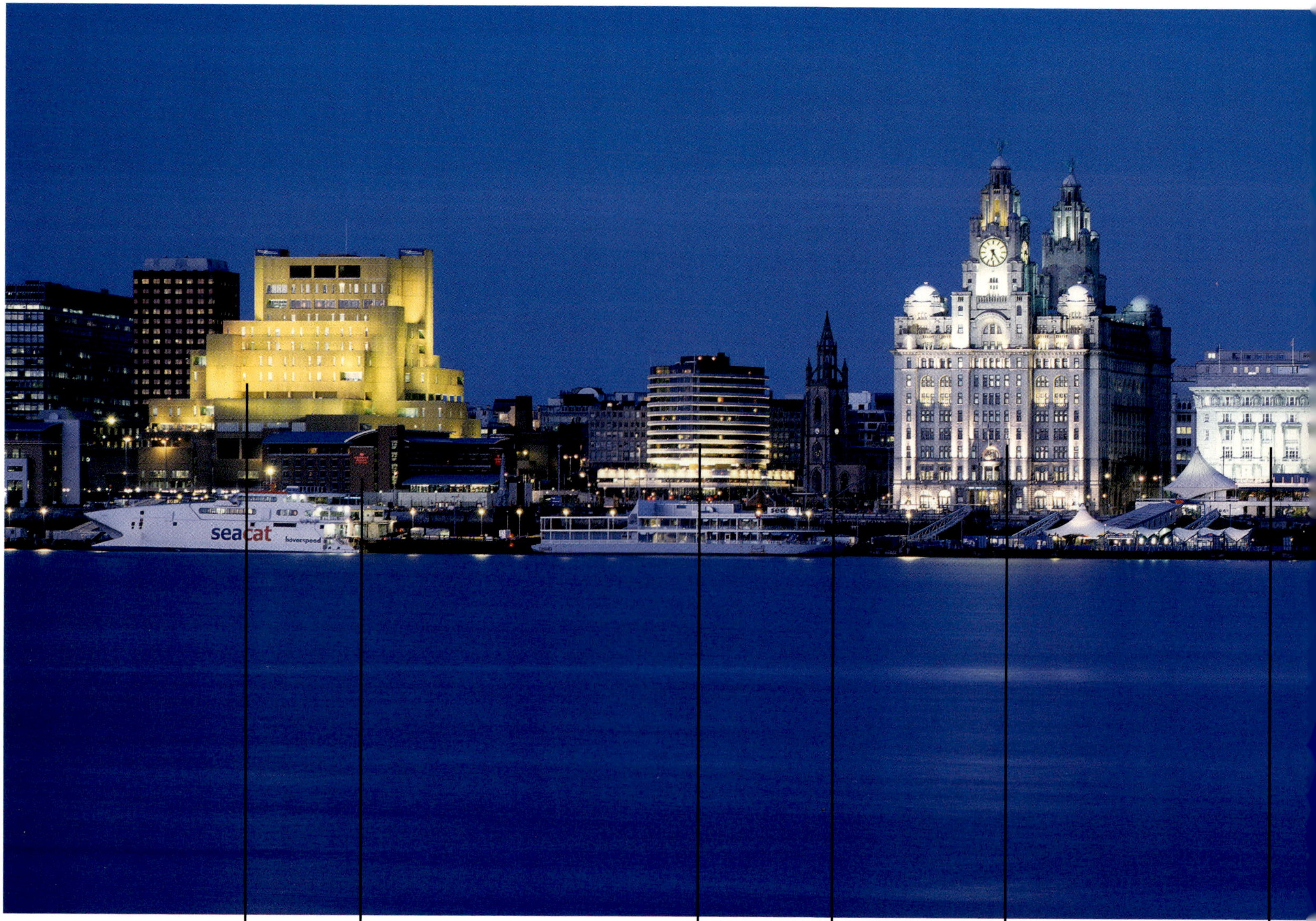

Liverpool Waterfront at Dusk

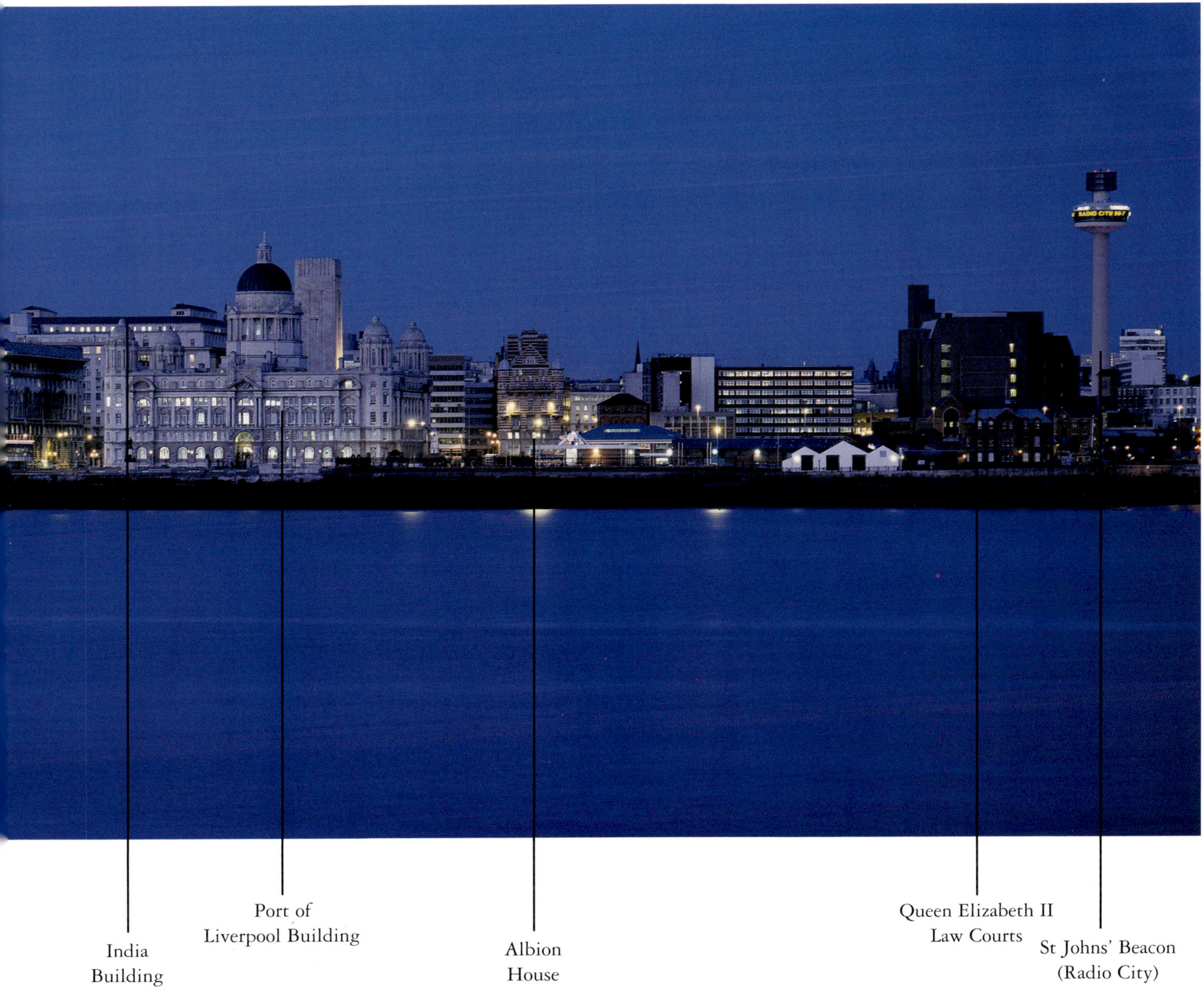
India
Building
Port of
Liverpool Building
Albion
House
Queen Elizabeth II
Law Courts
St Johns' Beacon
(Radio City)

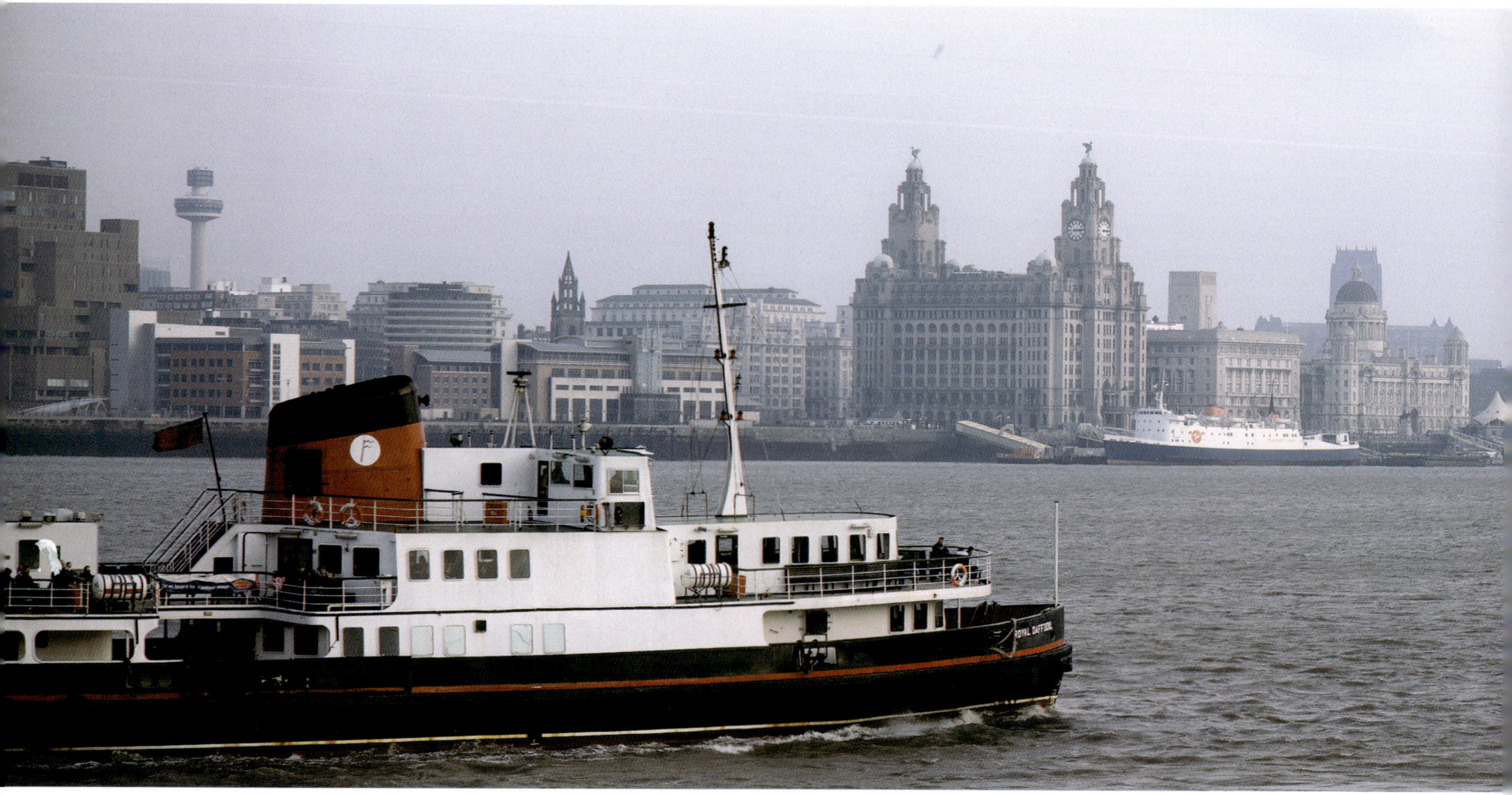

Mersey Ferry

The *Royal Daffodil* glides into the Woodside landing stage on another circular journey. In the background is the Isle of Man Steam Packet Co. vessel *Lady of Mann*, the last of that class, built in 1976 and berthed at the Pier Head. The faster Seacat class has now taken over the majority of the journeys from Liverpool to the Isle of Man, though the *Lady of Mann* is often used in the winter months, when rough seas can stop the Seacats.

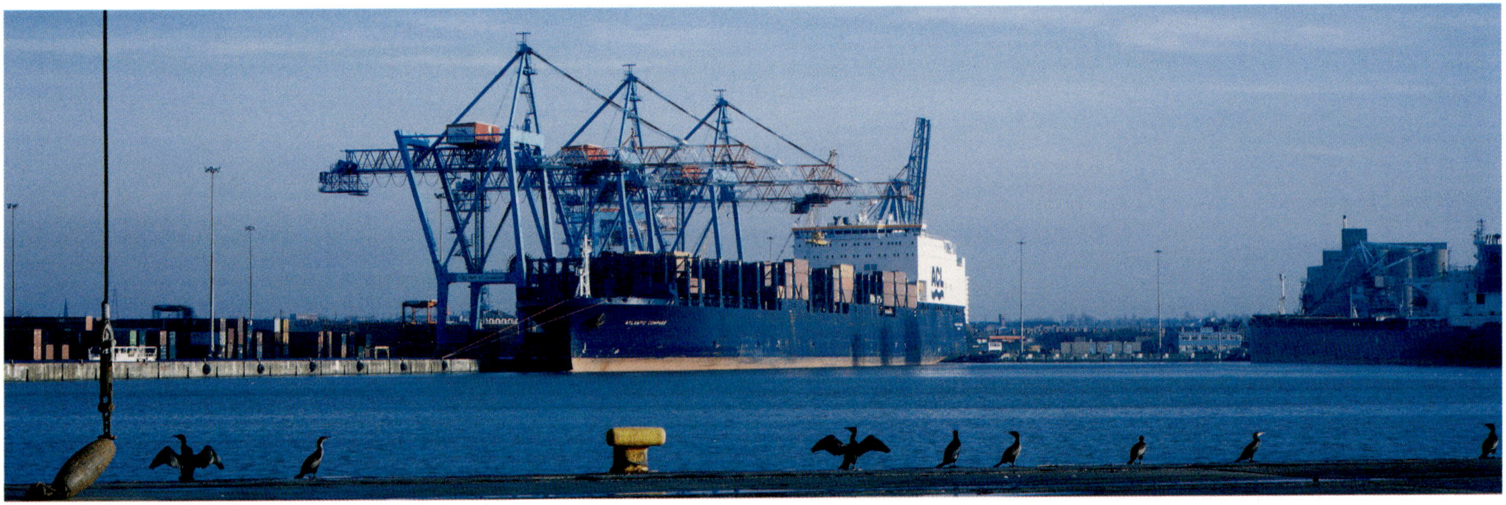

Royal Seaforth Container Base

The cormorants mirror the Liver Birds while the *Atlantic Compass* takes on its next cargo of containers. The Atlantic Container Line (ACL) has five ships plying between the UK, Europe and North America; the *Atlantic Compass, Conveyor, Companion, Concert* and *Cartier* are what is known as third generation vessels or G3's.

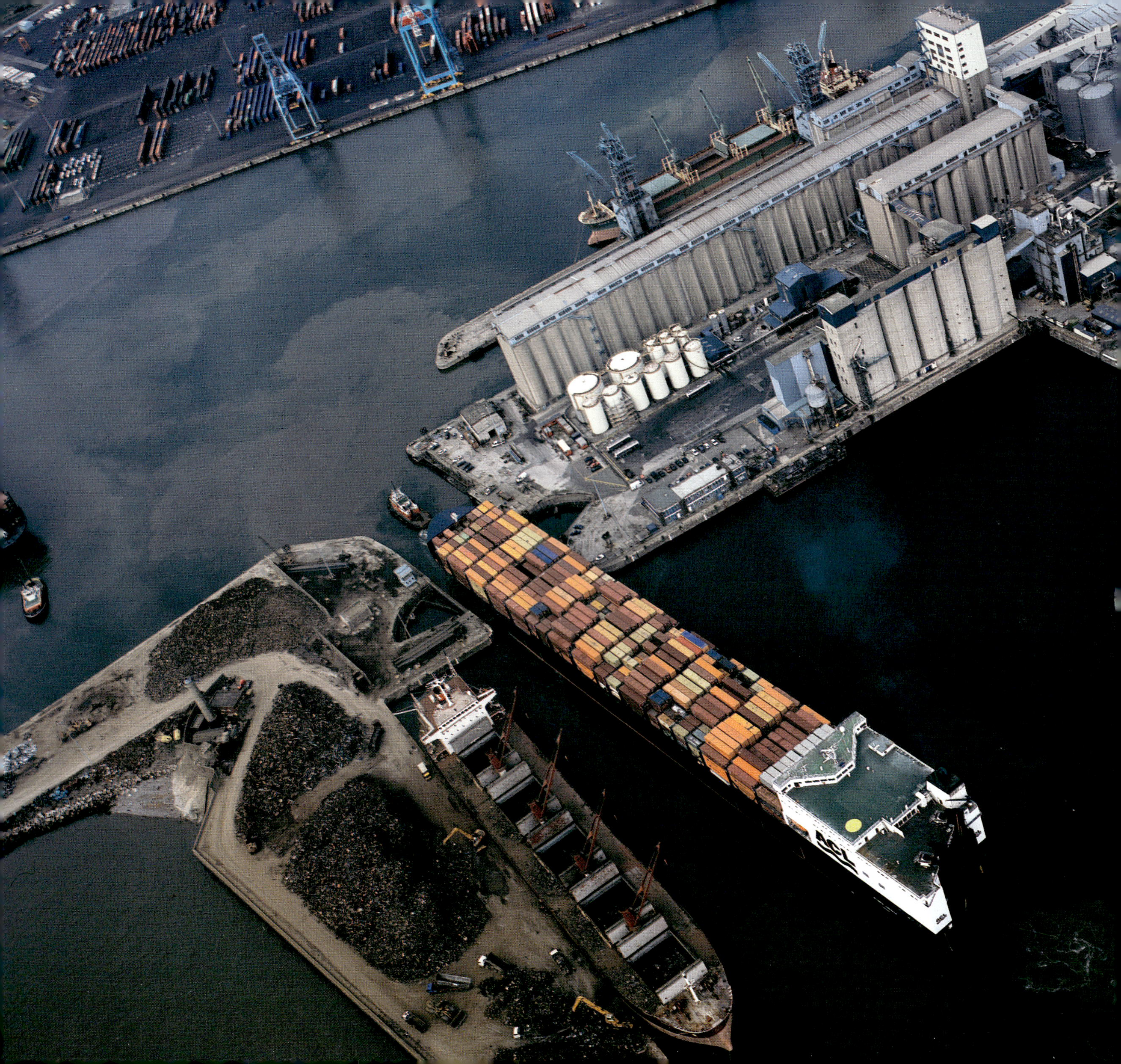
ACL

Entering the container base at Royal Seaforth *(left)*

Due to the Mersey's tidal restrictions, vessels can only dock during a two-hour window before high water. Each vessel stays for either twelve or twenty-four hours, subject to the volume of containers or export vehicles. Five vessels run a five-week transatlantic service departing from Liverpool on Saturday or Sunday for the United States and Canada, arriving at Halifax, Nova Scotia on Saturday or Sunday the following week. Next port of call is New York, followed by calls at Baltimore, Portsmouth and then Virginia before returning north to New York and again Halifax. After a six-day passage headed for Europe, the vessels call at Liverpool, Antwerp, Bremerhaven, and Gothenburg before heading back to Antwerp then on to Liverpool again.

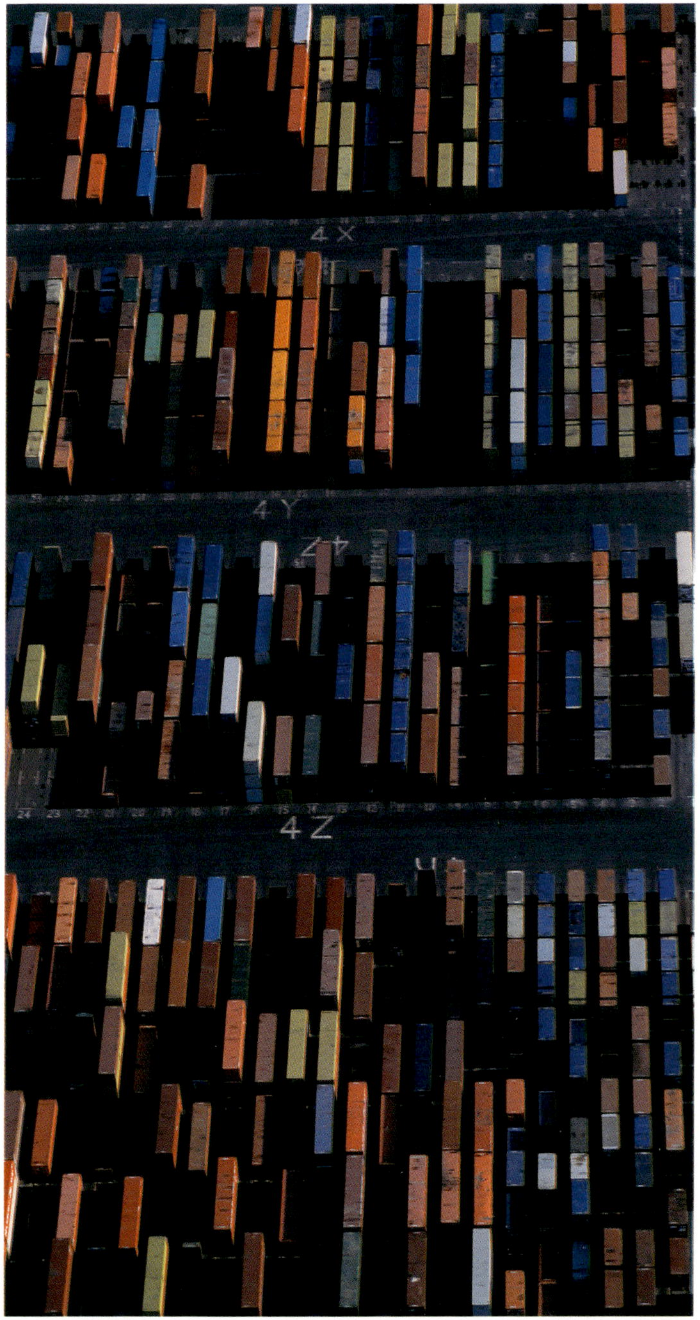

Containers awaiting loading

These days, satellite global positioning systems locate containers for the crane operators and keep track of loading operations. Each year approximately 500,000 containers make their way through Royal Seaforth container base.

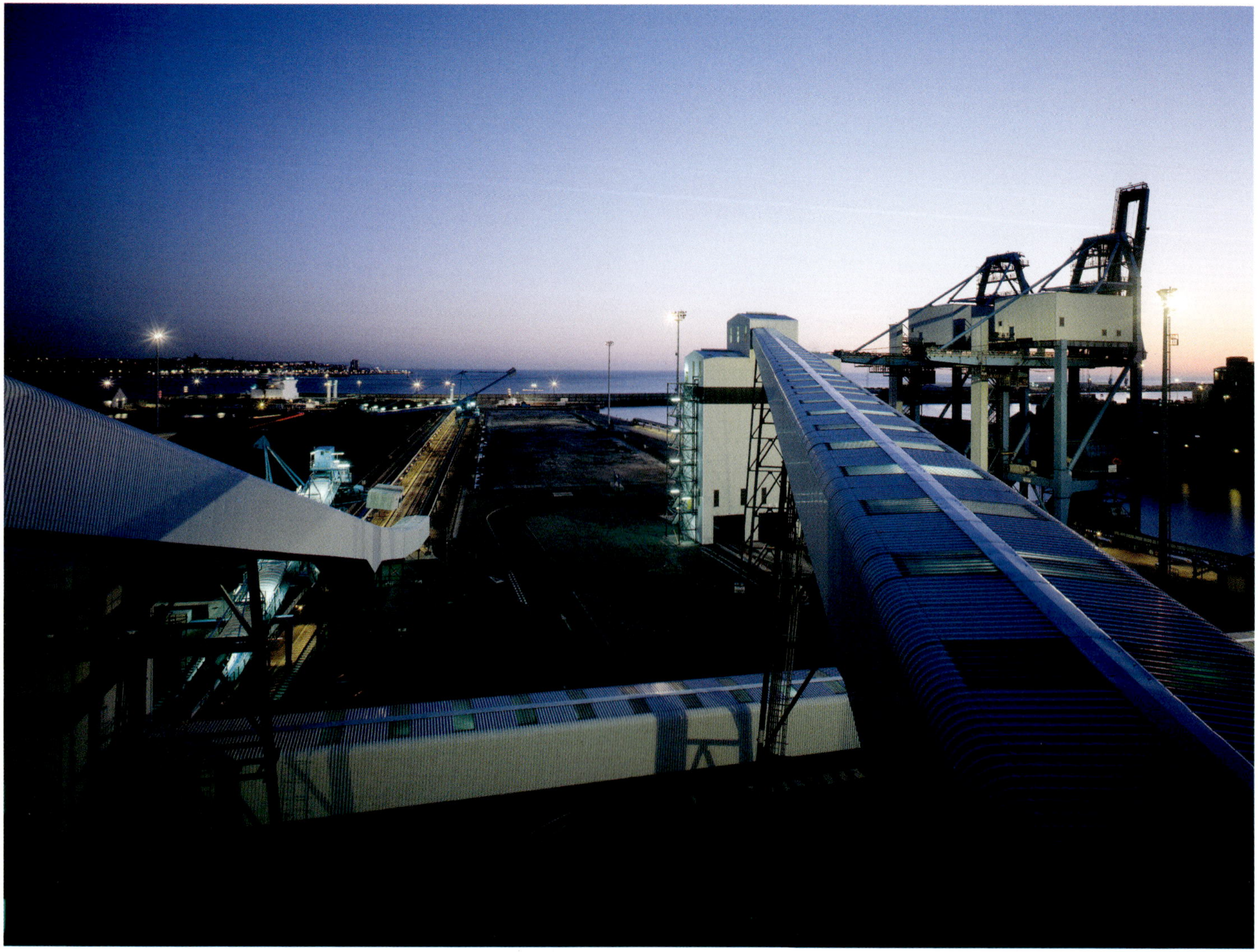

Gladstone Dock

South of Seaforth is this fully-automated coal-handling facility. Opened in 1913, it was originally designed to berth the largest transatlantic liners in its 58 acres of water space and 3 miles of quays.

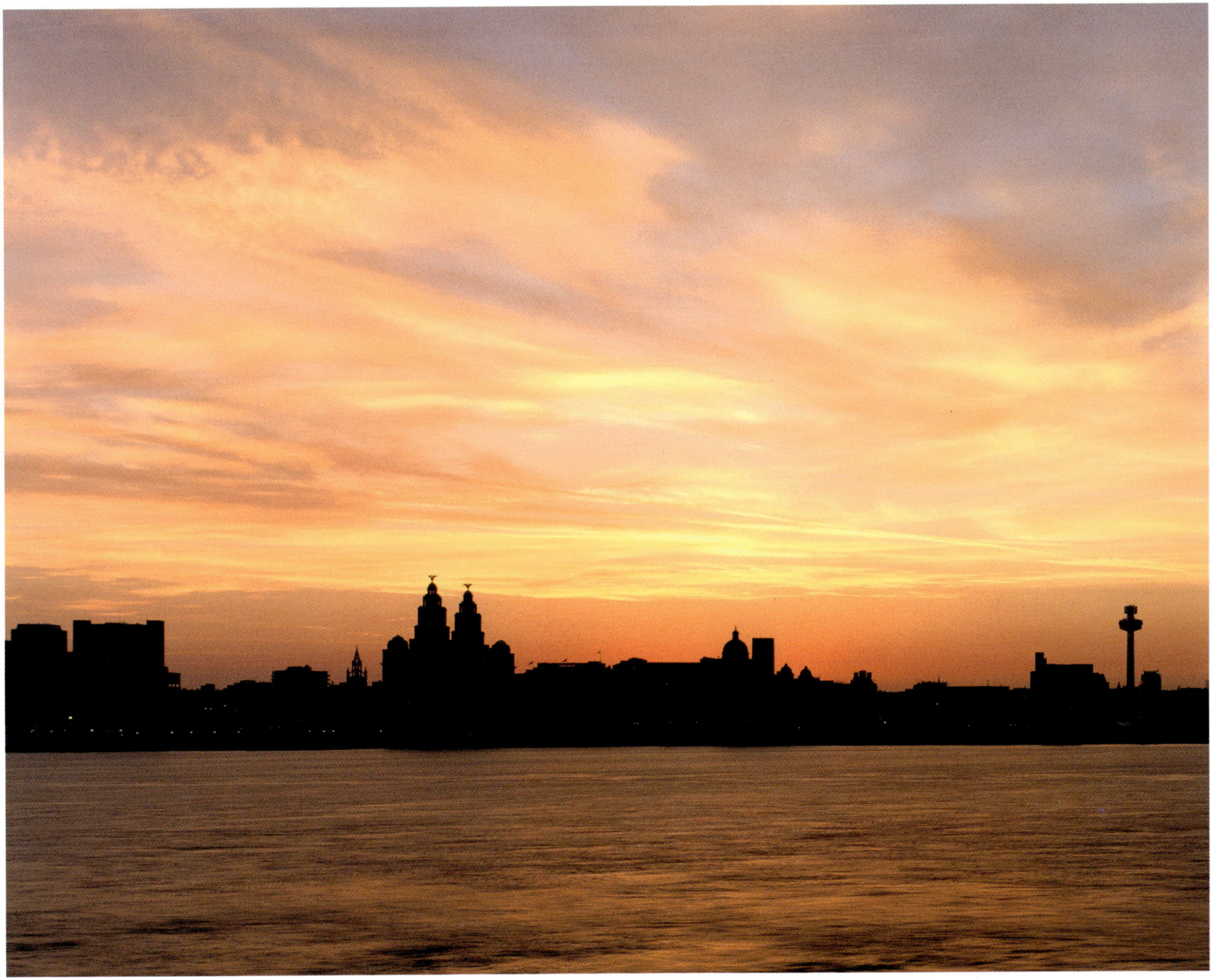

Sunrise over Liverpool
An early morning view, taken at 5am on a summer's day from near the Woodside landing stage of the Mersey ferries.

Sunrise over Liverpool
Just twenty minutes after the previous image was taken, the sky was transformed as the sun came into view over the Queen Elizabeth II Law Courts.

The Old Haymarket

This is a completely new development, but it uses the design of the previous Old Haymarket buildings. The Observatory is a modern office block completed around the same time as Haymarket as part of the modernisation of the area in 2002.

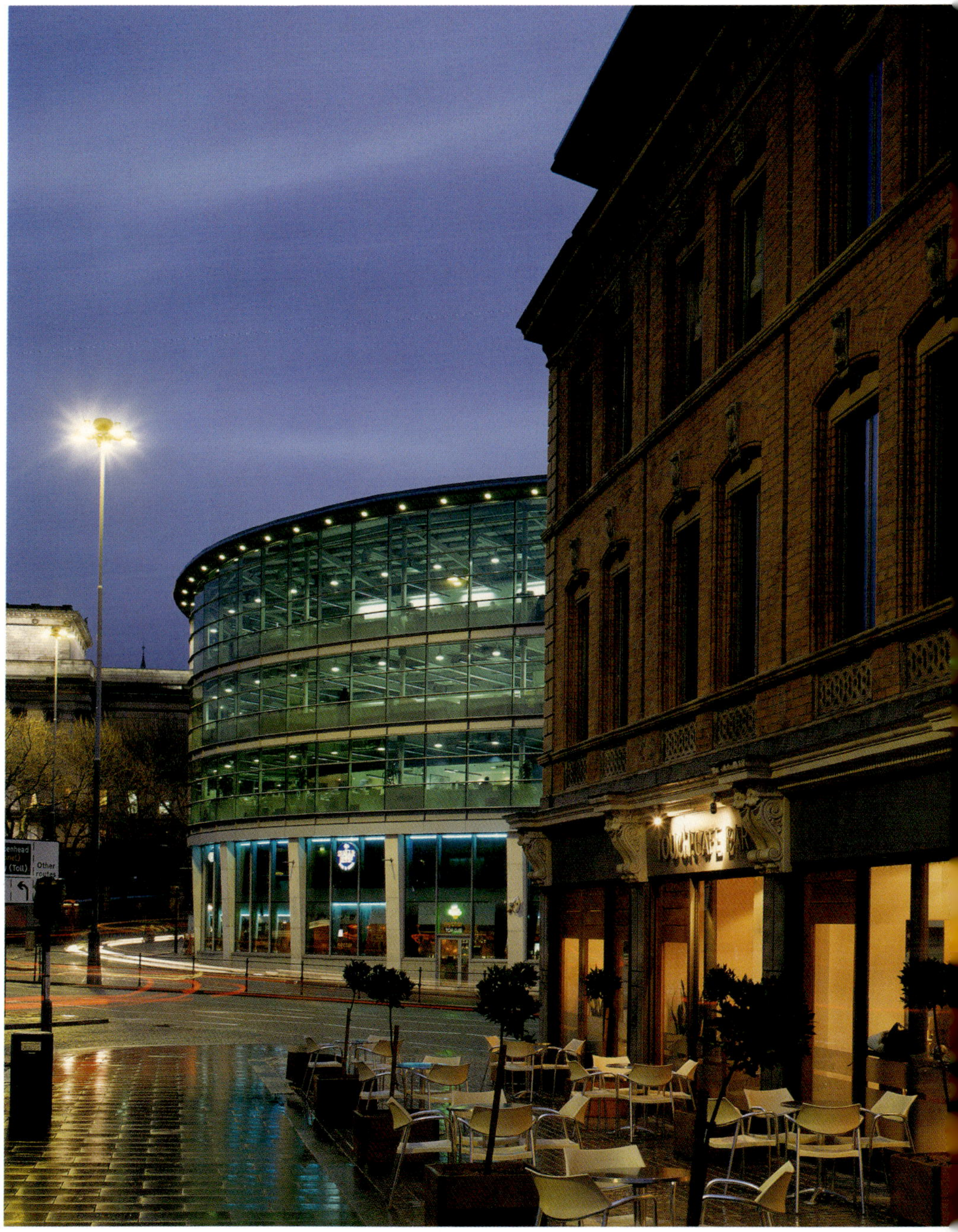

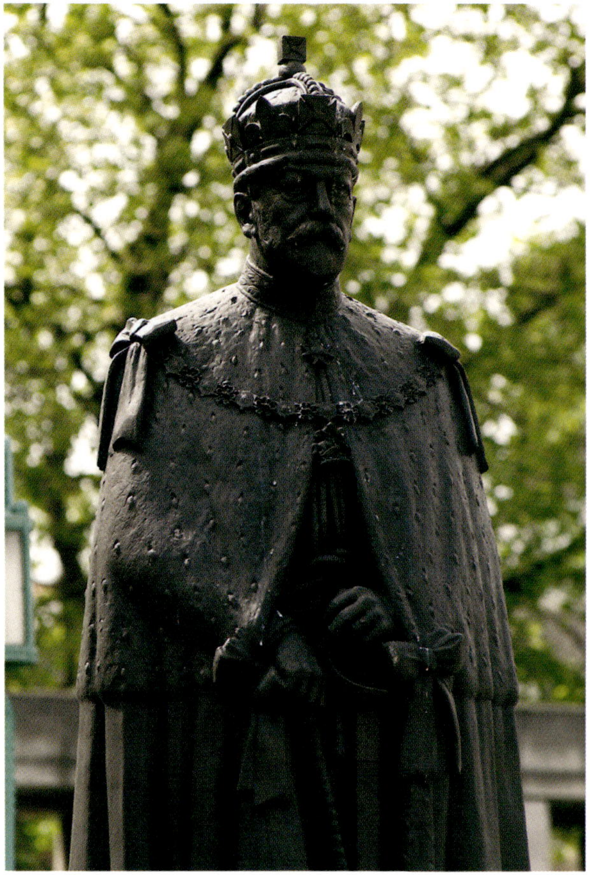

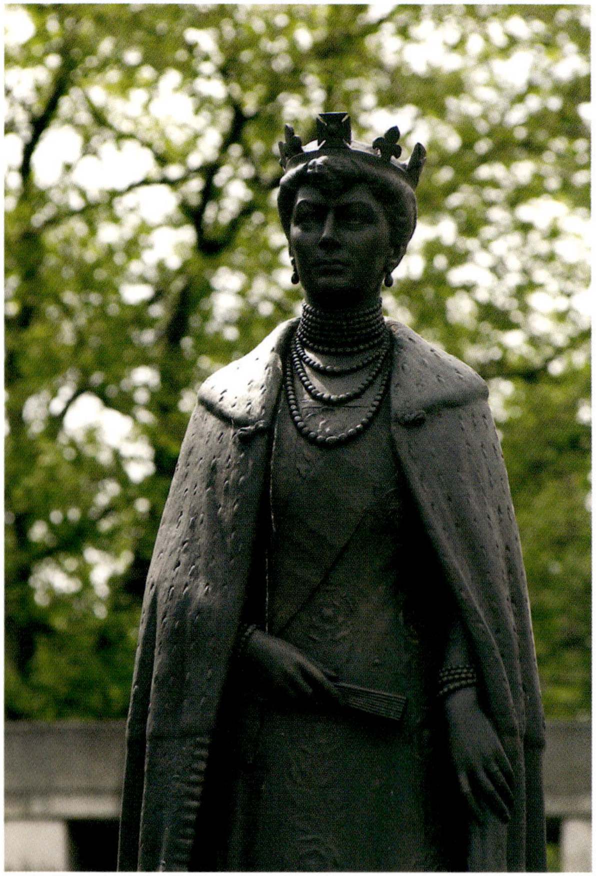

Queensway Tunnel

The 'old' tunnel was opened by King George V on 18 July, 1934. Above the tunnel entrance on Dale Street stand the statues of the King and Queen Mary. They were sculpted by Sir William Goscombe John in 1938, and were put into their present position in 1994. The Mersey Tunnel is over 2 miles long and cost £8m to build, with 1700 men employed in its construction, 17 of whom died. A total of 1.2m tons of rock, gravel and clay were excavated, some of which went to build the Otterspool promenade.

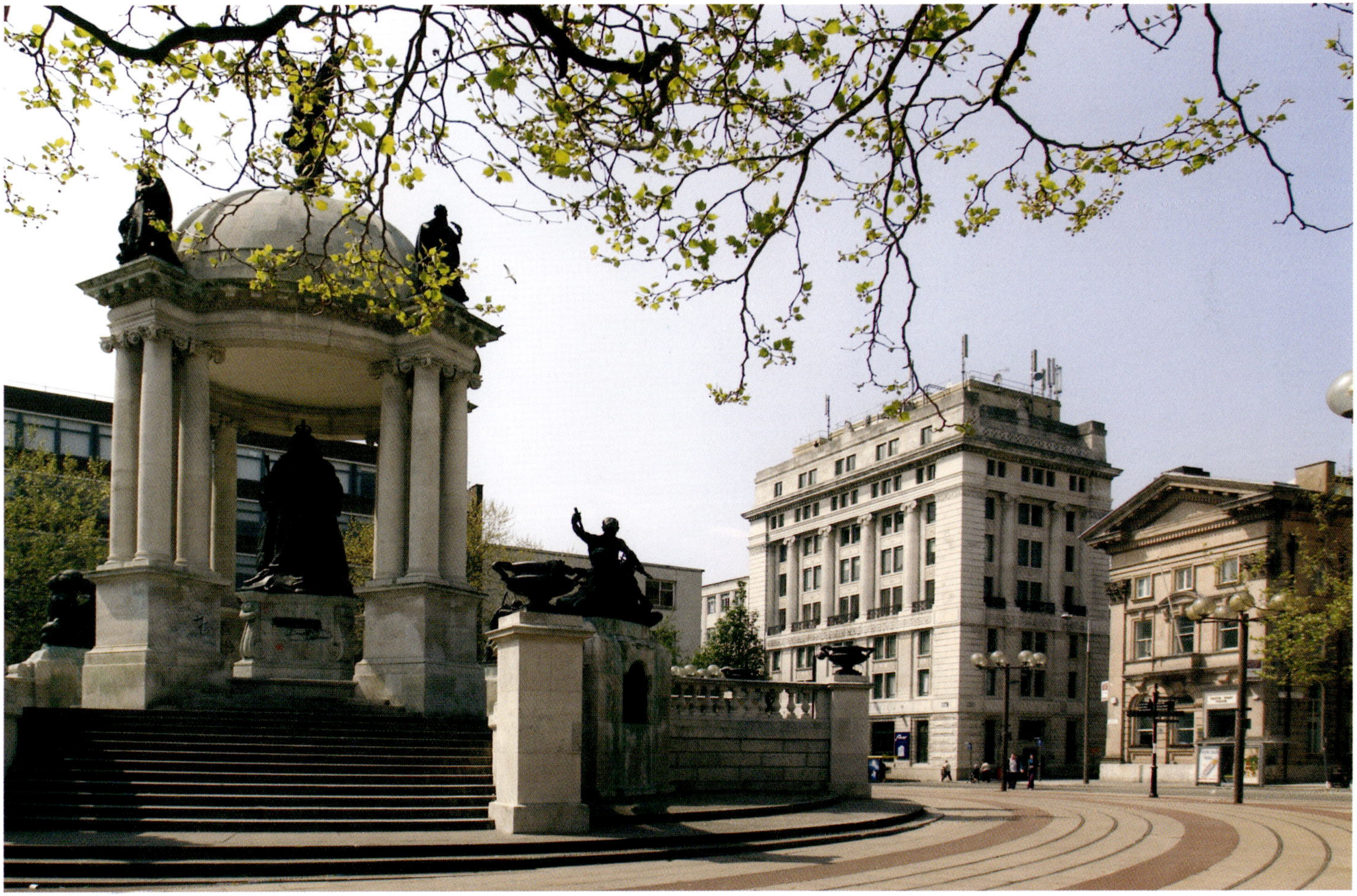

The Queen Victoria Monument

The Queen Victoria Monument stands in Derby Square adjacent to the Queen Elizabeth II Law Courts. The monument was installed 1906 on the site of Liverpool Castle, the last remains of which were demolished in 1726. The monument survived relatively unscathed during the May Blitz of 1941 on Liverpool, while the buildings around were devastated.

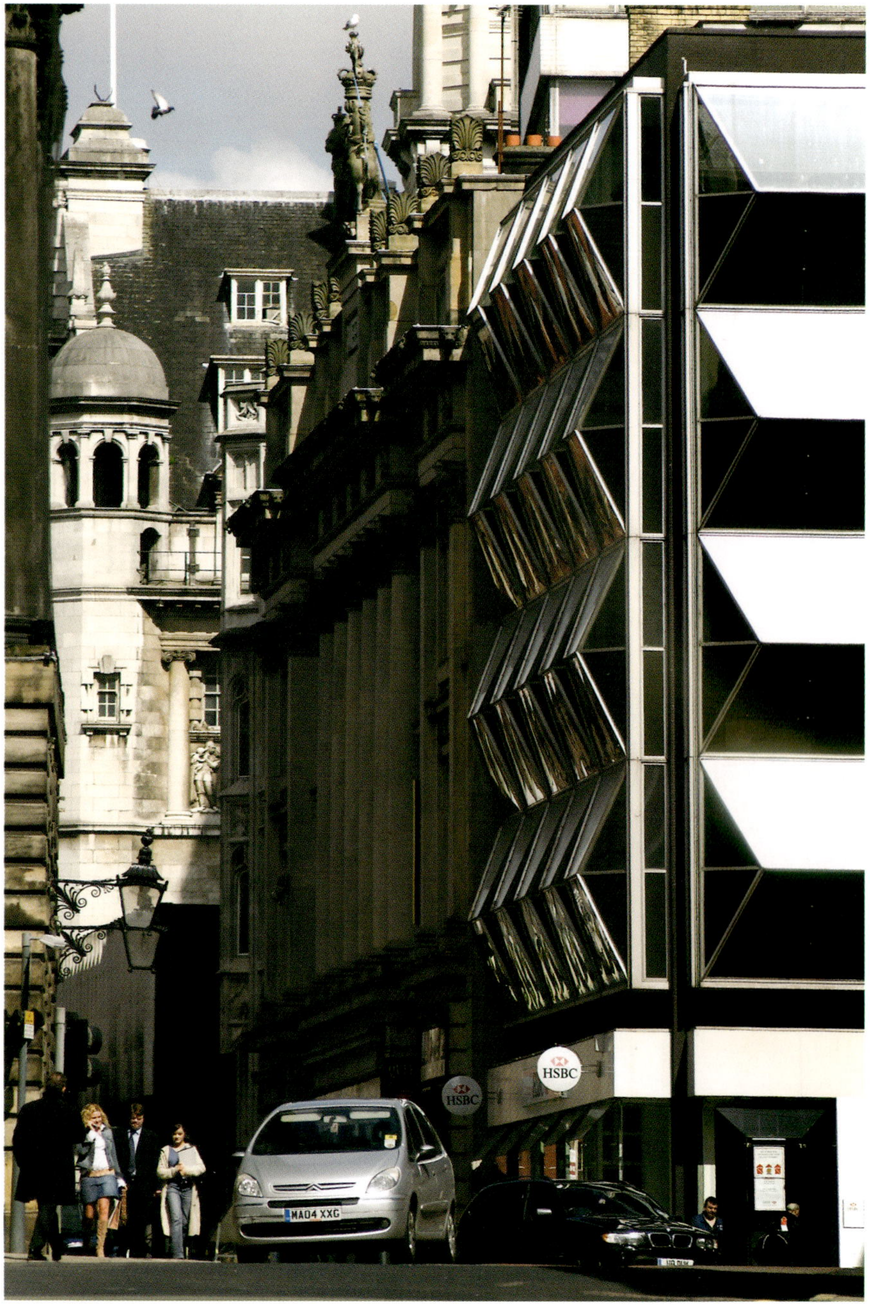

HSBC Bank

This modern office block of 1971 opposite the Town Hall on Dale Street stands happily among buildings many years its senior. Its façade consists of 28 identical faceted windows of reflective glass, framed in stainless steel.

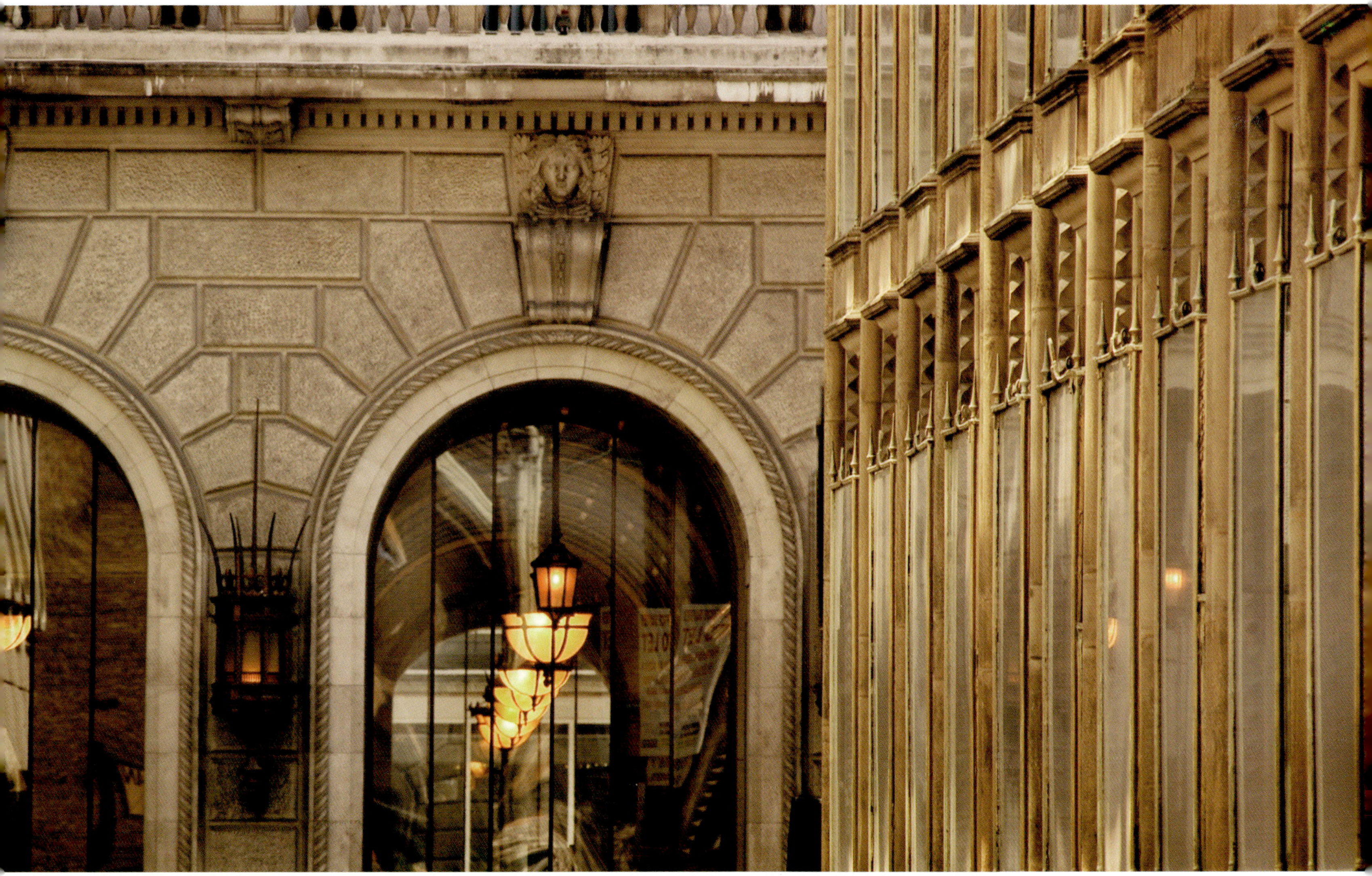

Oriel Chambers

Another view of this immensely-important building, with its tall oriel windows and slender cast-iron frames. Looking down Covent Garden towards India Building and its central mall.

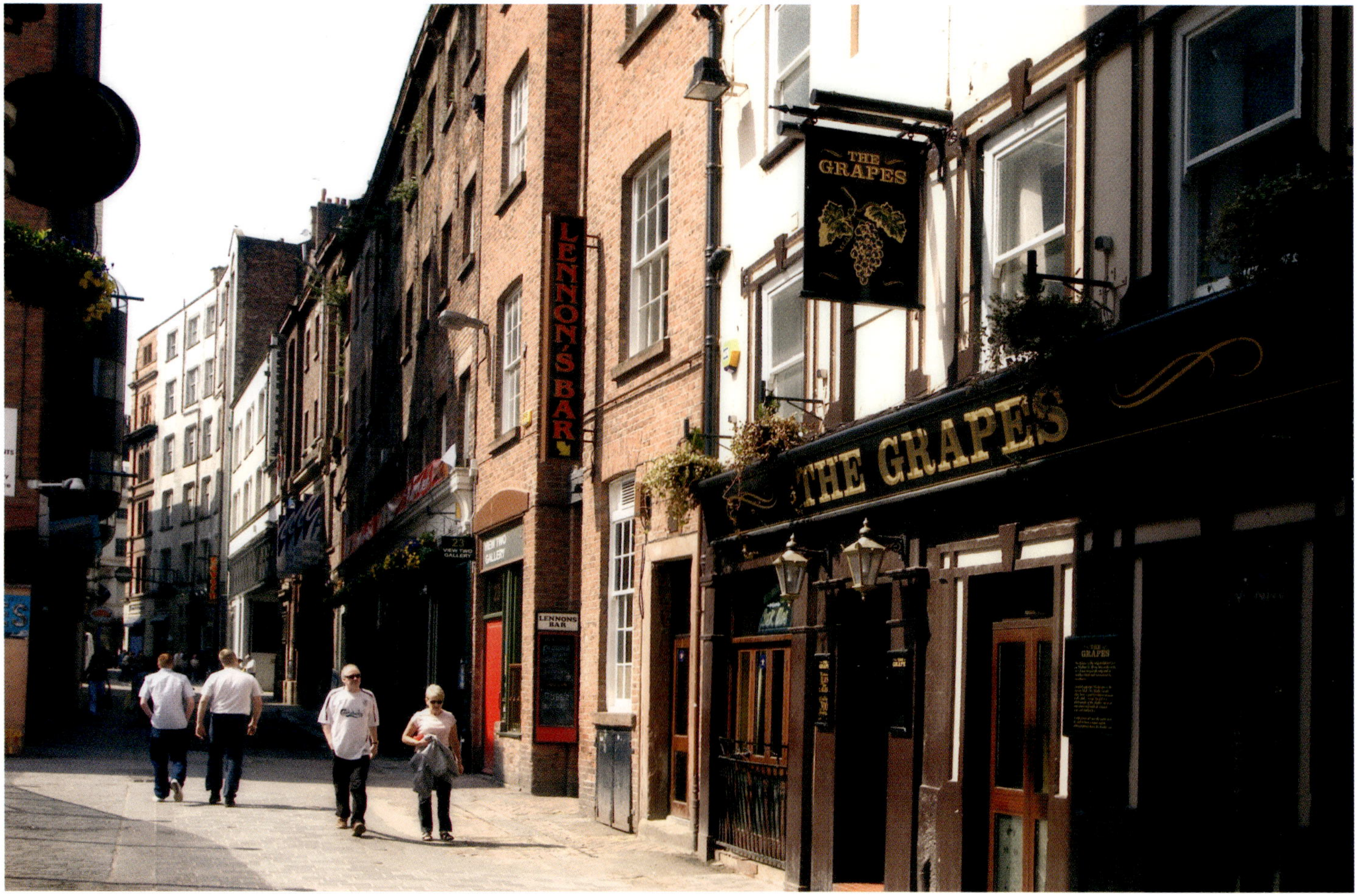

Mathew Street

Mathew Street is the birthplace of the Beatles, and one of the most visited streets in Liverpool. The original Cavern Club has long since been demolished, but there are still memorabilia shops, galleries and pubs in this famous landmark street.

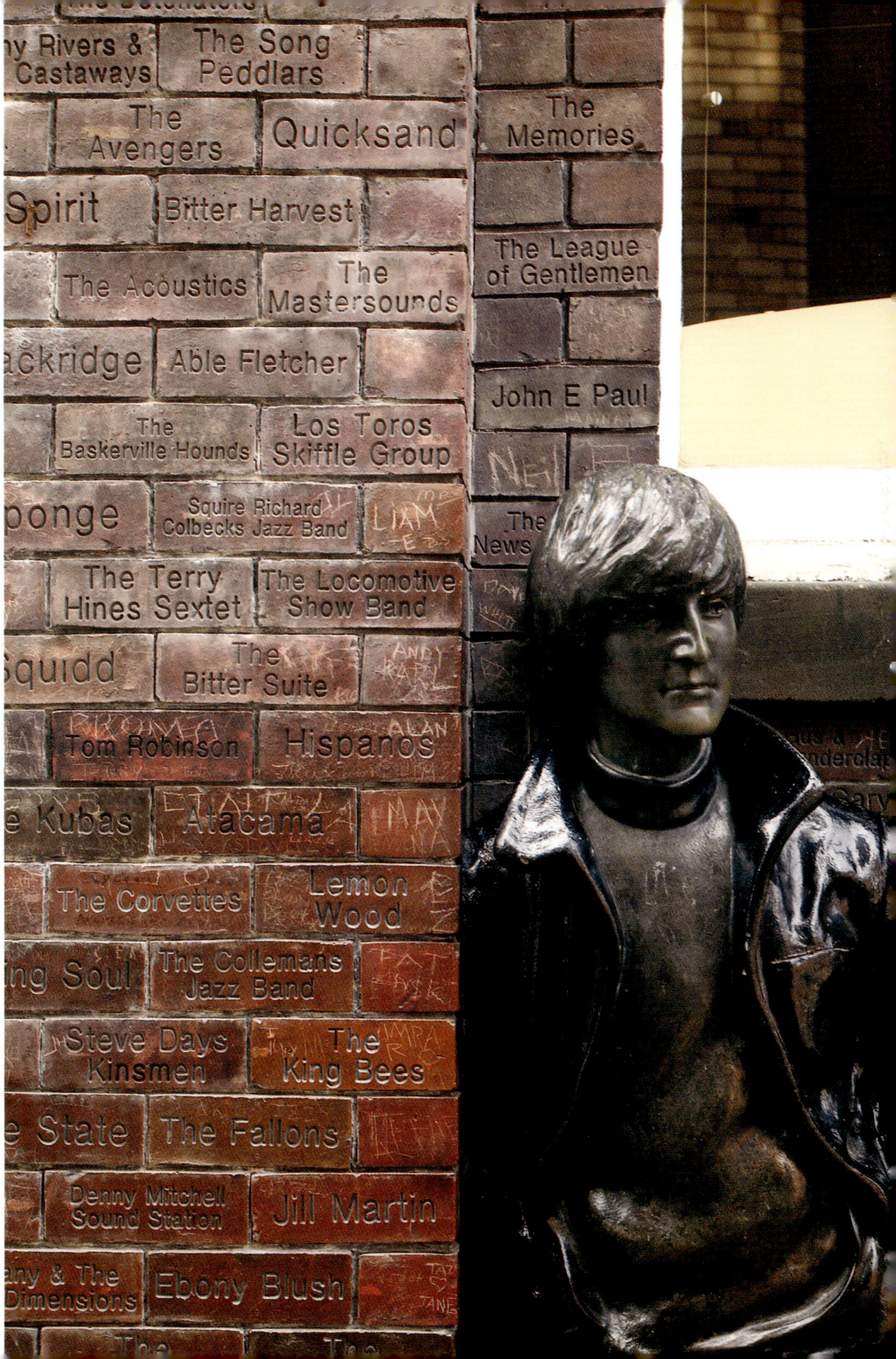

Statue of John Lennon
Positioned against 'The Cavern Wall of Fame' in Mathew Street, each of the bricks (behind) is inscribed with the name of a group or singer who appeared at the famous Cavern Club – the birthplace of The Beatles.

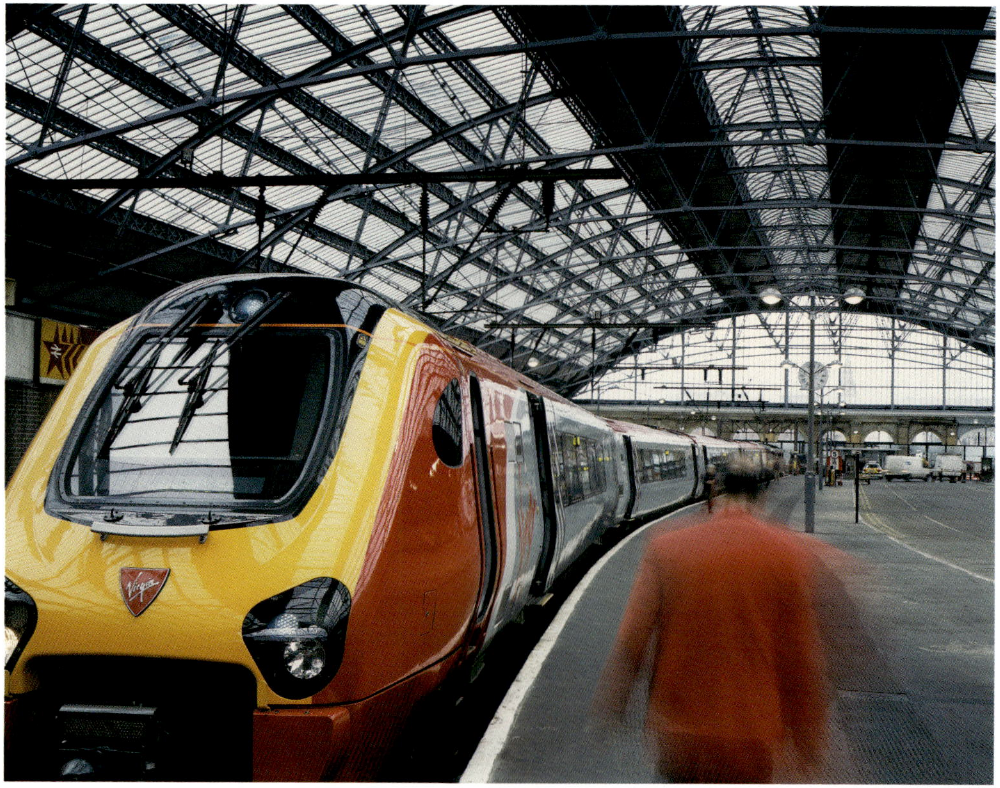

Lime Street Station

Lime Street is the main rail terminus for Liverpool. The present building is the third of three stations to be built on this site. Lime Street was completed in 1879 and it has recently been refurbished. The first station was built in 1836 to a design by John Fowler, and the second was built in 1851. At the time of its erection, the arch of the first engine shed spanned 200 feet, and was the largest arch in the world.

Mercury Court ***(right)***

Originally fronting the Exchange Railway Station, Mercury Court was a hotel and offices above ground floor shops. Exchange Station was the terminus of the Lancashire and Yorkshire Railway, which closed in 1977. The façade of 1888 now fronts a range of modern offices.

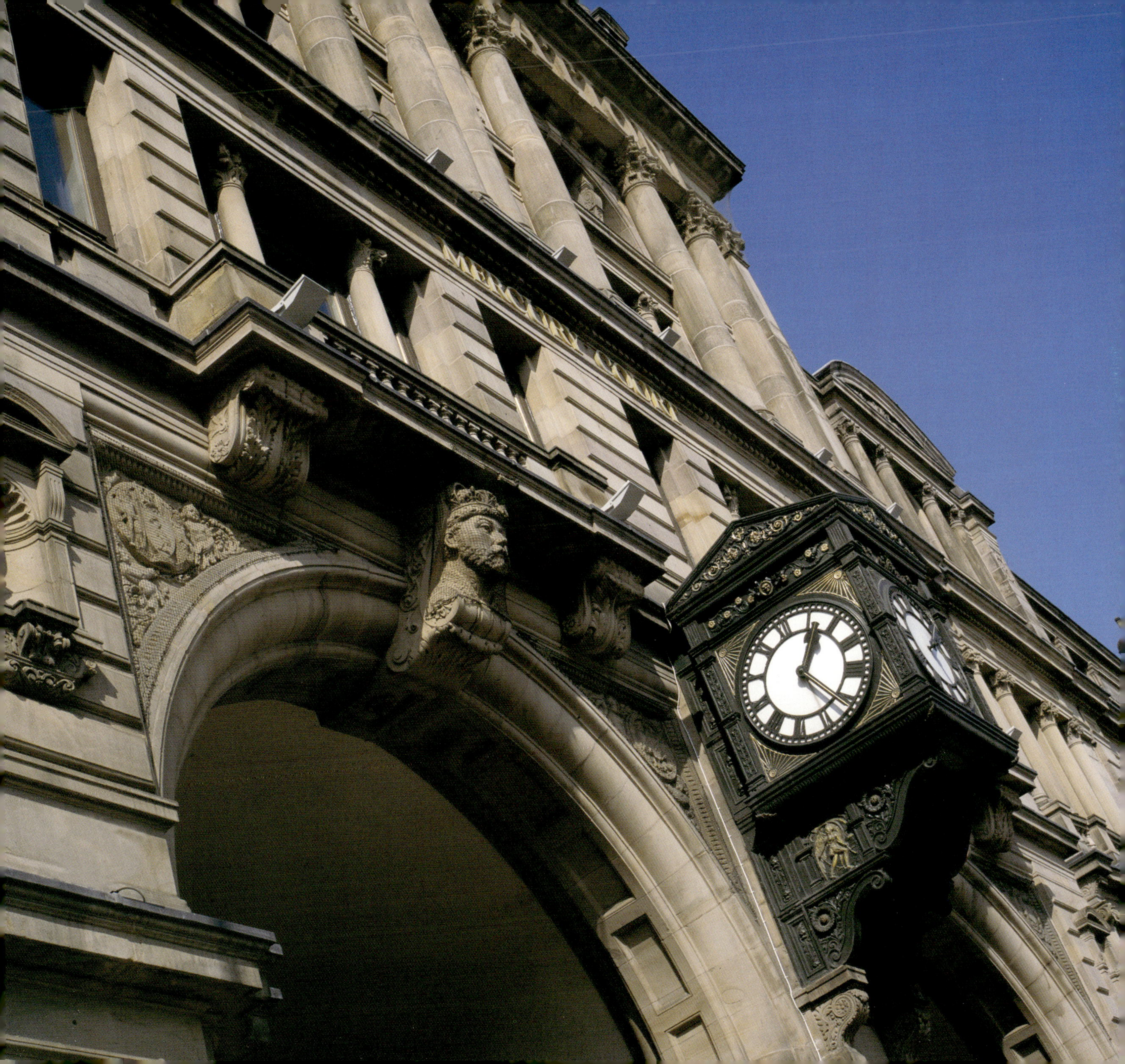
MERCURY COURT

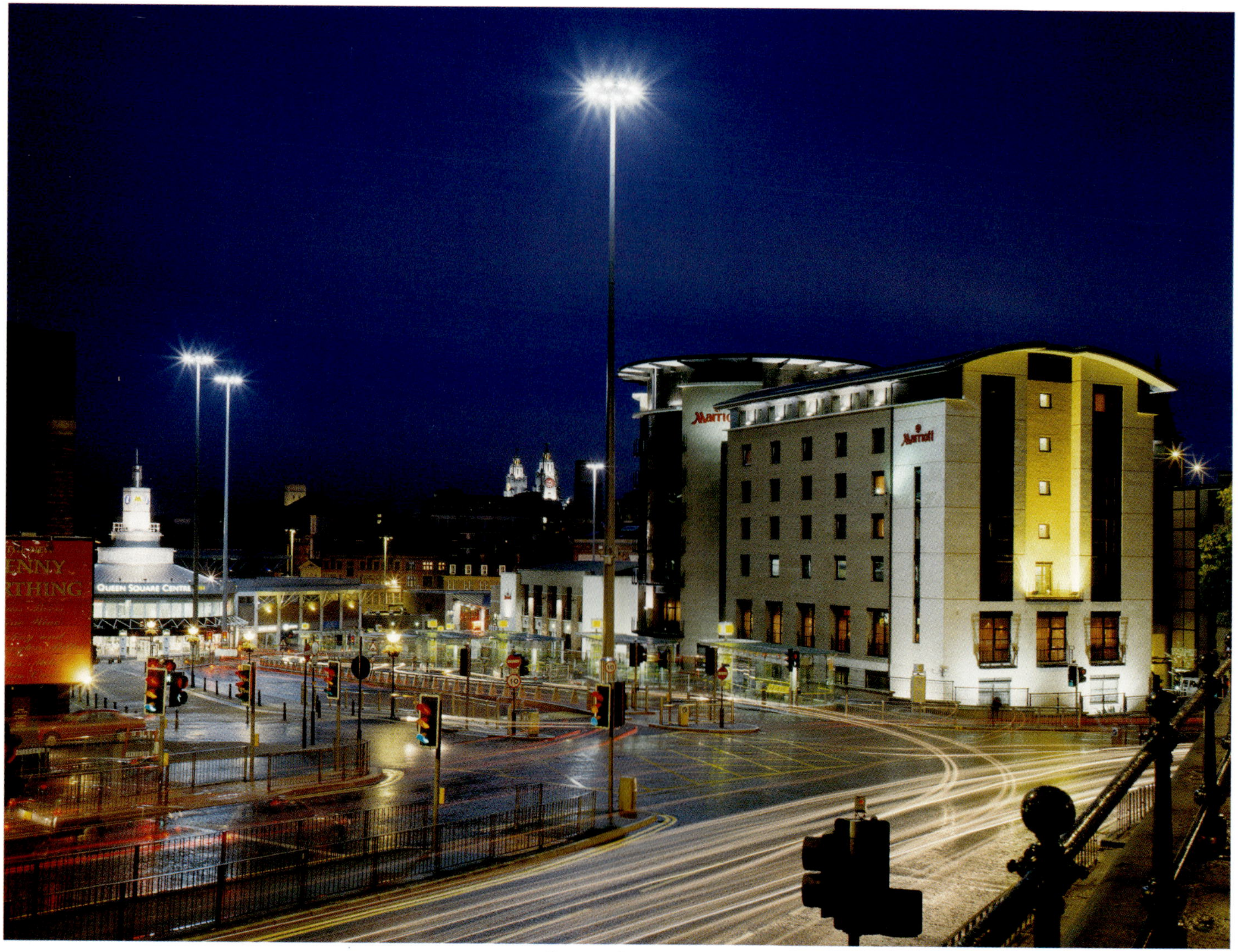

Queen Square

Queen Square as seen from St George's Plateau. The Marriott Hotel stands on the corner of the square opposite the Royal Court Theatre. The Visitor Centre can also be seen on the left hand side of the picture. Behind the centre is Williamson Square and the Playhouse Theatre.

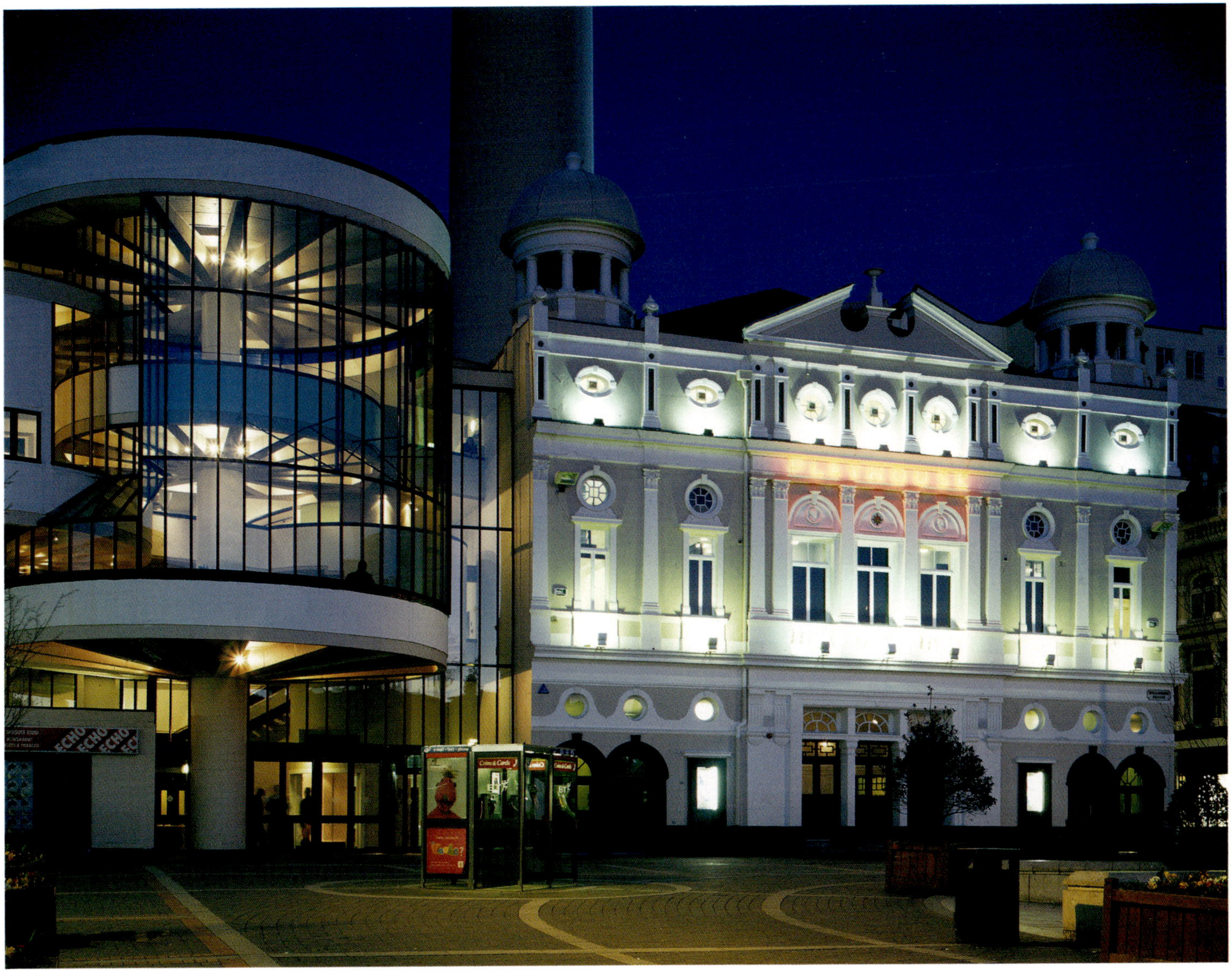

Playhouse Theatre

The Playhouse Theatre in Williamson Square opened in 1911 and has been extended and refurbished a number of times since. Originally named the Old Star Theatre, it was remodelled by Professor Stanley Adshead for the Liverpool Repertory Theatre.

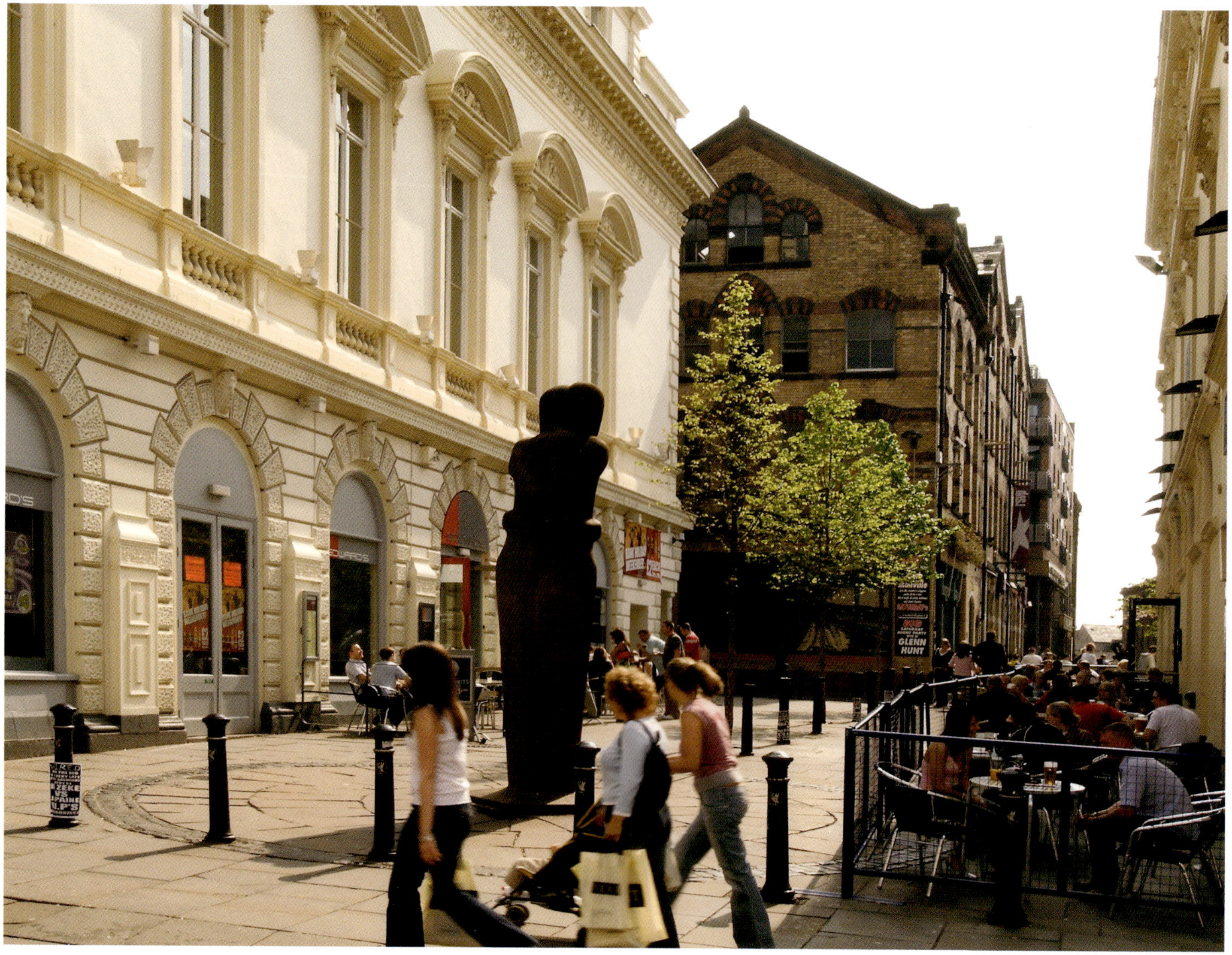

Concert Street leading to Concert Square

The sculpture 'Reconciliation' is one of three identical pieces by Stephen Broadbent; the others are located in Glasgow and Belfast. Concert Square is now a thriving open-air café and bistro area, just off Bold Street.

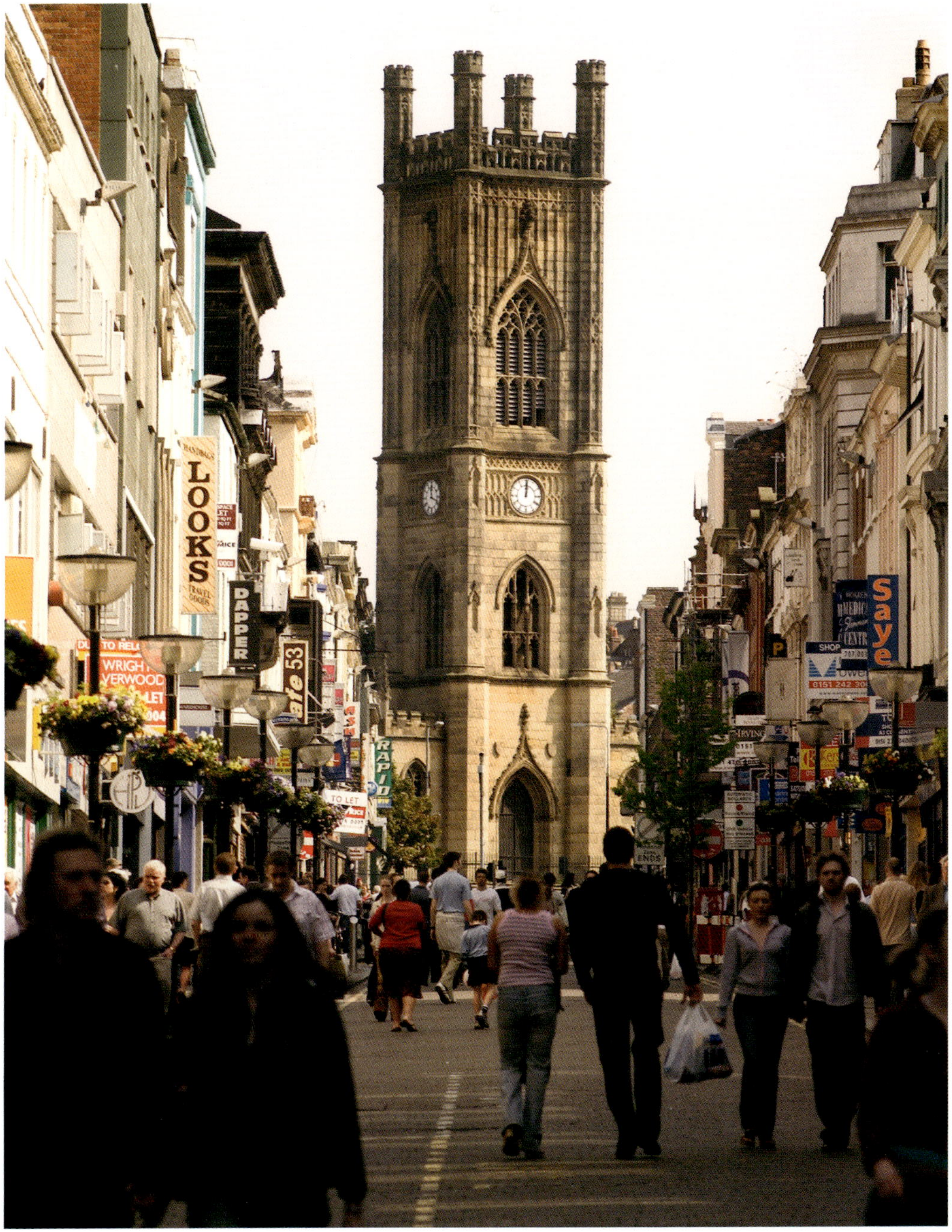

Bold Street
St Luke's Church dominates this view up Bold Street.

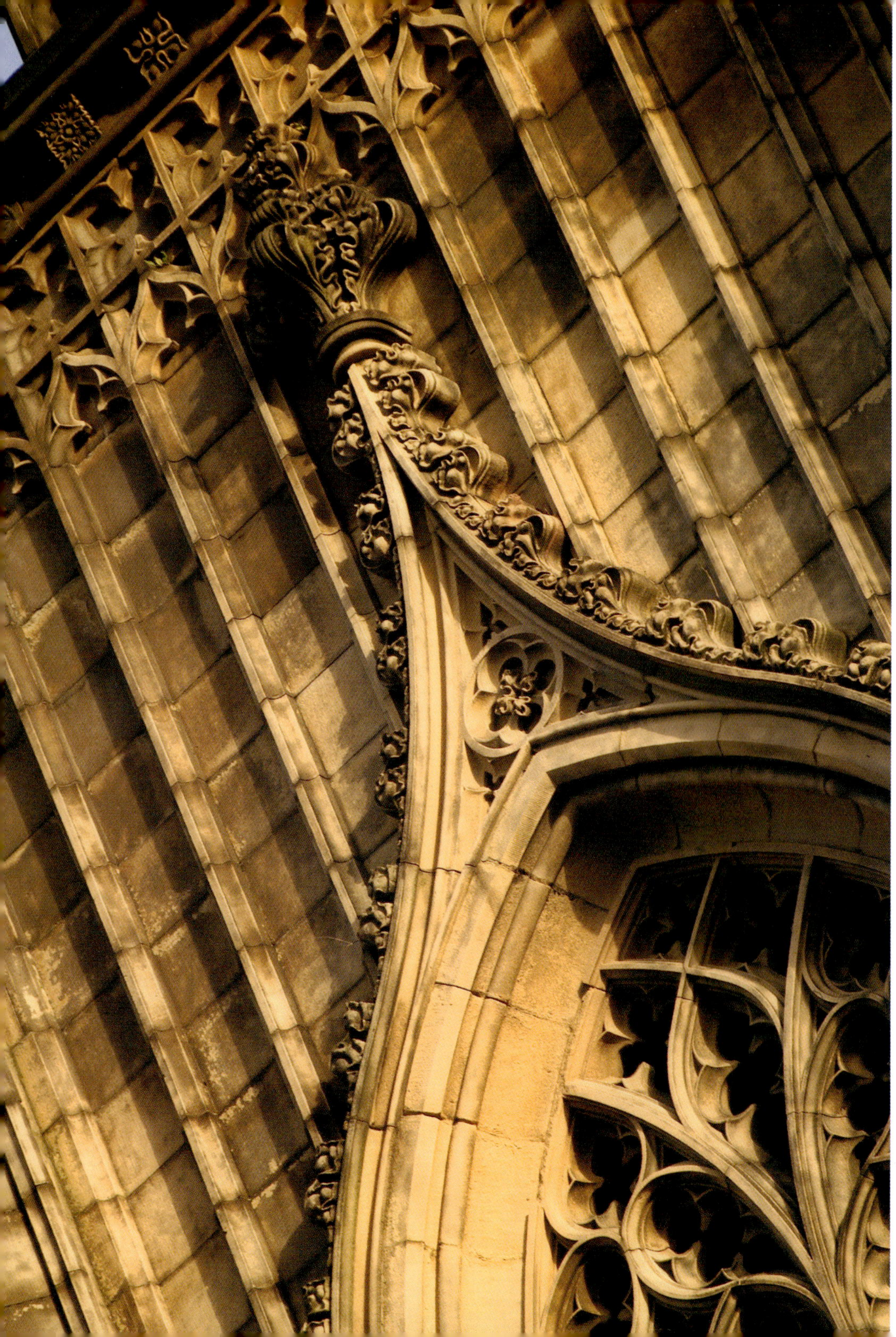

St Luke's Church

Commonly known as 'the bombed-out church', St Luke's is situated at the top of Bold Street on Berry Street. It was built in the years 1811-31 by John Foster the elder and John Foster junior. The tower contains one of this country's first cast-iron bell frames (1828) by George Gillebrand. The church is retained as a memorial to the Blitz on Liverpool during the Second World War.

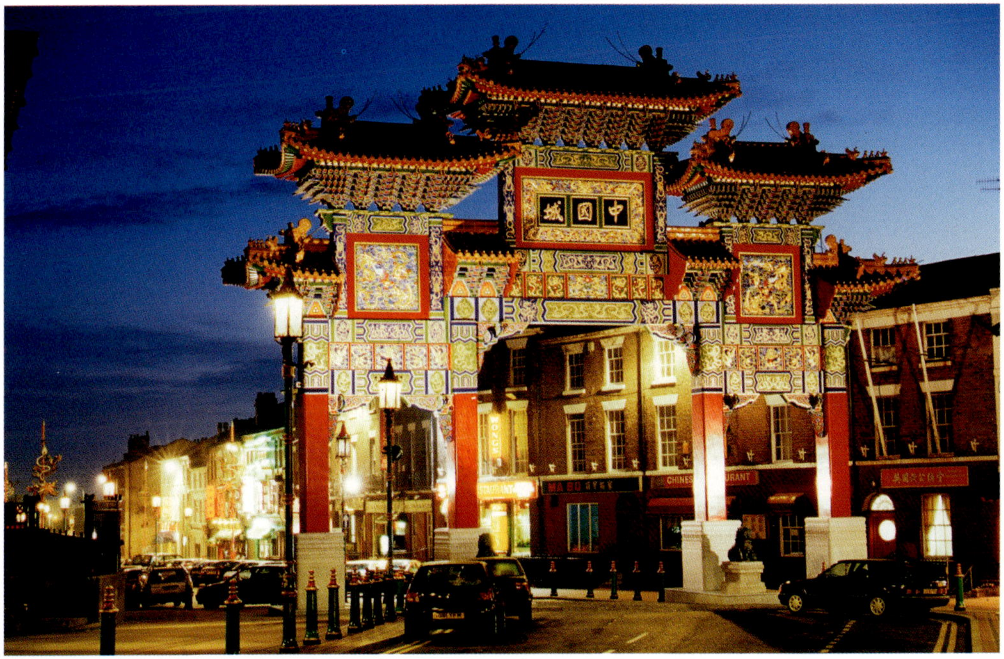

Chinese Arch

Designed and constructed in China by the Shanghai Linyi Garden Building Company, it was completed in 2000 and erected by Chinese craftspeople. The Chinese community is one of the oldest in the country, and has been in Liverpool for over a century.

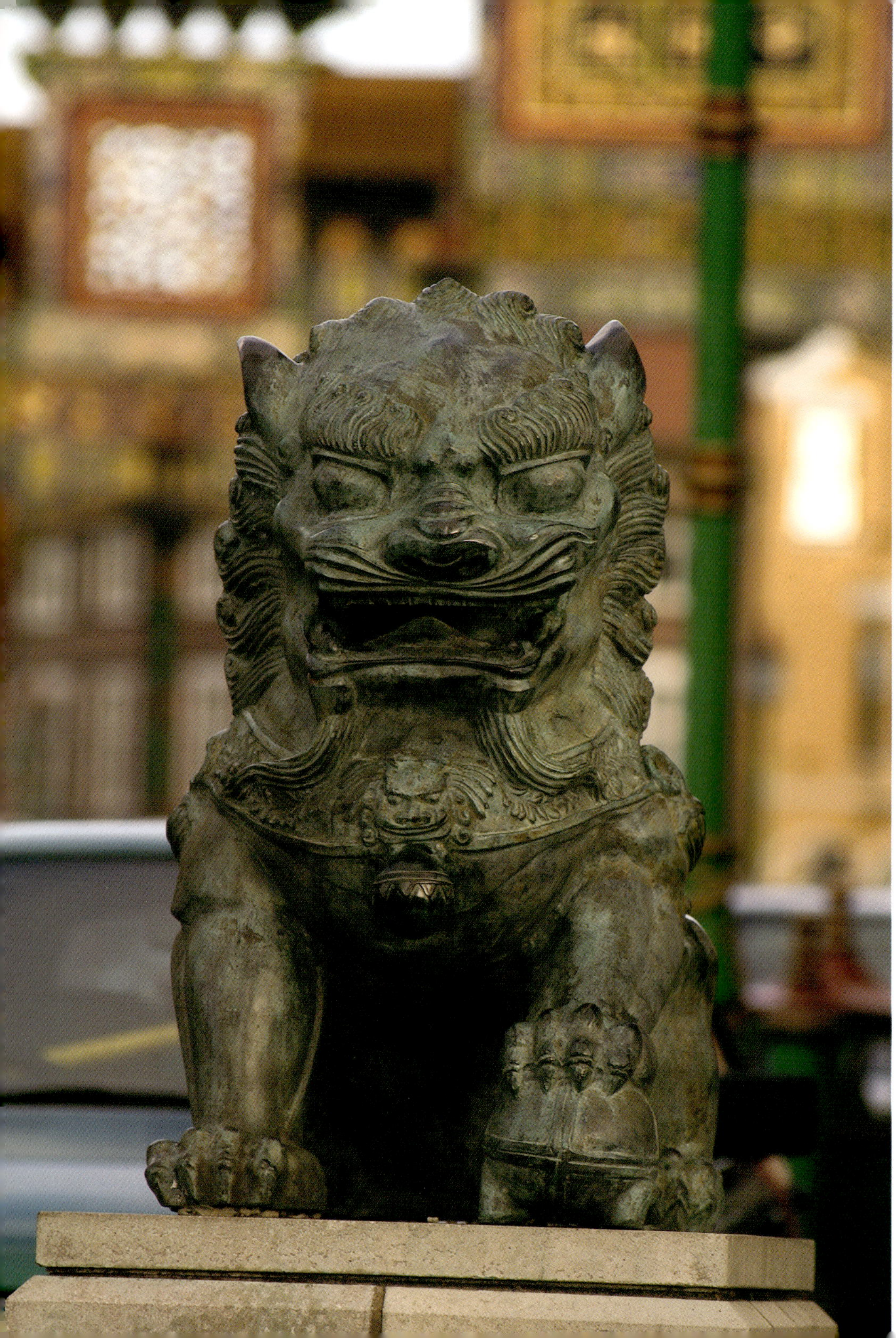

Chinese lion
In the background is the magnificent Chinese Arch at the entrance to Chinatown on Nelson Street. There are a number of these statues around Chinatown, always in pairs on opposite sides of the road. They traditionally represent guardians.

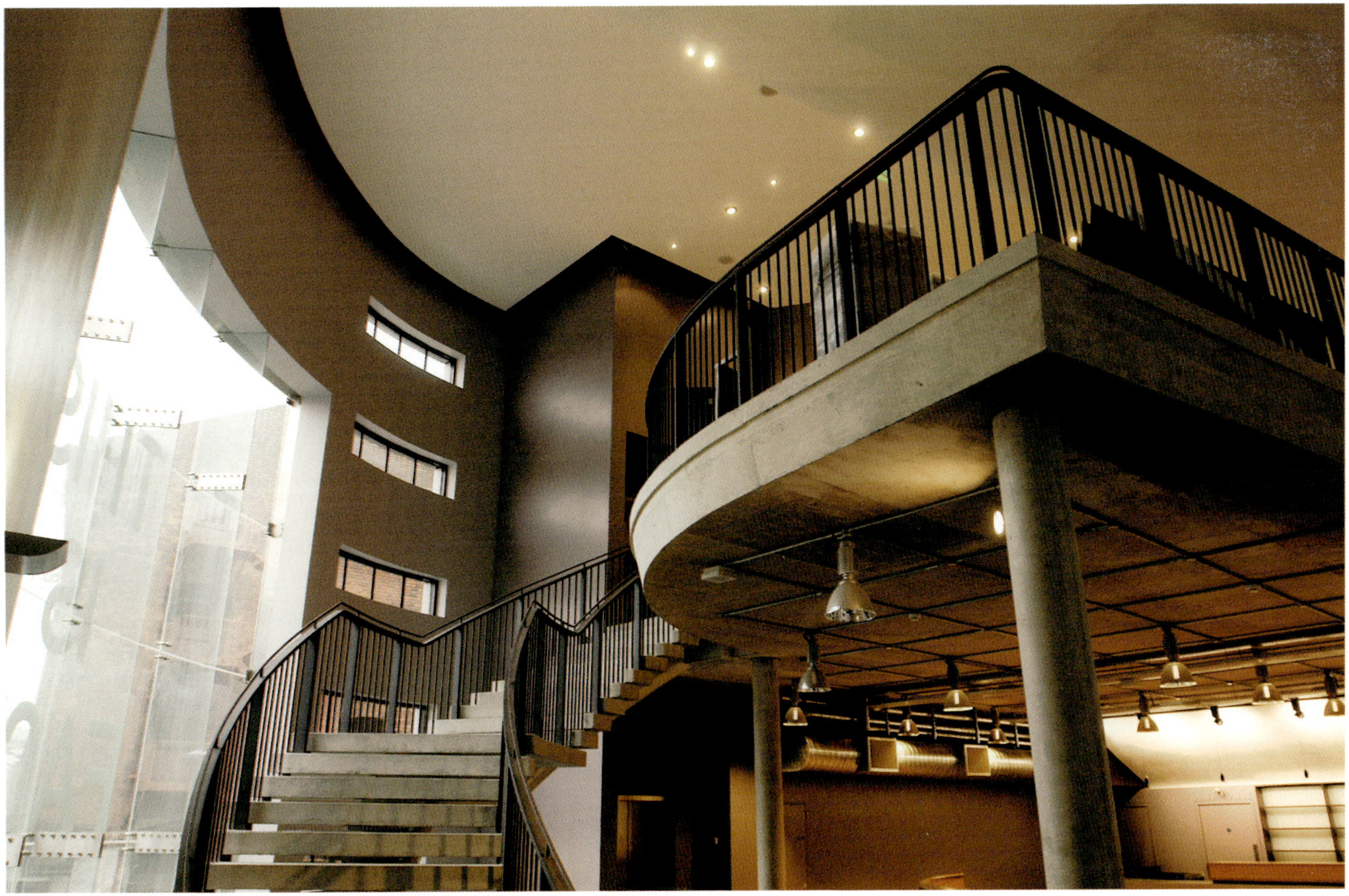

Facing the F.A.C.T.

The acronym stands for Film, Art, and Creative Technology. This new building on Wood Street opened in 2003, and is the UK's leading agency for the commissioning and presentation of film, video and new media art.

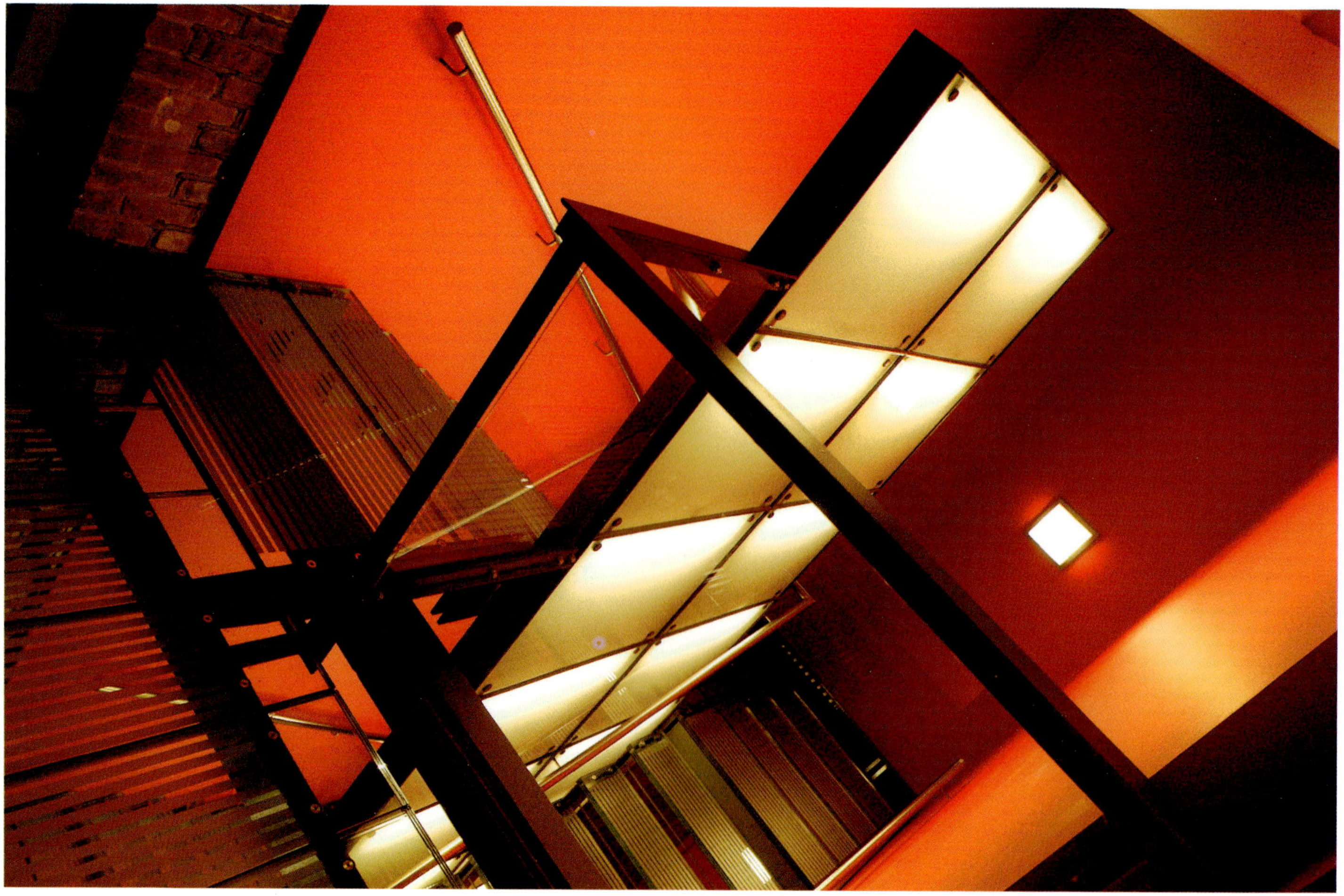

The Tea Factory, Wood Street

Once a rundown warehouse, this building on Wood Street now houses businesses, modern apartments and a café bar.

Tea Factory
The rear of the Tea Factory
on Fleet Street – a pleasant way
to spend a sunny afternoon.

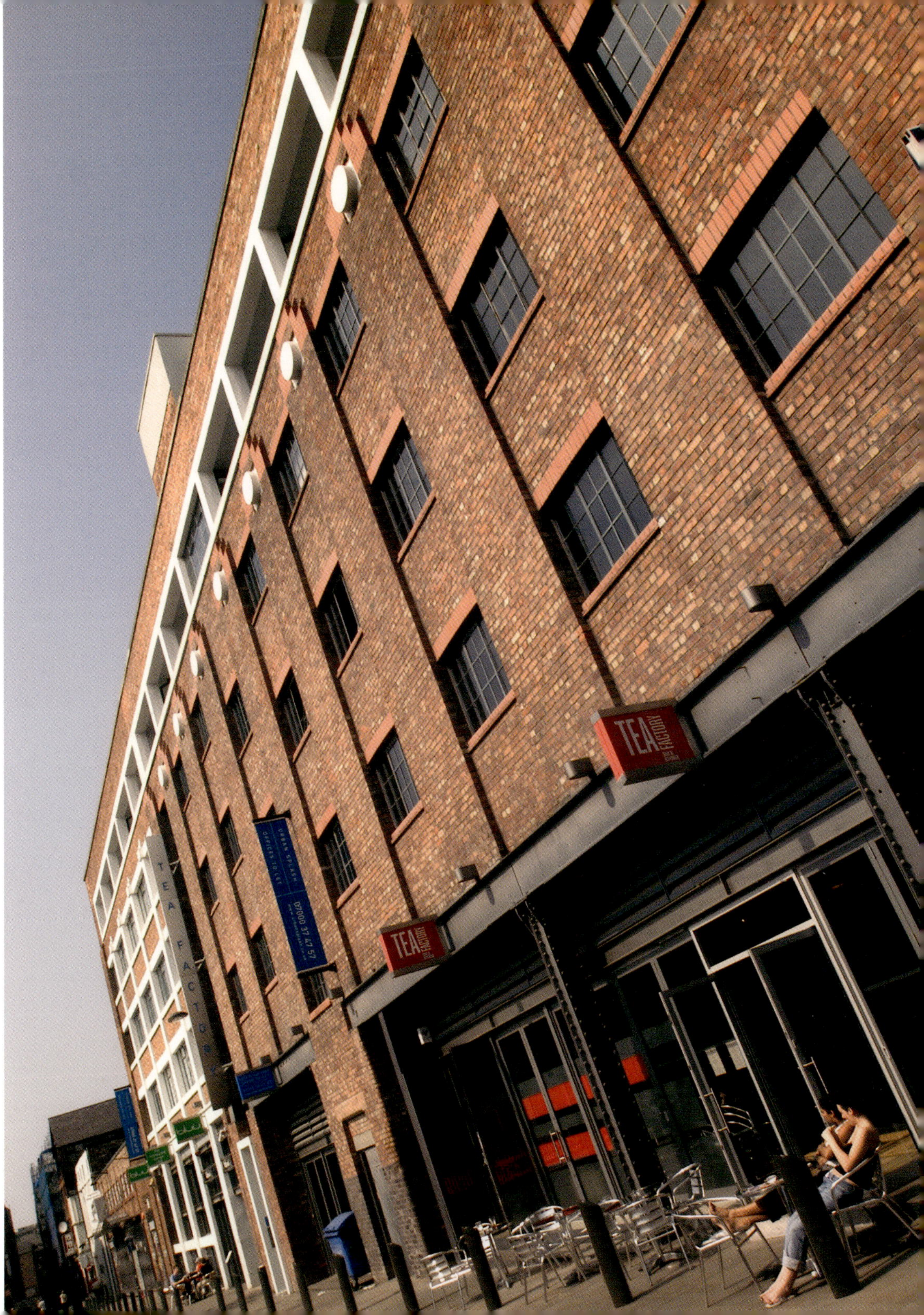

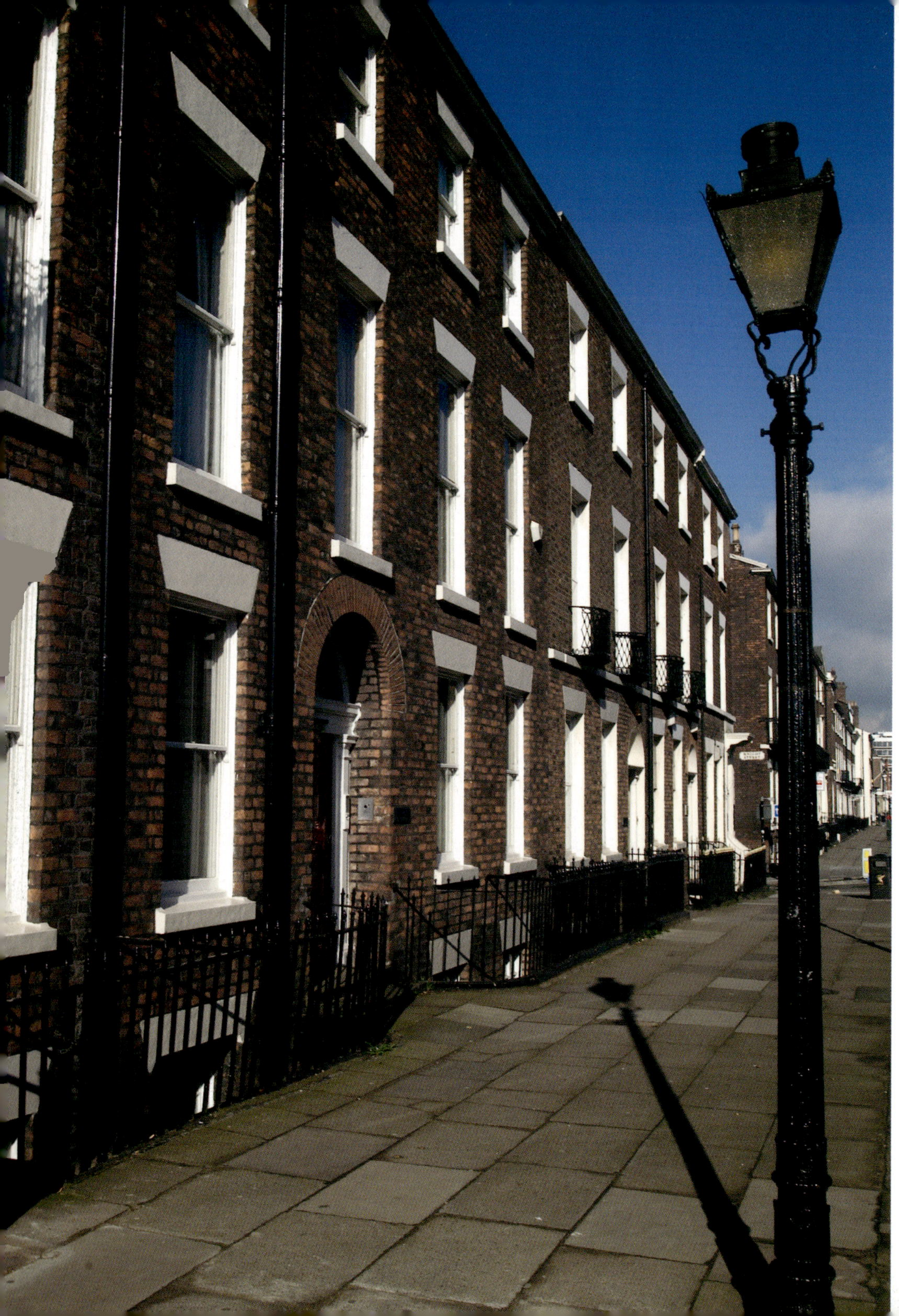

Aerial view of the Albert Dock *(right)*
Albert Dock boasts a collection of Grade I listed buildings. Opened in 1845 and designed by Jesse Hartley, with the coming of steamships it fell into decline and eventually closed in the early 1970s. Today, it is a bustling tourist attraction, featuring the Tate Liverpool, the Maritime Museum and many retail businesses and apartments.

Rodney Street
Rodney Street is the 'Harley Street' of Liverpool. Once the preserve of wealthy captains of ships and of industry, this fine street of mainly Georgian terraced houses was traditionally also occupied by Liverpool's leading doctors. Another famous resident was Liverpool photographer Edward Chambrè Hardman. His studio is now preserved by the National Trust and is open for guided tours. Hardman's house is situated at the end nearest the Anglican cathedral.

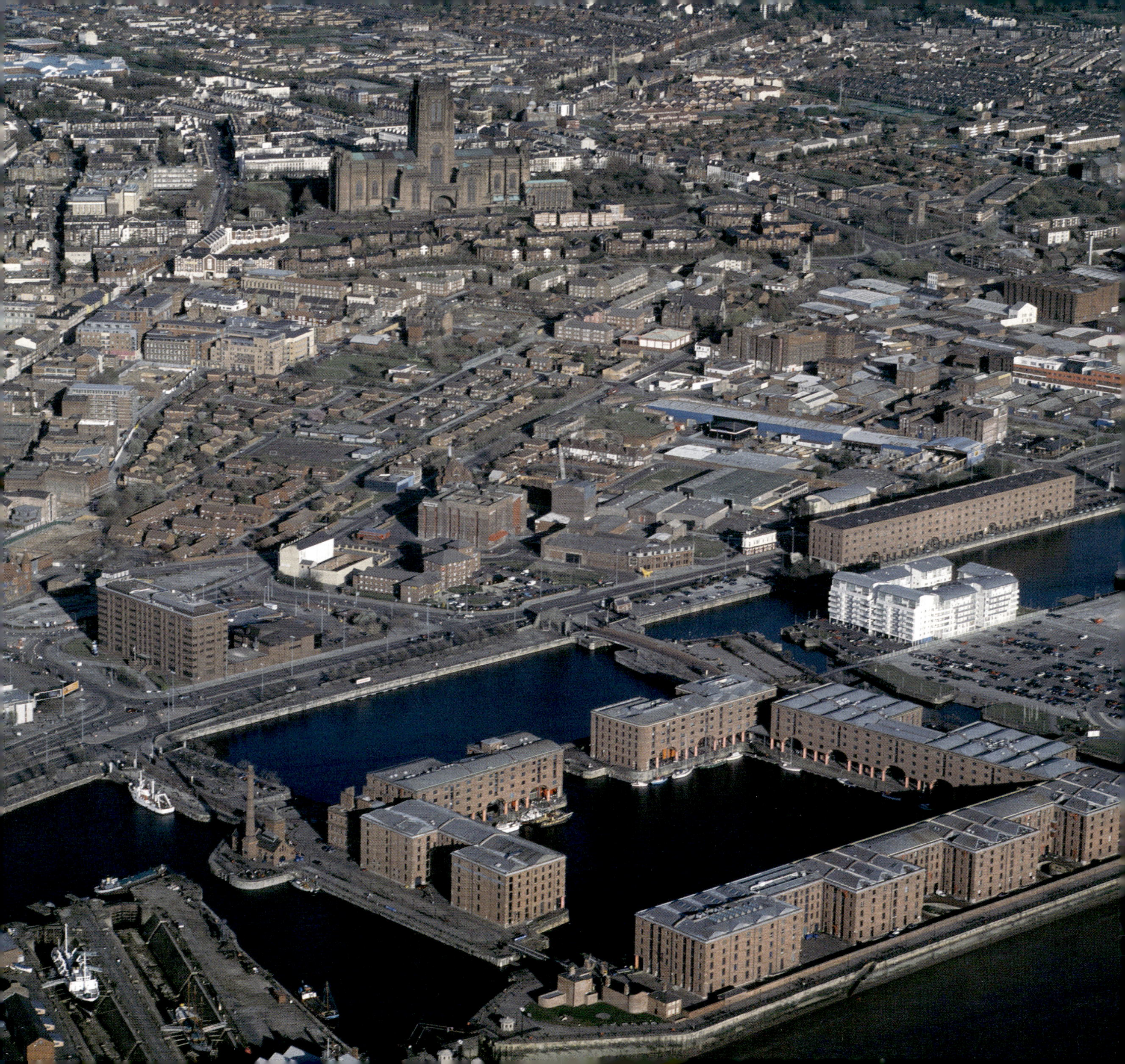

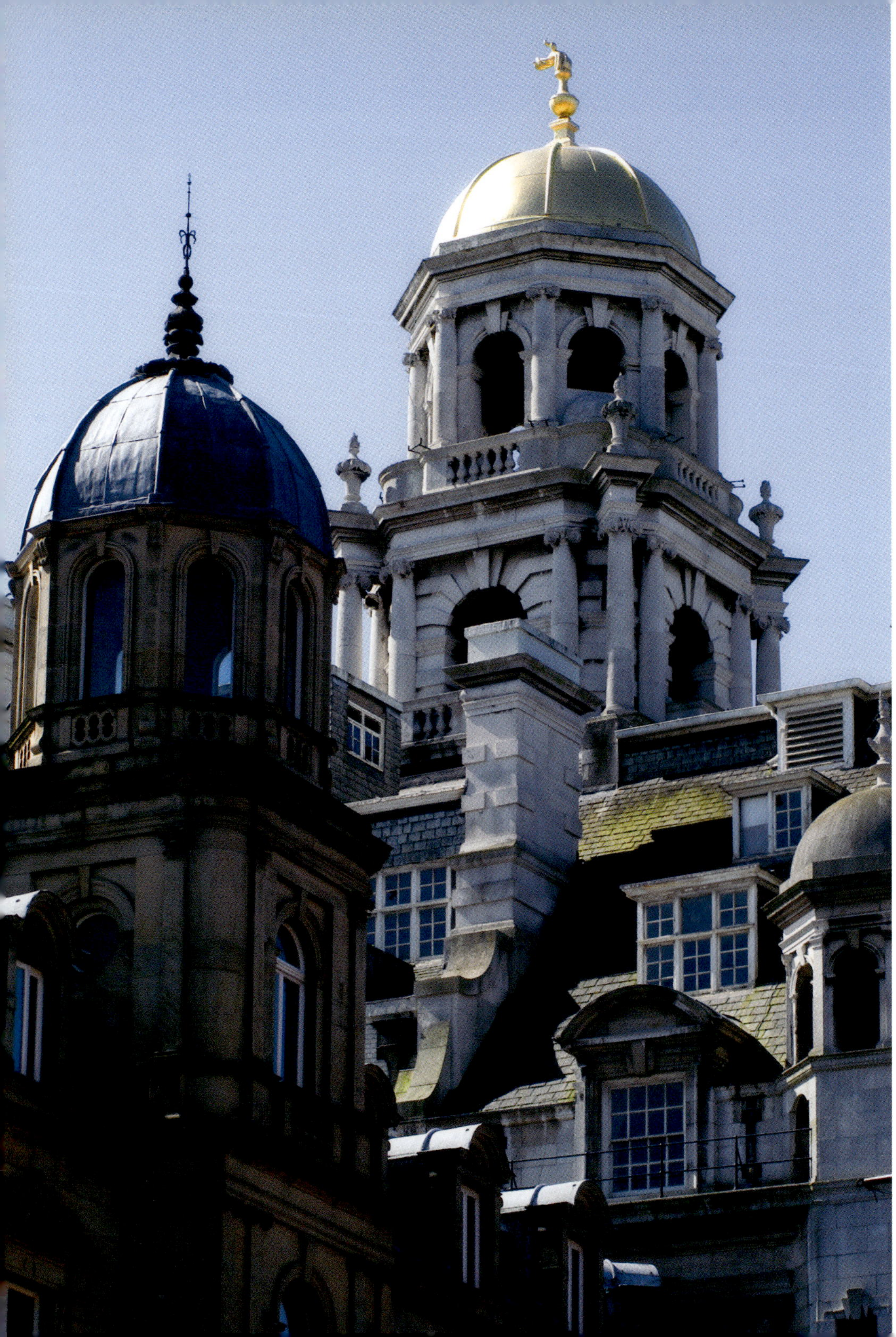

The Temple and Royal Insurance Building
Situated on Dale Street and North John Street, the Royal Insurance Building (built between 1896-1903) was the first to use a steel frame, which allowed the general office on the first floor to be free of columns. The Temple (built between 1864-65) was designed by J.A. Picton for the banker Sir William Brown.

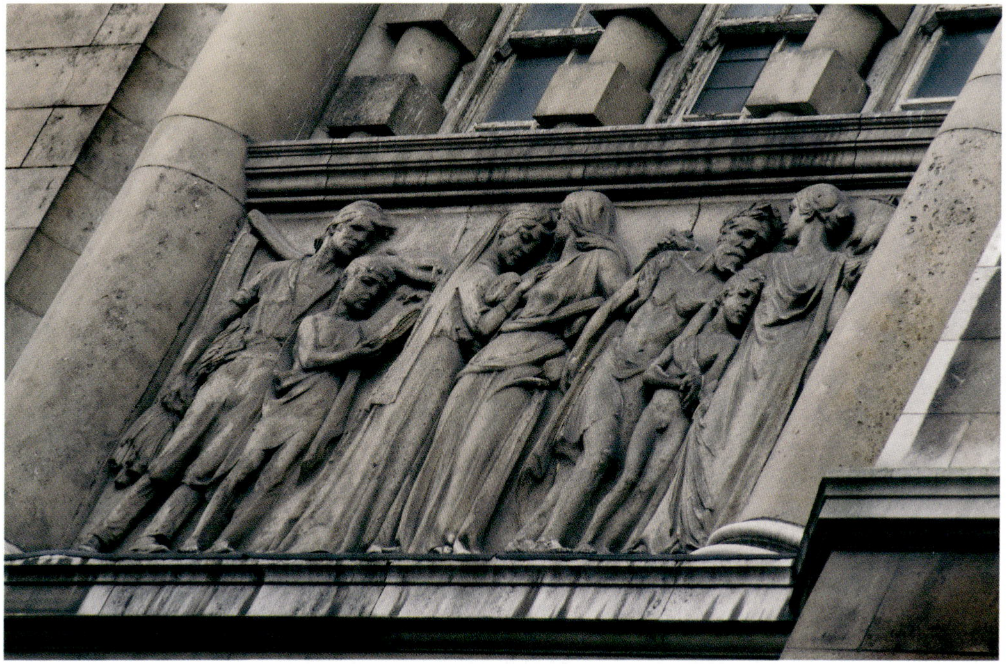

Sculpture on the Royal Insurance Building

One of five panels on the Royal Insurance Building. This one is on Prince's Street and shows the benefits derived from life insurance. 'Wisdom' is the central figure, who is seen comforting a widow. The sculpture is by C.J Allan and J. F Doyle, and the building was opened in 1903.

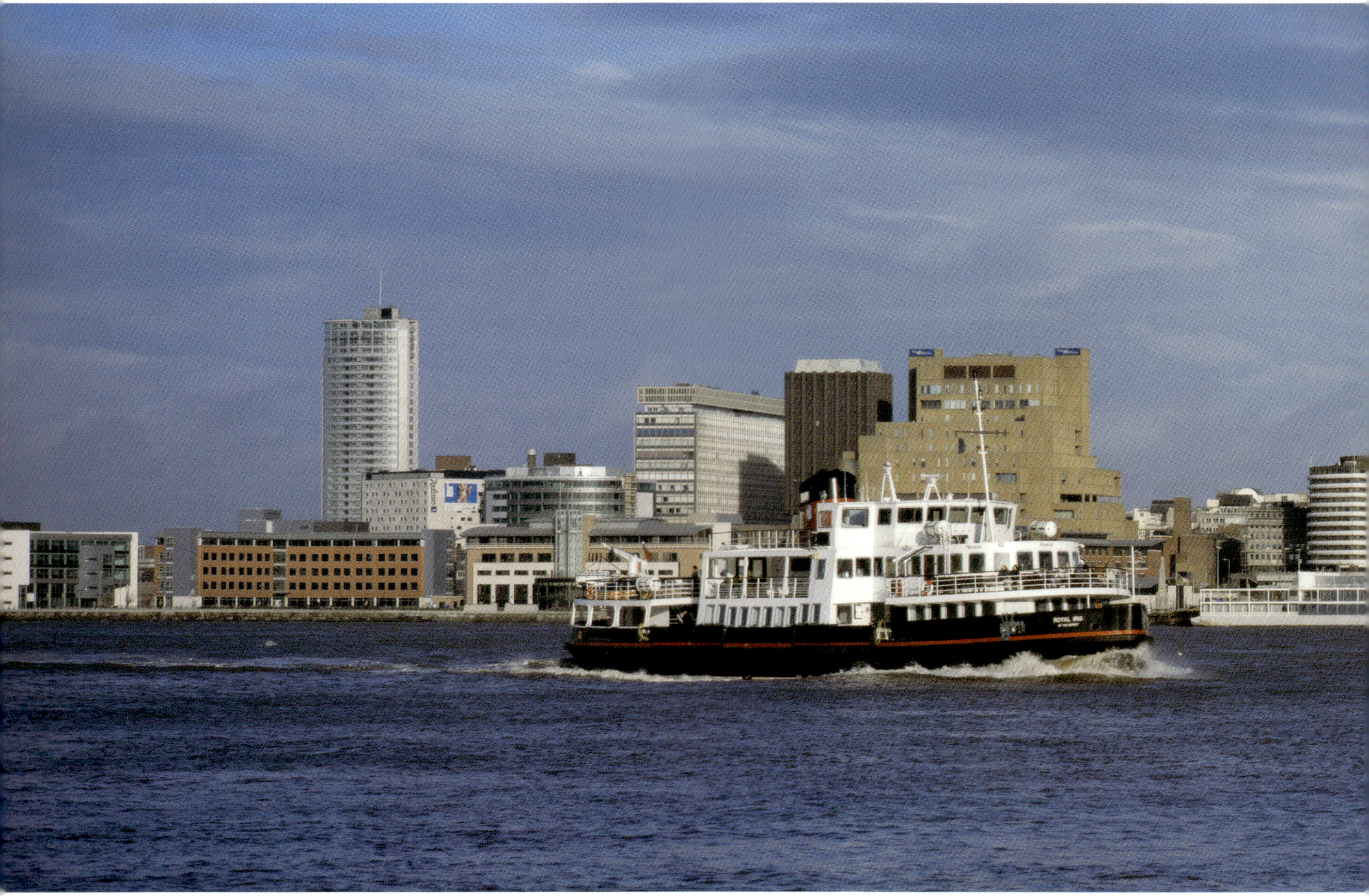

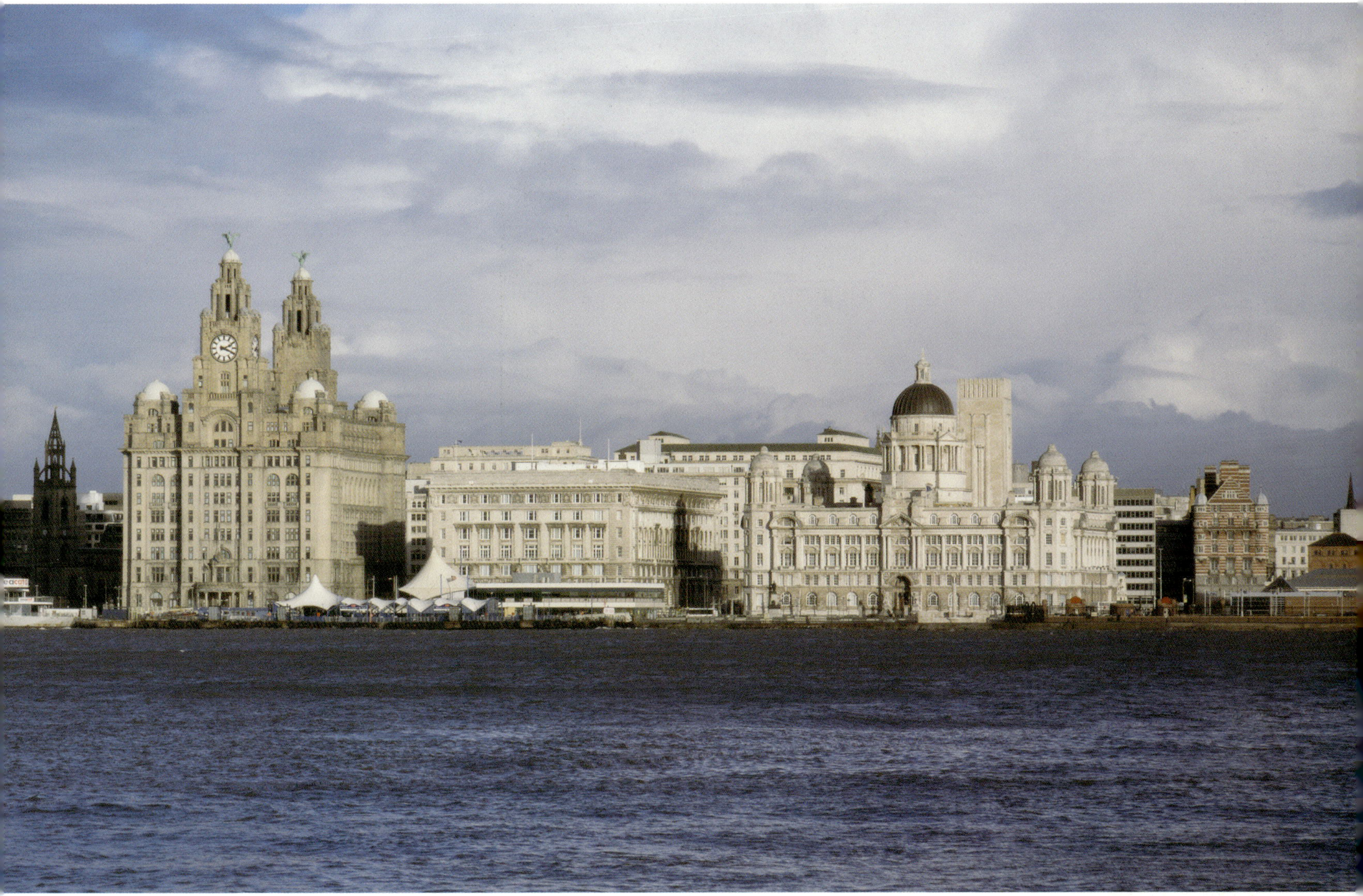

The Liverpool Waterfront with the ferry *Royal Iris of the Mersey*

The River Mersey has one of the largest tidal ranges in the world. Compare the height of the water line in this image to that on other waterfront images in the book. The difference between high and low tide is often more than 10 metres.

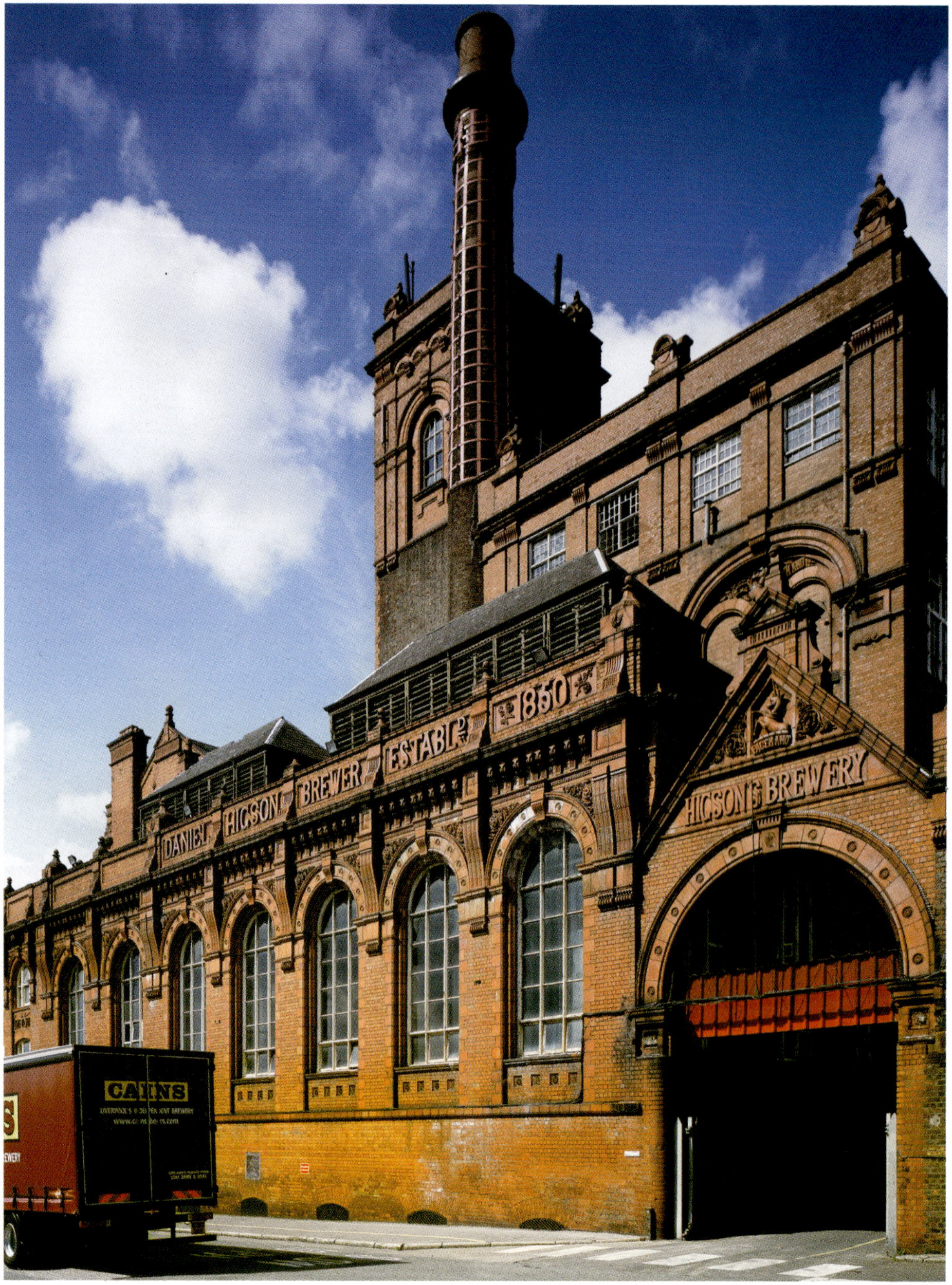

Cain's Brewery

Robert Cain founded this brewery but it was taken over by Higsons in the 1920s who inserted their own name into the building. The business is now back under the Cain's name. Robert Cain was also responsible for building the Philharmonic Hotel on Hope Street as an outlet for his beers.

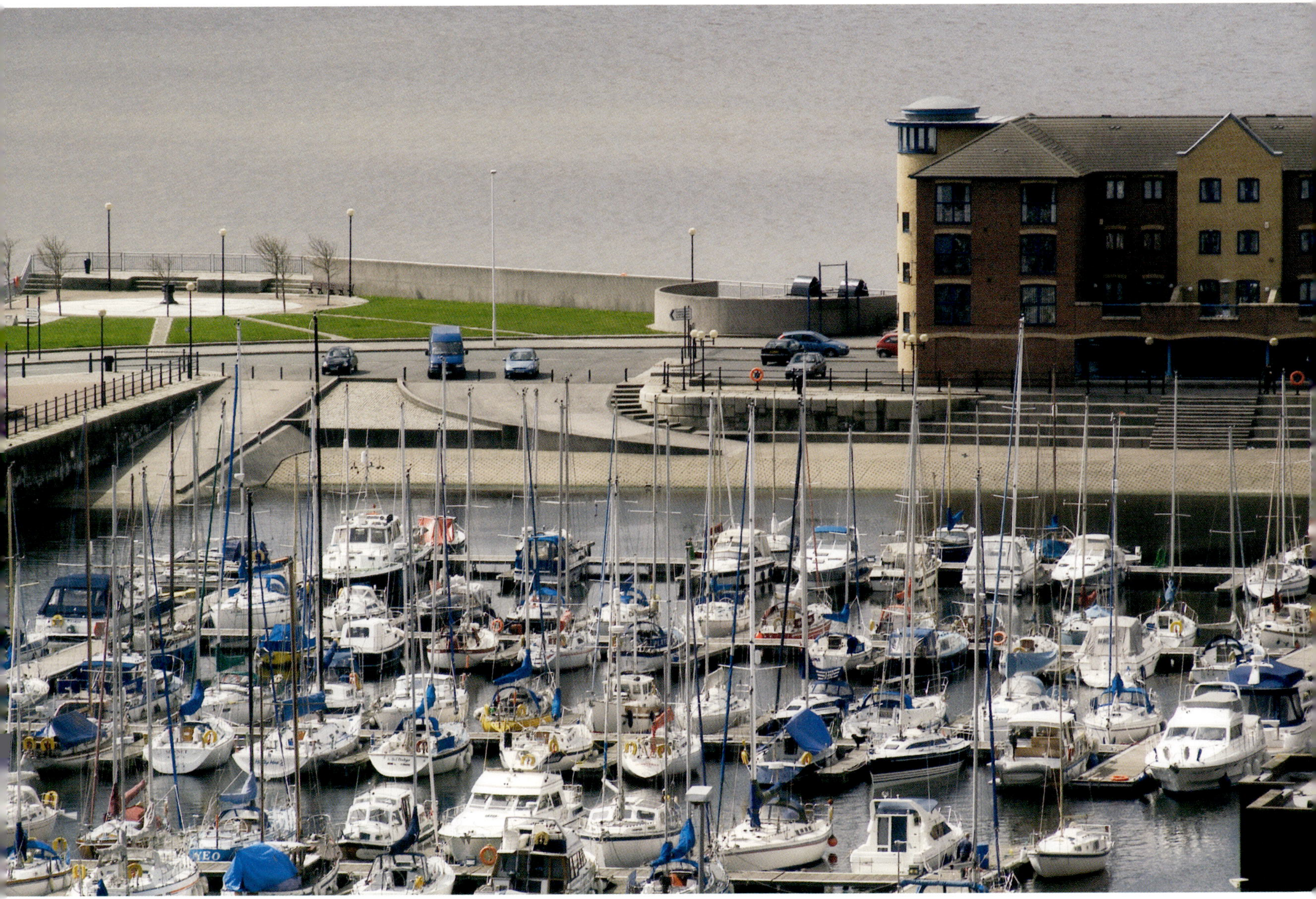

The Yacht Marina at Coburg Dock

This popular yachting marina lies to the south of the Pier Head.

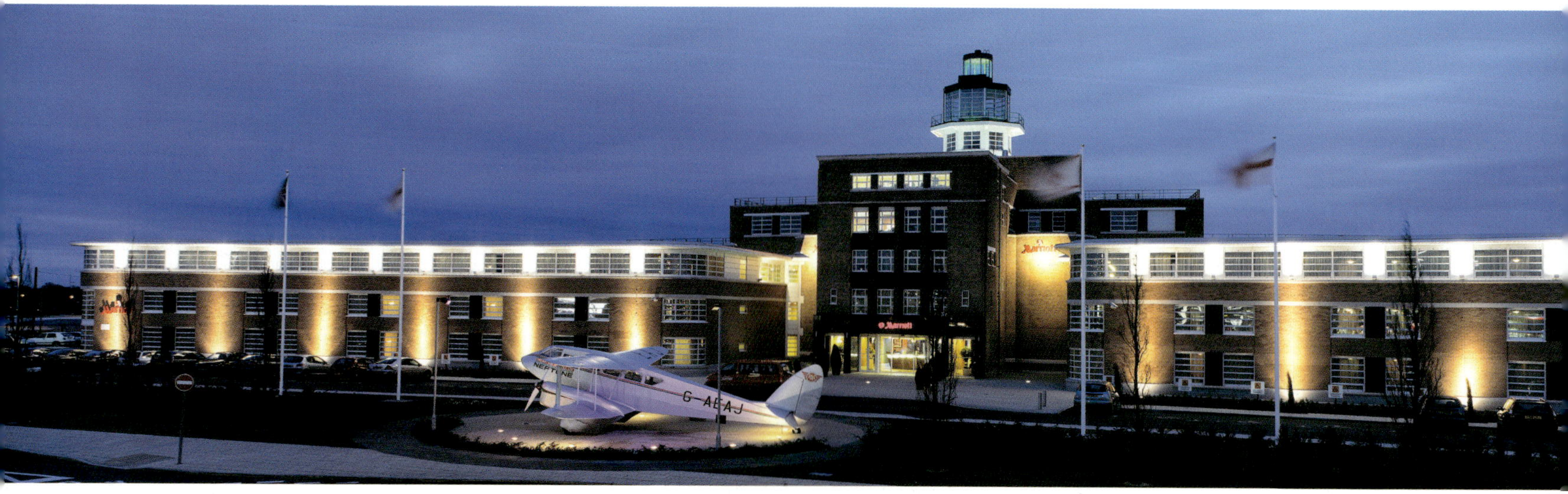

Speke Marriott Hotel

The old terminal building for Speke Airport, a Grade II listed building, fell into disuse in the early 1970s. The art deco building by Edward Bloomfield opened in 1939 and was refurbished in early 2001, when the adjacent hanger was turned into a sports and leisure facility. The terminal was replaced by a new one east of Speke Hall which opened in 1967, and is now called the Liverpool John Lennon Airport. An early passenger biplane, a Dragon Rapide, stands on the forecourt.

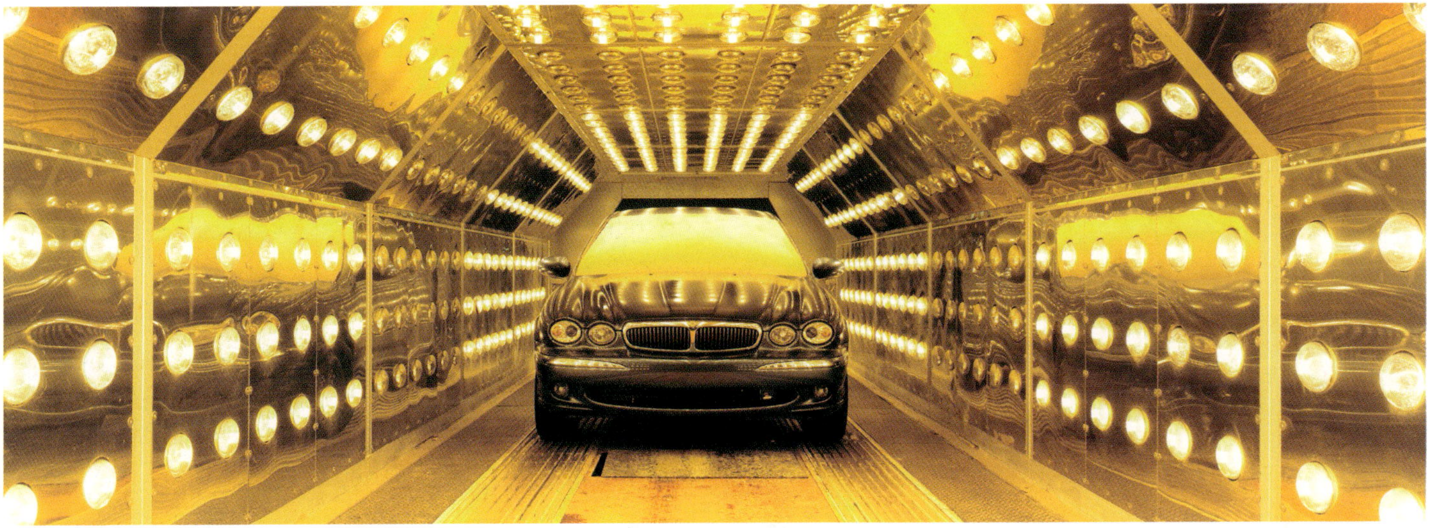

Jaguar Factory

Jaguar's Halewood plant has benefited recently from a £300m refurbishment and now employs over 3000 people. Liverpool has established a reputation as an international automotive centre, and is home to three of the world's leading vehicle manufacturers in the North West region. The Halewood plant at Speke has recently been nominated as Ford's number one assembly plant for quality worldwide.

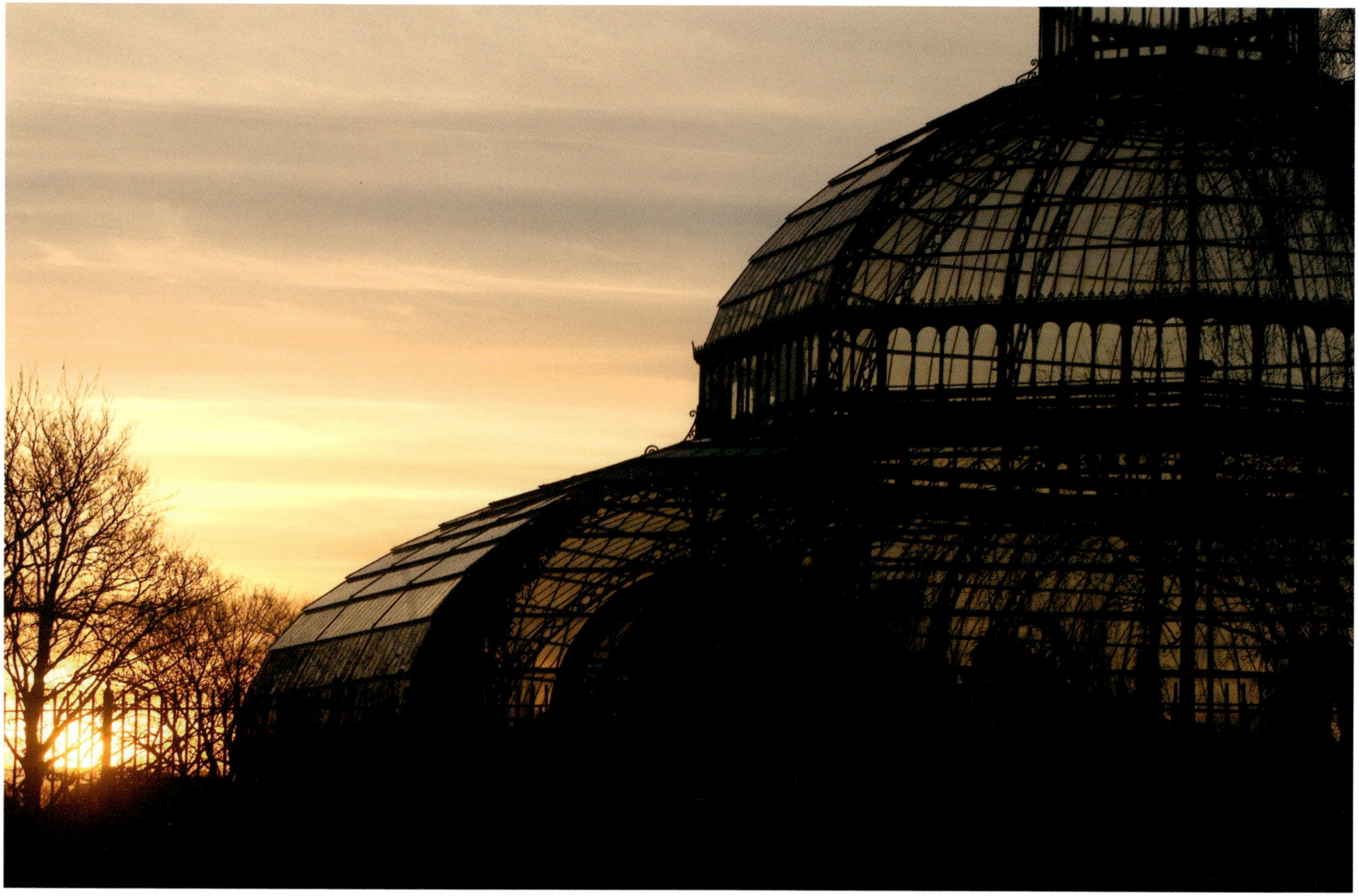

Palm House

The Palm House in Sefton Park was built in 1896. Now totally refurbished – a process in which every single piece of metal work was removed, renovated and then reassembled – the Palm House is a beautiful, relaxing building with many stunning features.

Statue of Linnaeus
This statue of Linnaeus, the pioneering Swedish botanist and the founder of modern taxonomy, stands outside the Palm House in Sefton Park.

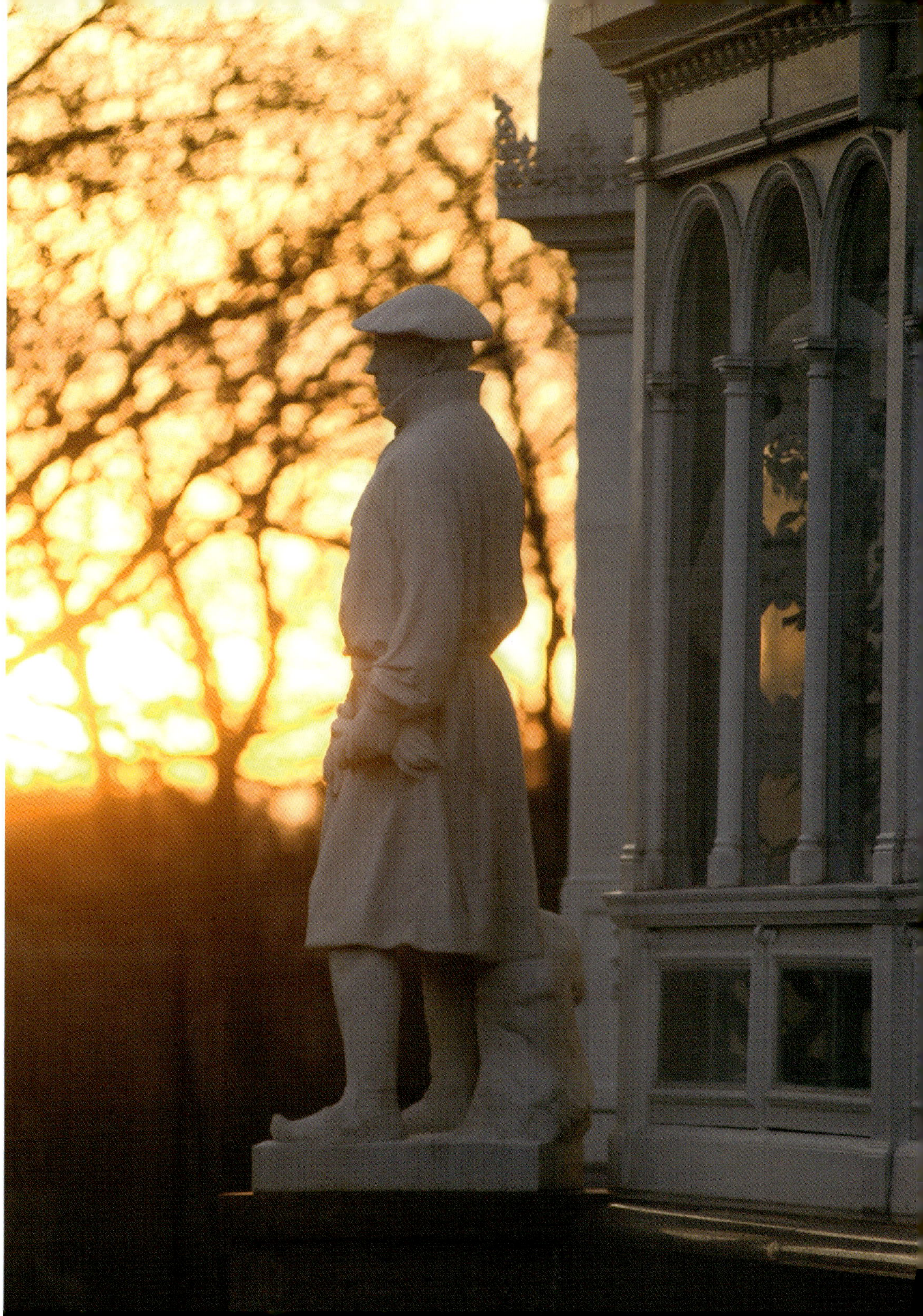

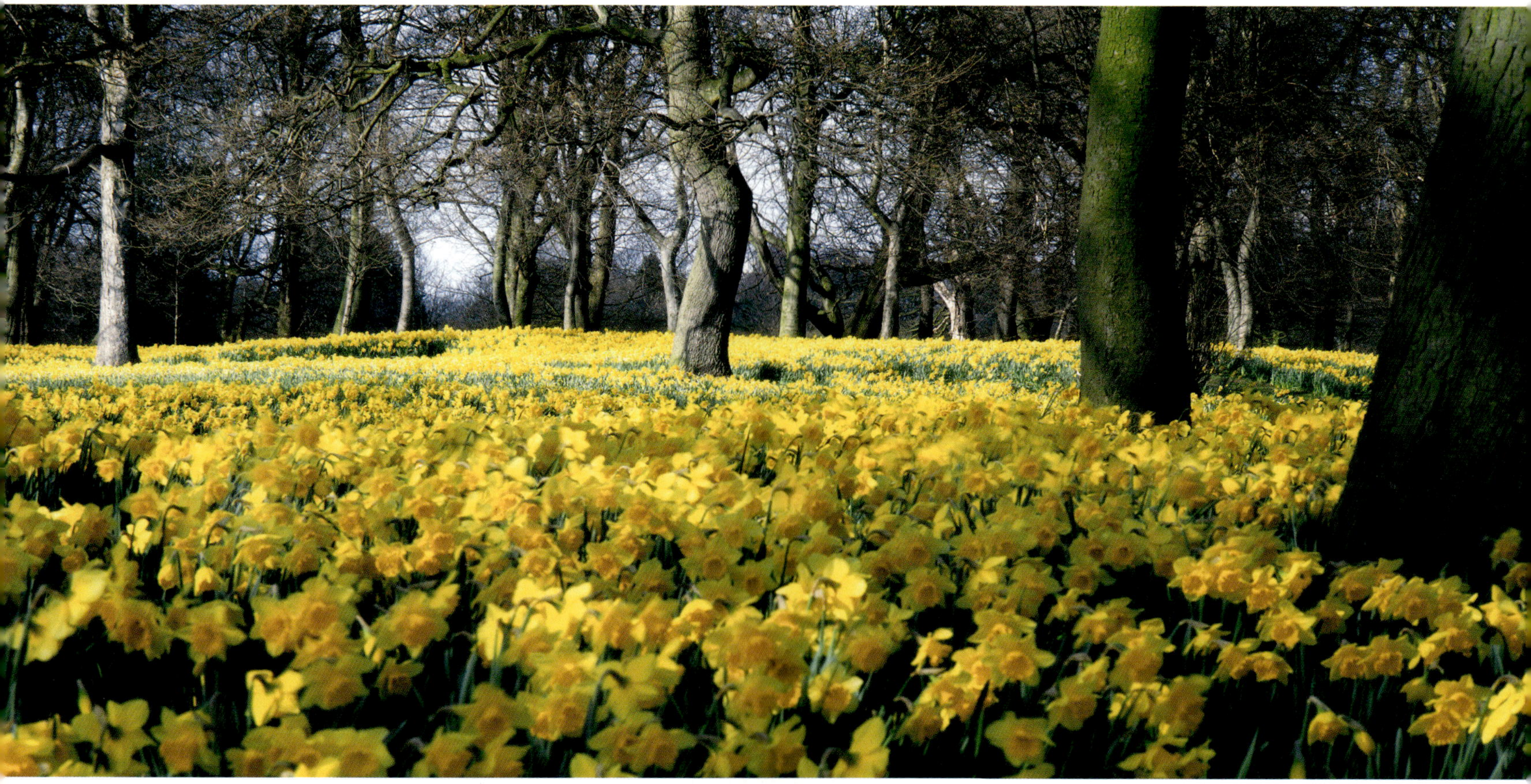

Marie Curie Cancer Care

The 'Field of Hope' in Sefton Park. These fields of daffodils come into bloom in early spring each year and this memorial in Sefton Park is one of many in the UK.

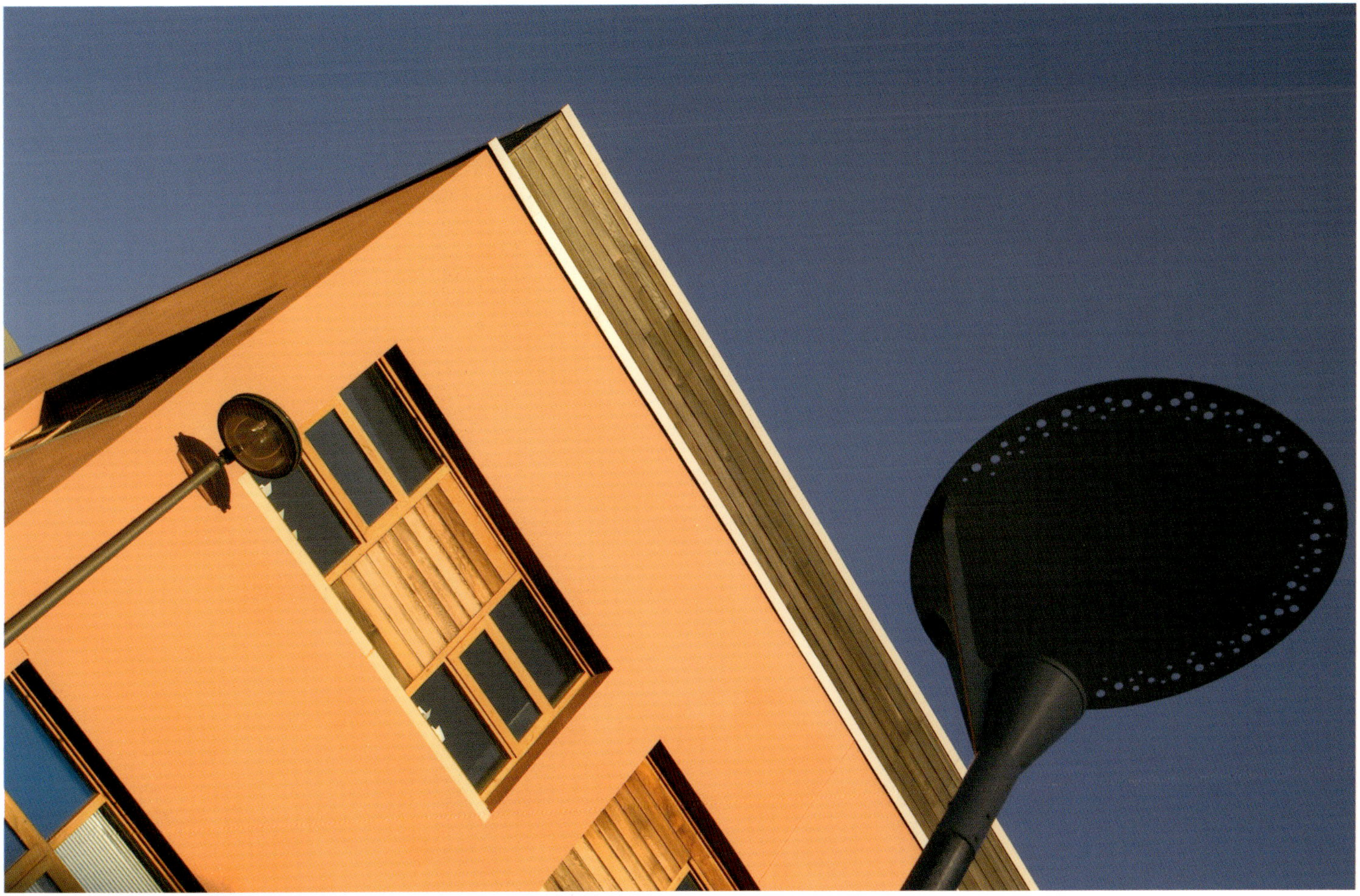

Campbell Square/Henry Street.
Many new buildings have replaced derelict warehousing in the Duke Street development scheme.

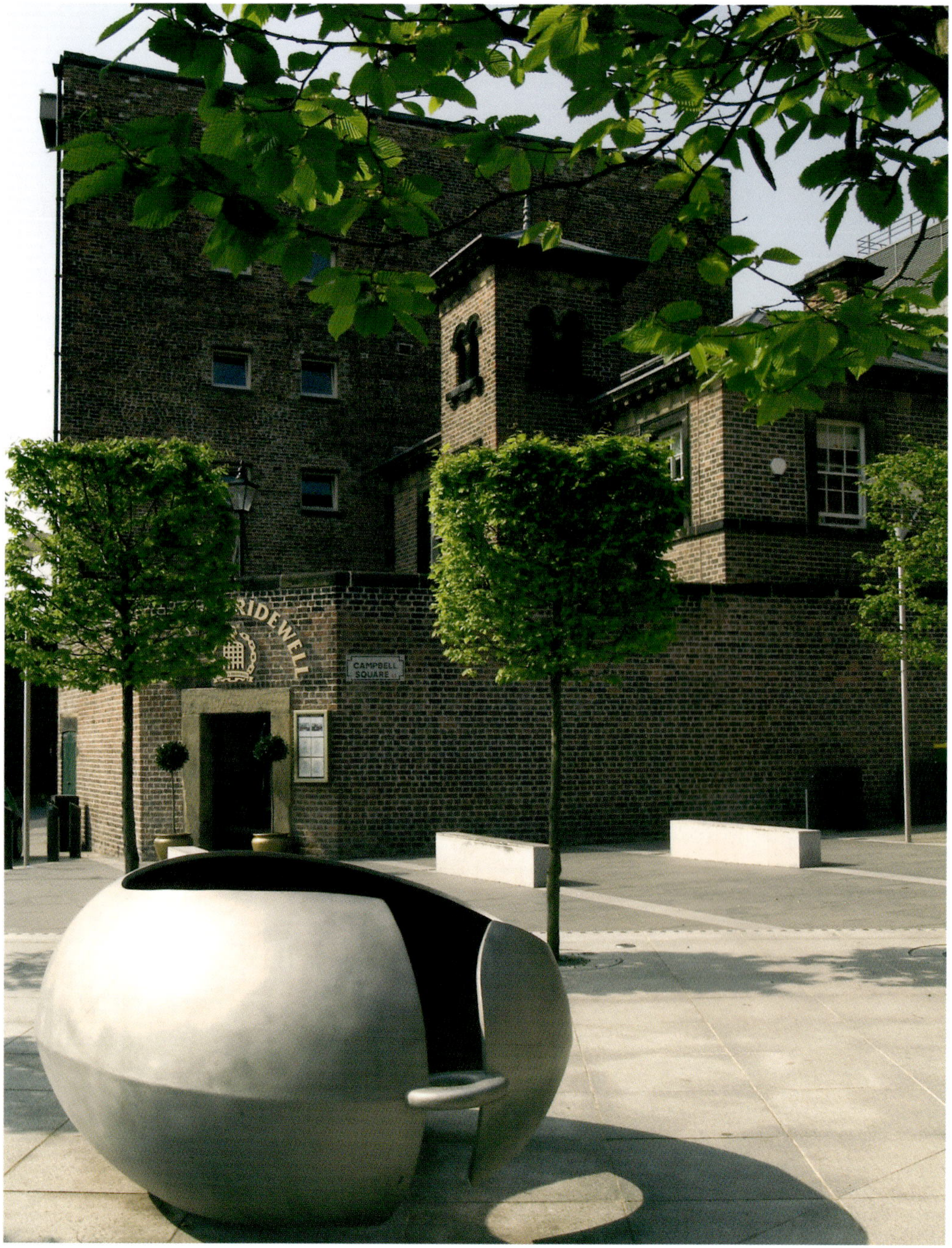

The Bridewell on Campbell Square
This is now a bistro and bar. Originally the Bridewell was built in 1861 and consisted of cells and police offices. The cells are still there, and you can enjoy your meal in them. 'Bridewell' is a generic term meaning 'house of correction'. To quote an old source, they were used 'for the correction of all strumpets, night-walkers, pickpockets, vagrants and incorrigible and disobedient servants'. The sculpture in the foreground is by Stephen Broadbent and is entitled 'Seed' 2002.

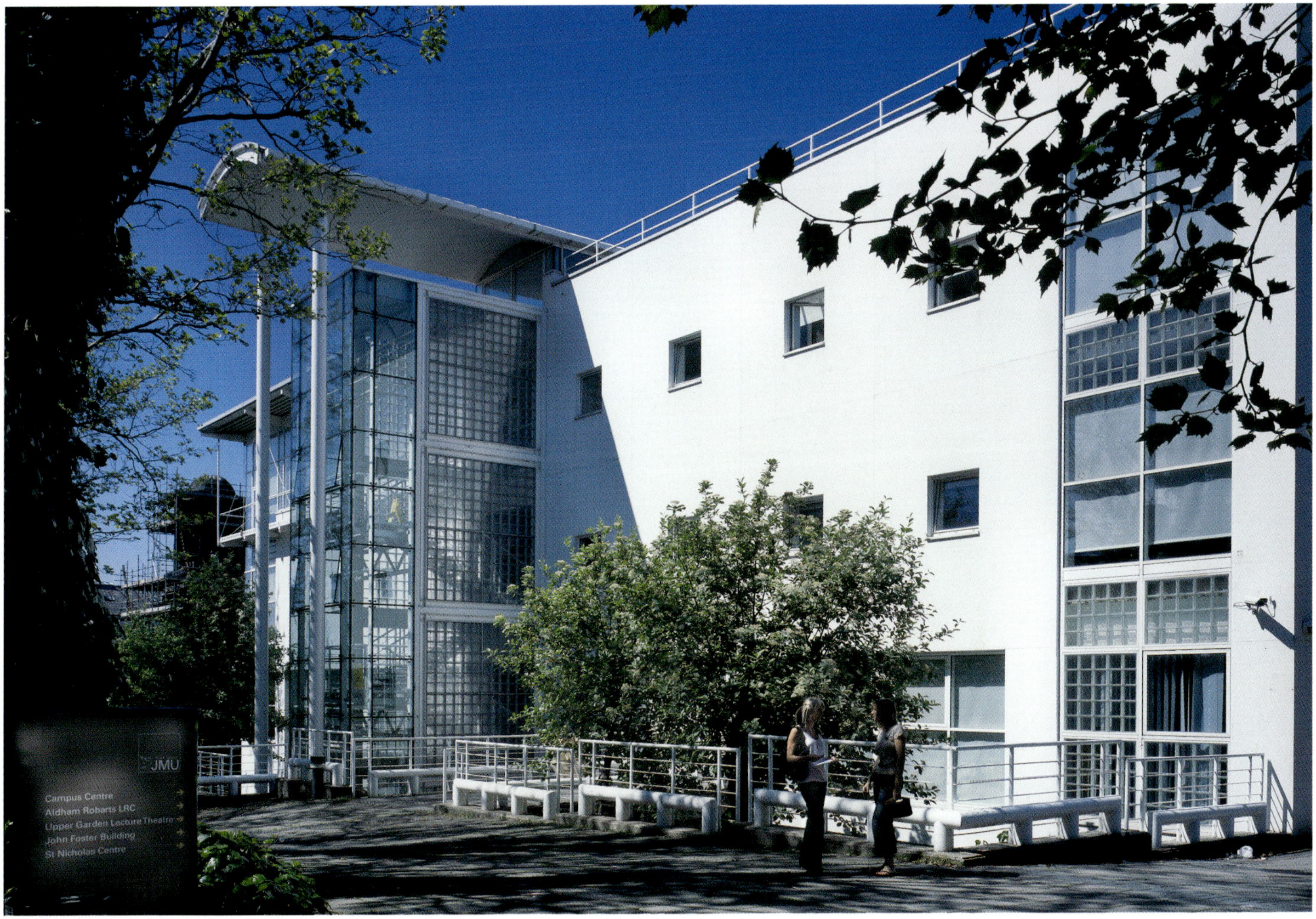

Aldham Robart's Learning Resource Centre

Liverpool John Moores University was the forerunner to the many modern university buildings which are now commonplace in Liverpool. This one was built in 1994 and the architects were Austin Smith Lord.

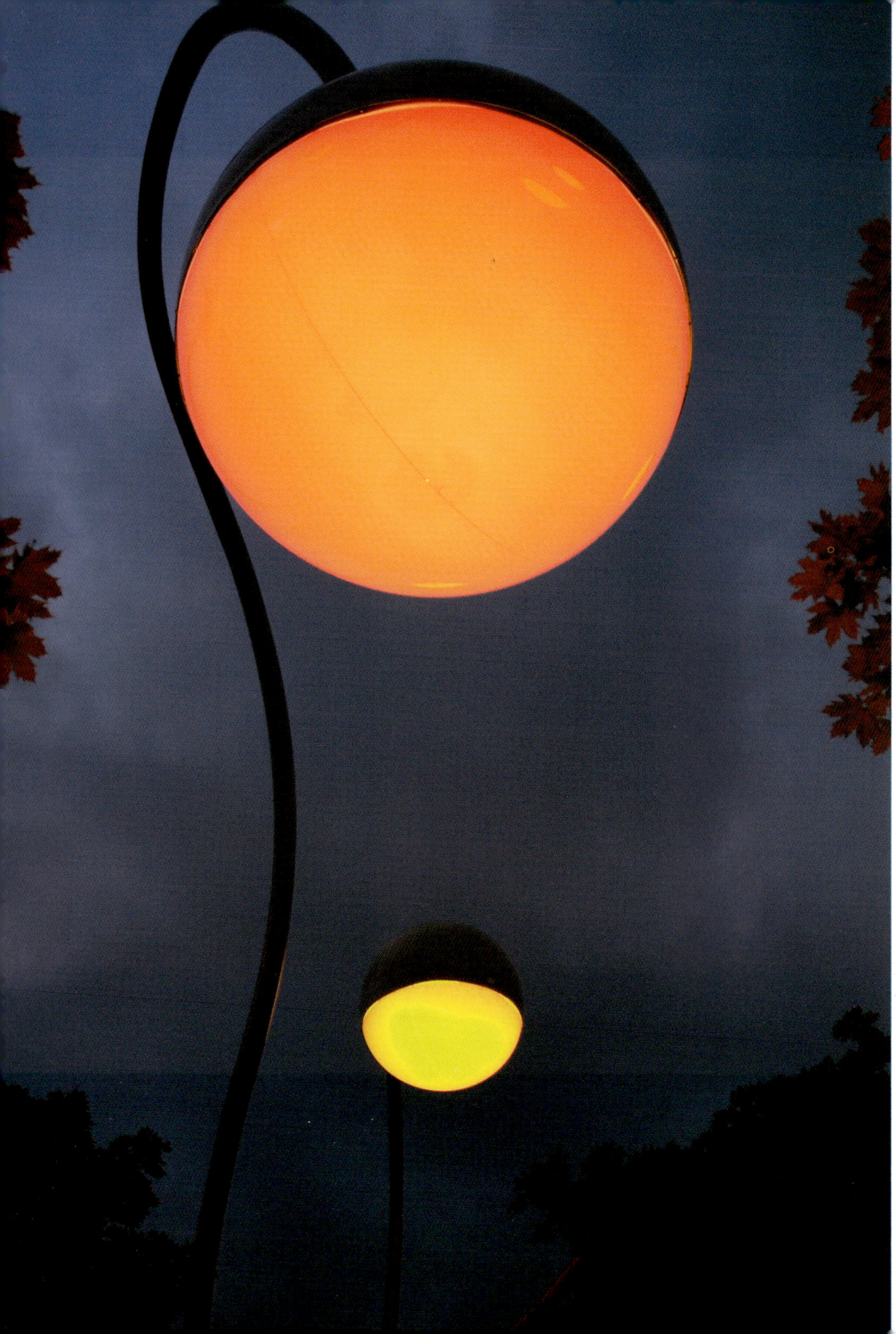

Penelope
Wolstenholme Square was the first square in Liverpool to have a central garden. The gardens were re-instated in 2002 and the modern sculpture consisting of eight illuminated globes was installed in May 2004.

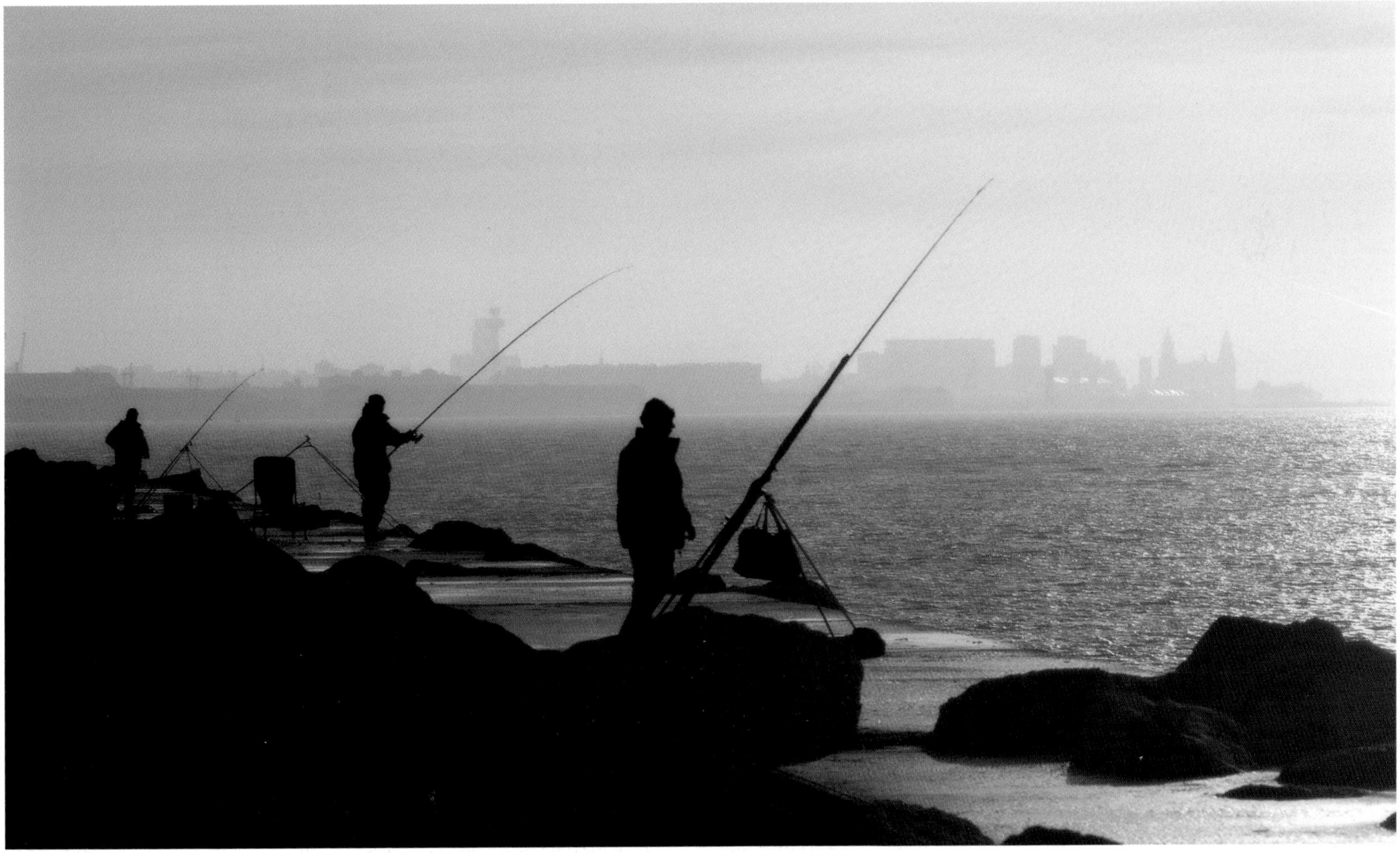

The mouth of the Mersey

Fishermen at Seaforth on an early January morning. Measures taken by the water company have improved the water quality in the Mersey to the extent that salmon have been caught, and commercial fishing has resumed around the mouth of the river.

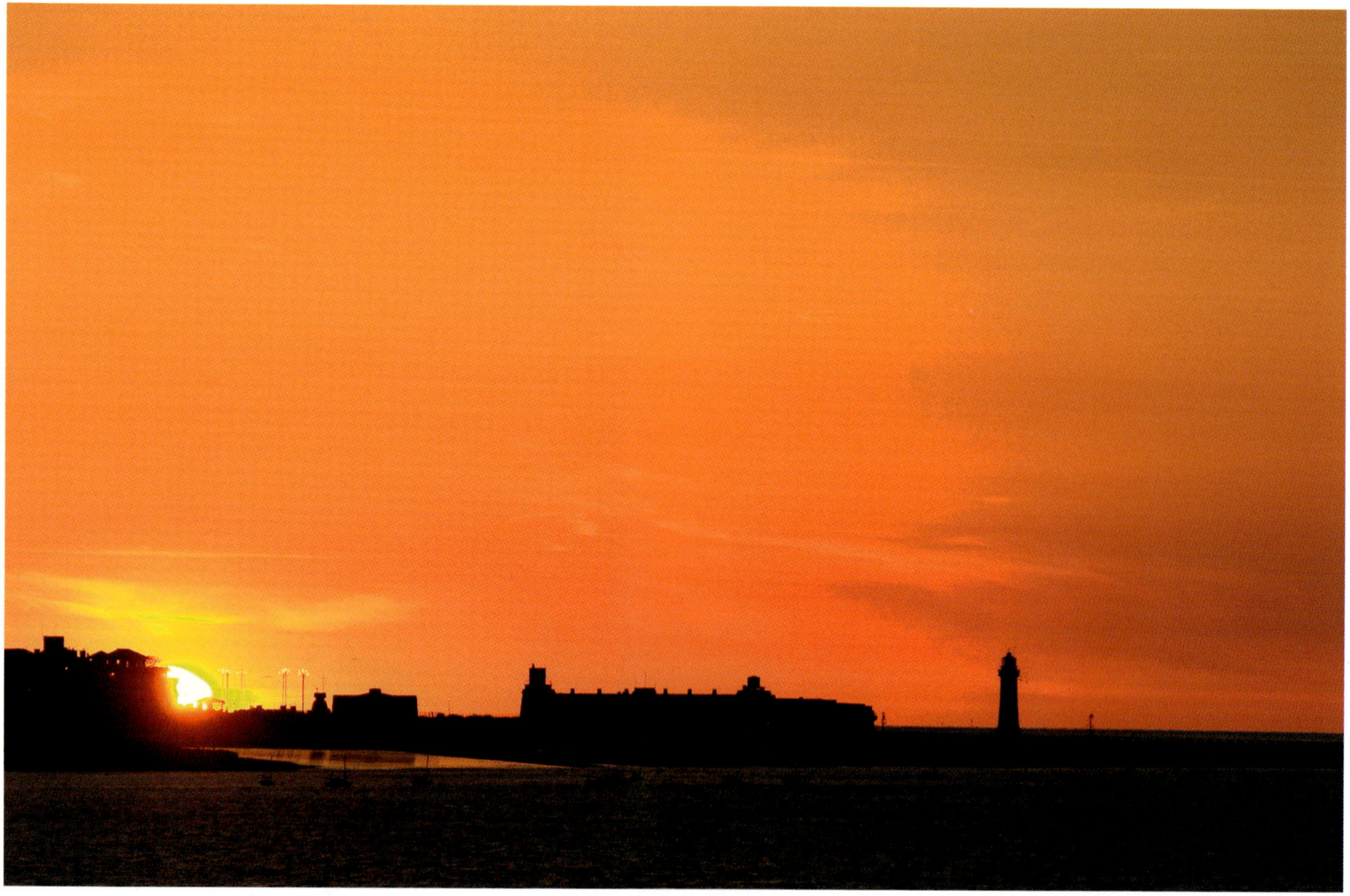

Fort Perch Rock

Situated on the tip of the Wirral Peninsula, the gun battery 'Fort Perch Rock' was built in 1829. It was garrisoned by 100 men and eighteen 32lb guns, to protect the Port of Liverpool against marauding French ships – although it was never actually needed. The New Brighton Lighthouse of 1830 stands opposite the modern Coastguard Station at Seaforth, which now provides navigation guidance to shipping.

Seaforth Windfarm

The six turbines of the Seaforth Windfarm were built in 1999. Operated by Mersey Docks and Harbour Board, they are connected to the National Grid. The turbines have a combined project capacity output of 3.6mw.

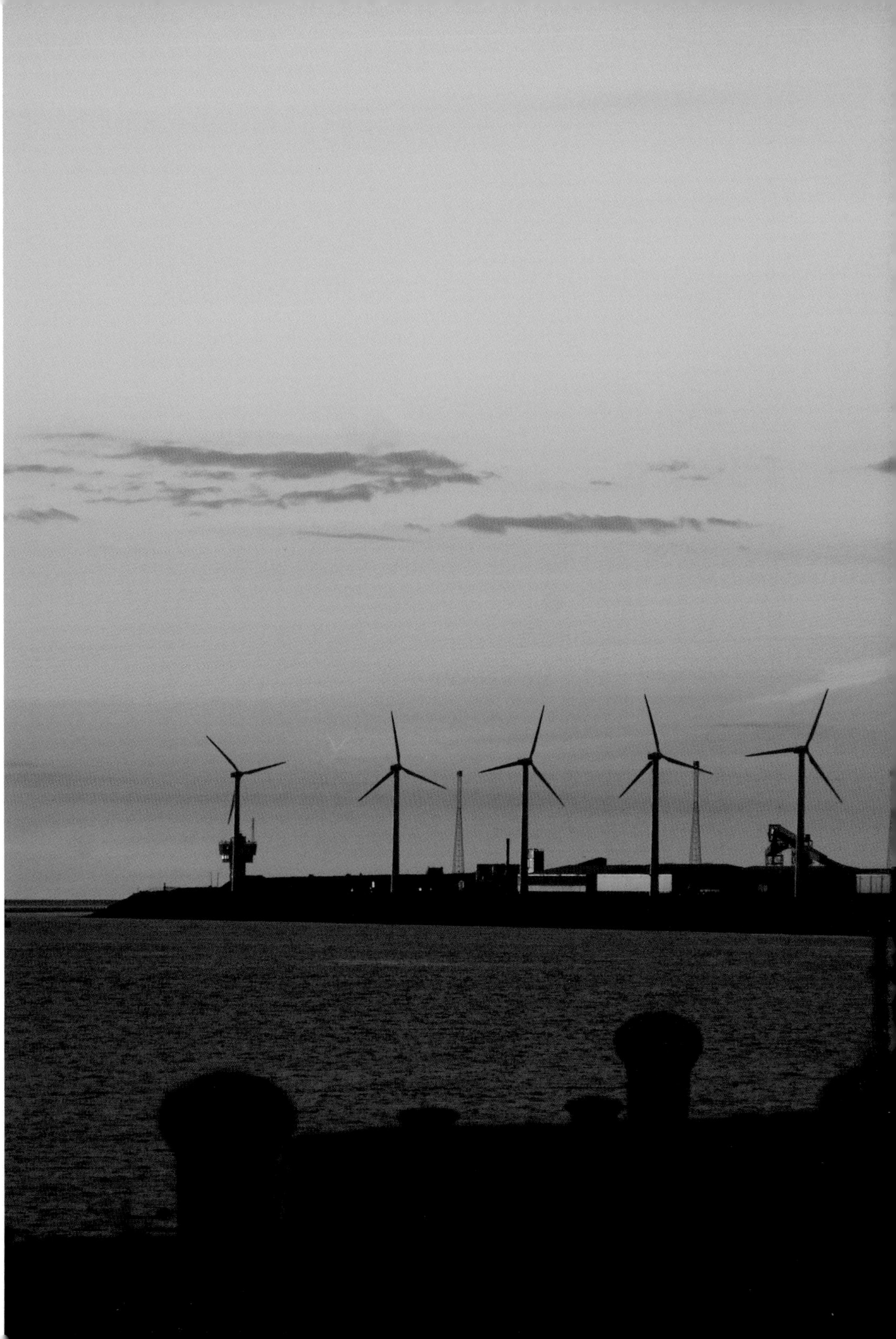

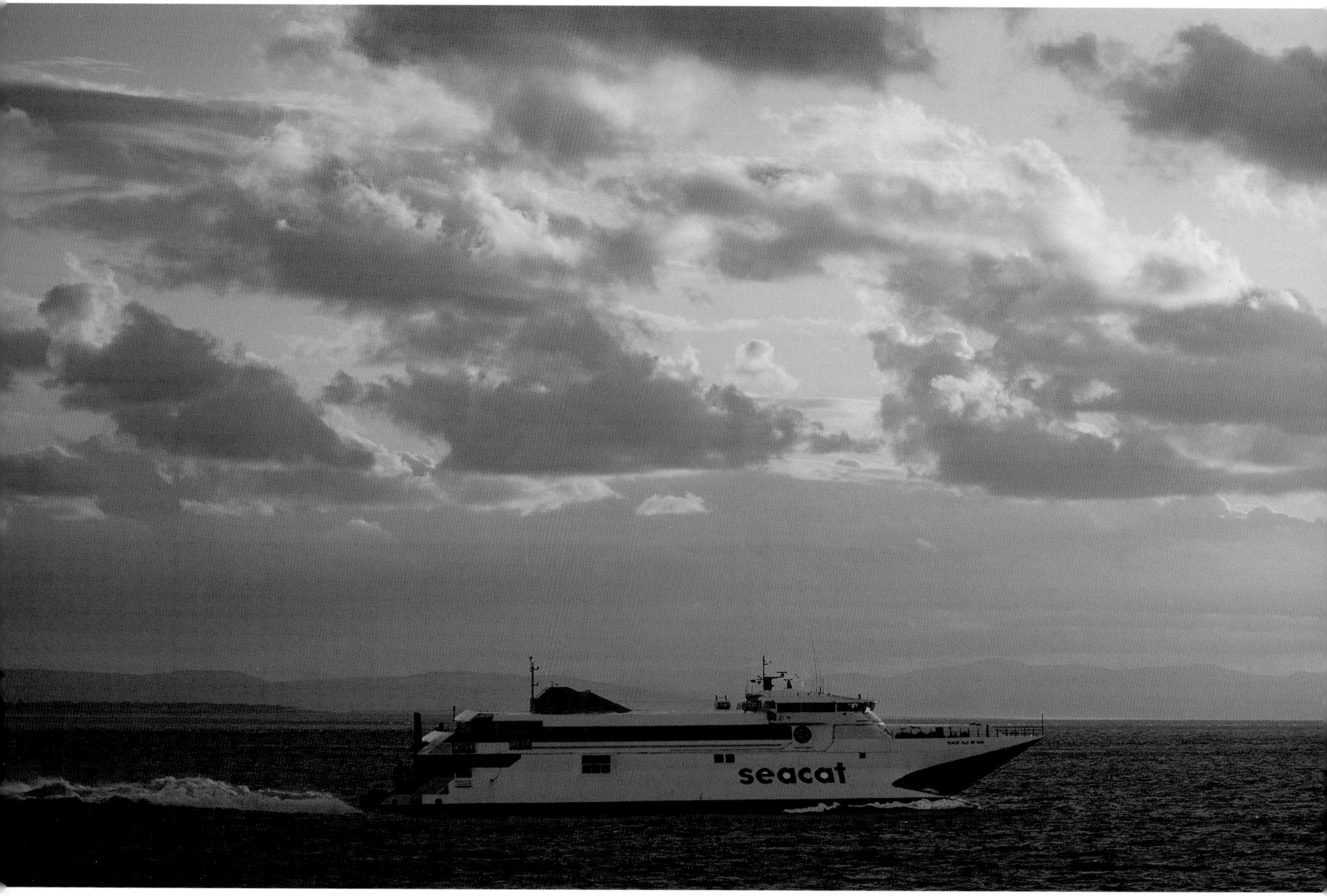
seacat

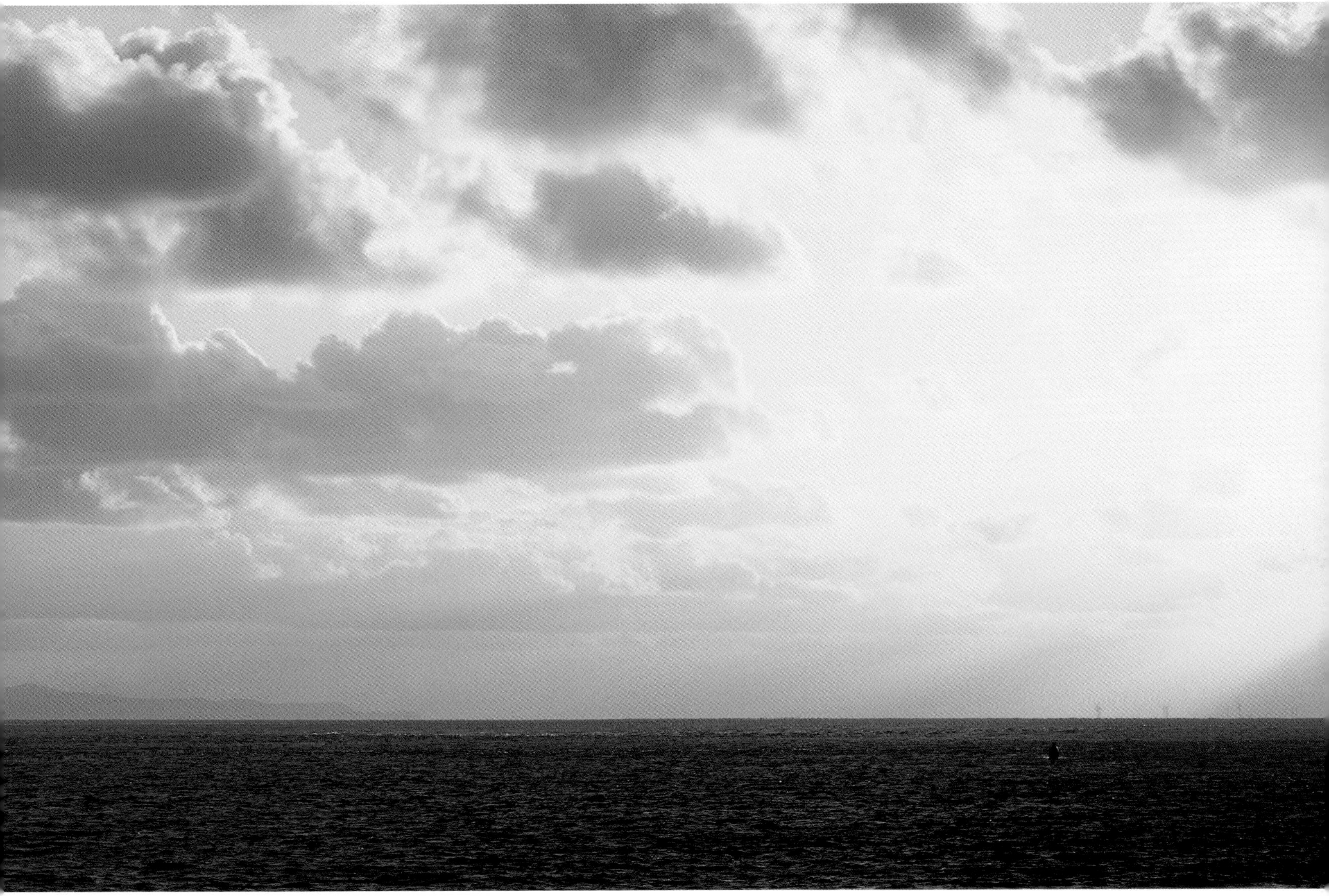

The Isle of Man ferry leaving the mouth of the Mersey

Operated by the Isle of Man Steam Packet Company, these daily services leave Liverpool for the Isle of Man and Ireland. Sailings take two-and-a-half hours to Douglas and under four hours to Dublin.

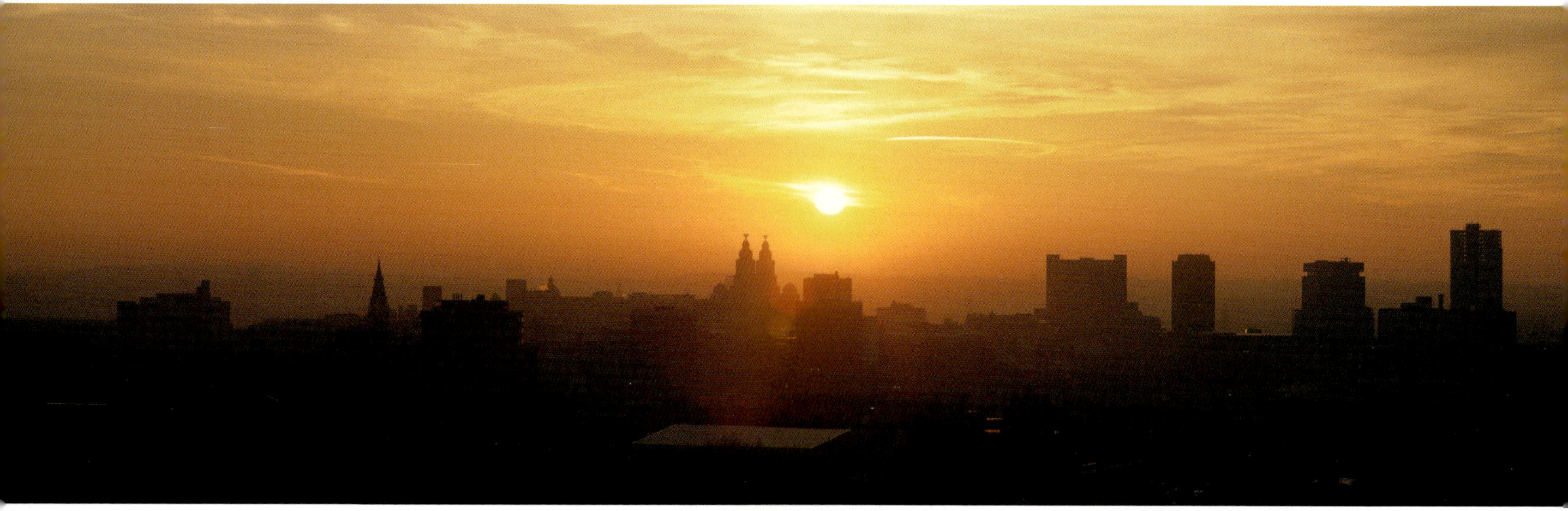

Winter sunset from Everton Brow